Authors in the Pantry

Authors in the Pantry

Recipes, Stories, and More

Sharron L. McElmeel

with Deborah L. McElmeel

LIBRARIES

U N L I M I T E D

A Member of the Greenwood Publishing Group

Westport, Connecticut • London

Library of Congress Cataloging-in-Publication Data

McElmeel, Sharron L.
   Authors in the pantry : recipes, stories, and more / Sharron L. McElmeel with
   Deborah L. McElmeel.
      p. cm.
   Includes bibliographical references and index.
   ISBN 1-59158-321-7 (pbk : alk. paper)
   1. Cookery. 2. Children's literature—Authorship. I. McElmeel, Deborah L. II. Title.
   TX652.M3654   2007
   641.5—dc22   2006033741

British Library Cataloguing in Publication Data is available.

Library of Congress Catalog Number: 2006033741
ISBN: 1-59158-321-7

First published in 2007

Libraries Unlimited, 88 Post Road West, Westport, CT 06881
A Member of the Greenwood Publishing Group, Inc.
www.lu.com

Printed in the United States of America

The paper used in this book complies with the
Permanent Paper Standard issued by the National
Information Standards Organization (Z39.48–1984).

10 9 8 7 6 5 4 3 2 1

The publisher has done its best to make sure the instructions and/or recipes in this book are
correct. However, users should apply judgment and experience when preparing recipes, especially parents and teachers working with young people. The publisher accepts no respon-
sibility for the outcome of any recipe included in this volume.

For E.J.M. and all those who have shared good times and good food at Hermit's Hill (1977–2007 and beyond).

Contents

Introduction

This book follows our earlier book, *Authors in the Kitchen,* which, like this one, is for lovers of food and books—and for teachers and librarians who wish to connect children with favorite authors through the common language of food. Among four brothers and another sister, my daughter Deborah grew up loving books and loving to cook. She experimented and refined her own recipes for all the favorites of family and friends. Her experience with food is long and varied. Her experience with books is equally as long. We both love books—but she's the cook.

As with our previous book, we have solicited stories and recipes for this cookbook from many of today's popular authors and illustrators. Some of the recipes are family recipes generously sent by an author; others are recipes developed especially to connect with an author's life story or book. To those recipes we have added anecdotes and bits and pieces of information that will help readers make literary connections to the food (and vice versa). The underlying purpose of the book is to give educators and book lovers the opportunity to connect with authors and books in a new and interesting way. We hope some connections will spur interest in learning more about a topic or subject.

Our thanks to each of the authors and illustrators represented here—some for their recipes, some for their stories, and some for both. Each sent correspondence that allowed us to connect an idea with them or their book. Several created some special "cooking" photographs and sent them along for inclusion in this book—special thanks to Marsha Diane Arnold, Stephanie Calmenson, Carol Otis Hurst, Sandy Lanton, Ann Morris, and Robin Pulver.

Roger Bradfield, Craig Brown, Wendy Anderson Halperin, Loreen Leedy, Nicole Rubel, Claudia Rueda, and Linda S. Wingerter each sent along illustrations for their section —a special addition to their comments and stories.

A warm hug and a thank you to illustrator and culinary advisor, Deborah L. McElmeel. Her sketches can be found on most pages in this book, and many of the recipes (those not submitted by the author or illustrator) were developed or adapted by her.

Although this book was not intended as a cookbook for children, some of the recipes are simple enough for children to execute with an adult supervisor. However, the real purpose is to offer recipes and suggestions of connections that adults who wish to promote literacy might use in the classroom, in the library, or at home. Parents might mix up a batch of pickle chiffon pie and then read to their children Jolly Roger Bradfield's book *Pickle Chiffon Pie* before exploring the list of other "pickle" books. Or they might create a special "literacy-connected" birthday dinner, based on their child's favorite book. Educators and librarians can also use the recipes to enhance lessons and programs. Enjoy real food and connect to the books for the children. And if you don't wish to cook, just use the "food" information to help young readers make connections to books. Knowing that a raisin pie is a funeral pie (see Penny Colman's chapter) and why it is called a "funeral pie" connects to a study of early pioneer days, and other eras such as the Depression era. Young readers may be interested in the origin or history of other traditions or in where specific foods are raised and how they are used. Each of the food dishes are indexed so you can find literary connections by the food, or you can find the author or illustrator and then find the food connection. Within each author or illustrator section, we have included booklists for more reading and bits and facts about related topics. The indices include a theme/subject index, a book title/author index, and the recipe index.

Read, share, and enjoy.

Sharron L. McElmeel

Sue Alexander—Fudge

Later, when Goblin went home,
he thought about eating fudge.
He thought about eating it
for breakfast, lunch, and dinner.
"I'll do it!" he said.

—From *Witch, Goblin, and Ghost Are Back*
by Sue Alexander

Sue Alexander

Birthday: August 20

Favorite place: Los Angeles, California

Favorite foods: potato chips, lamb chops

Family:

    Spouse—Joel Alexander

    Sons—Glenn and Marc

    Daughter—Stacey (married to Andy)

Home:

    Childhood—Born in Tucson, Arizona; spent childhood in Chicago, Illinois

    Now—Canoga Park, California (part of Los Angeles)

To fellow writers and illustrators, Sue Alexander is known as a major and vital part of the Society of Children's Book Writers and Illustrators (SCBWI). She was the first member to join SCBWI and has been vitally involved with the organization since its origin in 1971. To readers, she is a vital author who has written numerous books for young readers.

Alexander's interest in stories began when she was in elementary school. She wrote stories and told them to her classmates. But as an adult, she did not think about writing for a living until she had married and became mother to three children. Food shows up in her books about the World Famous Muriel and in the books about Goblin and his friends Witch and Ghost.

"Goblin ... [likes] fudge," as he demonstrated in 'Ghost's Fudge' in *Witch, Goblin, and Ghost Are Back*, says Sue Alexander.

"That story began with two separate incidents involving my daughter, Stacey, and my son, Marc. Stacey adored strawberries and refused to believe that there was such a thing as eating too many of them—until the day, after having eaten three boxes of strawberries in one sitting, she wound up with an itchy rash all over—face, arms, chest—and a stomachache.

"Marc developed a passion for homemade fudge. Not mine, since I had never made fudge in my life—but his best friend Tim's mother's concoction. One day, at Tim's house, Marc ate fudge for lunch and brought some home to have for dinner. (I subsequently got Tim's mother's recipe and made fudge for Marc.)

"Since, in the other books about Witch, Goblin, and Ghost, I had already established Goblin's liking for fudge, fusing the two incidents into a story in which Goblin eats so much fudge that he winds up with a stomachache seemed just right for the character that I'd created and enjoyed writing about."

—Sue Alexander

MAGIC RECIPES

There are some recipes that have some great results from some interesting ingredients—many omitting certain normal ingredients so they are dubbed "magic."

Here is a cookie bar recipe with no eggs, no flour, no mess, and cookies made with ice cream that disappears.

Magic Cookie Bars

- 1/2 cup butter
- 1 1/2 cups graham cracker crumbs
- 1 can sweetened condensed milk
- 6 ounces semisweet chocolate chips
- 3 1/2 ounces of flaked coconut
- 1 cup crushed walnuts

In a 9 x 13 inch pan, melt 1/2 cup butter and sprinkle the graham cracker crumbs over the melted butter. Pour the sweetened condensed milk over the crumbs and top with semisweet chocolate chips, flaked coconut, and walnuts. Gently press the chips, coconut, and walnuts into the cracker crumbs. Bake at 350 degrees F for 25 minutes or until brown. Cool. Cut into 12 large bars or 24 smaller squares.

Magic Cookies with Disappearing Ice Cream

- 1 pound butter
- 4 cups flour
- 1 pint softened ice cream
- 3/4 cup sugar
- 1/4 cup walnuts or pecans (finely chopped)
- 2 tablespoons cinnamon

Cut 1 pound butter and soften into 4 cups flour until thoroughly blended.

Add 1 pint softened ice cream and work the ice cream into the flour mixture. Add more flour if needed to make the dough easier to handle. Shape the dough into a cigar shape, 2 to 3 inches in diameter. Wrap in plastic wrap or aluminum foil and refrigerate overnight. The dough will be hard.

When ready to bake, preheat oven to 350 degrees F.

While oven is preheating, combine the sugar, nuts, and cinnamon. Take the tube of cookie dough from refrigerator. Cut in half horizontally twice to create four equal quarters; then cut 1-inch slices to create wedges of cookie dough. Roll each wedge in the sugar and nut mixture. Roll into a ball and then flatten the ball on a cookie sheet. Repeat until all the dough and sugar mixture have been used. Bake on a cookie sheet for 20 minutes or until browned.

Selected Books Written by Sue Alexander

Behold the Trees. (Arthur A. Levine/Scholastic, 2001)

Nadia, the Willful. (Pantheon, 1983)

One More Time, Mama. (Cavendish Books, 1999)

Small Plays for Special Days: Holiday Plays for You and a Friend. (Clarion, 2003)

Who Goes Out on Halloween? Level 1 (Bank Street Ready-To-Read). Illustrated by G. Brian Karas. (Gareth Stevens, 1998)

Witch, Goblin and Ghost Are Back. (Knopf, 1985)

Witch, Goblin and Ghost's Book of Things to Do. (Pantheon, 1985)

World Famous Muriel and the Magic Mystery. Illustrated by Marla Frazee. (HarperCollins, 1990)

Goblin's Fudge Recipe

(Courtesy of Tim's Mother)

Ingredients

- 2 tablespoons butter
- 1 1/2 cups of sugar
- 1/2 cup evaporated milk
- 2 cups semisweet chocolate chips
- 2/3 marshmallow cream
- 1/2 teaspoon vanilla

With a little bit of butter, grease a square (8 x 8 inch) pan on the bottom and sides. Set the pan aside.

Put the rest of the butter, the sugar, and the evaporated milk into a large cooking pot. Put the pot on the stove at a medium heat. Stir constantly with a wooden spoon. Keep stirring for 5 minutes after the mixture begins to bubble.

Remove the pot from the heat. Pour the chocolate chips into the mixture and stir until they are melted and thoroughly mixed in. It will feel stiff.

Add the marshmallow cream and continue to stir. Then add the vanilla. Stir until both the marshmallow cream and the vanilla are integrated into the mixture.

Spoon the mixture into the pan. Smooth it out as much as possible. Put the pan in the refrigerator for an hour. Cut into squares and serve.

Signature Recipe—Sue Alexander

Magic Books

Food is just one theme in Alexander's books. Magic also enters into several of them. In her *Witch, Goblin and Ghost's Book of Things to Do,* she asked her friend Sid Fleischman (a Newbery Medal–winning writer as well as a professional magician) to create a magic trick for Goblin to perform in the book. The illustration depicting "Mr. Mysterious" in the book bears an interesting resemblance to Fleischman. Another book with magic is *World Famous Muriel and the Magic Mystery.*

Learn Magic on Your Own

Bree, Loris. *Kid's Magic Secrets: Simple Magic Tricks & Why They Work.* (Marlor Press Inc., 2003)

Ho, Oliver. *How to Read Mind and Other Tricks.* Illustrated by Dave Garbot. (Sterling, 2002)

Ho, Oliver. *Young Magician: Magic Tricks.* Illustrated by Dave Garbot. (Sterling, 2003)

Leyton, Lawrence. *My First Magic Book.* (Dorling Kindersley, 1993)

Setteducati, Mark. *The Magic Show with Cards.* Illustrated by Steve Ellis. (Workman Publishing, 1999)

Berthe Amoss—Pralines

Berthe Amoss

Birthday: September 26

Favorite place: New Orleans and Pass Christian, Mississippi

Favorite foods: seafood

Family:

    Spouse—Walter James Amoss, Jr. (James)

    Sons—Jim, Bob, Billy, Mark, Tom, John (six daughters-in-law)

    Grandchildren—Nine grandsons and three granddaughters

Home state:

    Childhood—Louisiana

    Now—Louisiana; New Orleans and Pass Christian, Mississippi

After growing up in Louisiana, Berthe Amoss studied art at the University of Hawaii and later in Bremen, Germany, and Antwerp, Belgium, before settling down again in Louisiana where she is involved in many literacy ventures. She has taught children's literature at Tulane University and authored and illustrated books. She has been publisher, illustrator, writer, mother, and storyteller. She founded More Than a Card, Inc. (MTC), a press that produced several books with a Cajun flavor. She has also started a new line of children's books, The WORD Among Us, that produces books with a religious theme, and she is the president of Cocodrie Press. Her six sons are grown; she has six daughters-in-law and a dozen grandchildren (three times as many boys as girls). *Tom in the Middle* came about because of the antics of her three youngest sons, Mark, Tom, and John.

When she retold her version—or rather the Cajun version—of "Little Red Riding Hood," Berthe Amoss used her own name as part of Little Red Riding Hood's name, Marie Berthe Aspasie Philomen. It is mostly one of her granddaughters that inspired the female pig in *The Three Little Cajun Pigs*. In Amoss's version, Cochon, the third pig saves her brothers Pudgy and Chubby by making a hot pot of gumbo. The gumbo is so hot that when the alligator drops into the pot, he immediately jumps out and howls his way home.

M'sieur Cocodrie shows up in several of Amoss's books. Because Cocodrie looks similar to a crocodile, readers might assume the name is French for crocodile. However, Cocodrie (pronounced co-co-dree) means "alligator"— the animal with the broad snout and only the teeth of the upper jaw showing. Although some crocodiles do live in the United States, they are found only in the southern tip of Florida, in saltwater environments, whereas alligators can be found in various freshwater environments throughout the southeastern United States. South Florida is the only place in the world where both alligators and crocodiles can be found.

CREOLE COOKING

Berthe Amoss's ancestors arrived in New Orleans from France. The French immigrants are thought to have begun seasoning their food with spices and seasonings already being used by the Choctaw Indians. Africans who later came to the area added their own herbs and vegetables. And when the Spanish arrived, they brought peppers and new combinations of foods to add to the cook pot. As each culture contributed new combinations and seasoning alternatives, the Creole version of cuisine emerged.

Booklist

Selected Books Written and Illustrated by Berthe Amoss

A Cajun Little Red Riding Hood. (MTC Press, 2000)

The Cajun Gingerbread Boy. (MTC Press, 1994)

Delicious Dishes: Creole Cooking for Children. With Dulaney Montgomery. (MTC Press, 1991)

The Three Little Cajun Pigs. (MTC Press, 1999)

Tom in the Middle. (HarperCollins, 1988; reillustrated)

Creole Seafood Gumbo

Since Cochan (in *The Three Little Cajun Pigs*) is a pig, she much prefers to make a seafood gumbo in her cooking pot—no sausage, no ham. A recipe for seafood gumbo is supplied in Amoss's book; but here's another one that might be just "hot" enough.

Cook 1 cup of rice in 3 cups water—enough to make 3 cups cooked rice. (Use directions on the package.)

Melt 3/4 stick butter, and use it to sauté the following:

- 2 cups chopped green onion
- 2 cups sliced okra
- 1 cup chopped white onion
- 3 blue crabs (discard top shell, cut into 4 pieces)

Remove from heat.

Put the following in a separate pot and bring to a boil:

- 2 cups raw peeled shrimp
- 2 cups raw shelled oysters
- 1 cup chopped tomato pulp
- 2 cups tomato juice
- 1 1/2 quarts fish stock

Let the seafood mixture boil for a minute, then add the mixture to the first pot with the crab meat.

In a small skillet put 1/2 stick butter and 3 tablespoons flour together; heat, stirring gently, until the mixture is a brown paste (this mixture is the roux).

Blend this brown roux with some of the gumbo mixture and 1 tablespoon file (powdered sassafras), then add the mixture to the gumbo.

Season with salt, pepper, and cayenne.

Serve each 1 1/2 cup gumbo in a bowl over 1/2 cup cooked rice. Serves 6.

PRALINES—SUGARED NUTS

In France almonds are often mixed with caramelized sugar, but when the French came to Louisiana, there were no almonds—but pecans were plentiful. There are several legends crediting the new praline candy to various Frenchmen, but they are simply legends. Perhaps, though, it was the Ursuline nuns who came in the eighteenth century, made the nutty treat with pecans and cane sugar, and named the treat after the Marechal de Plessin-Pralin. The word "praline" simply means "sugared" in French. Pralines are the treat that Little Red Riding Hood is hoping that her grandmère will make for her, but she has to use her basket of pecans to chase off M'sieur Crocodrie. So instead of making pralines, Grandmère reads Katrine a story of Little Red Riding Hood and promises to send home the secret recipe so her mother can make her some pralines.

Pralines

This recipe is said to have been lost for generations when a jealous stepsister hid it from Rosemonde. (A young girl in eighteenth-century Louisiana.) It is a "quick, easy way to make absolutely foolproof, mouth-watering pralines," says Amoss. One day Rosemonde's great-great-great granddaughter Rosie was cleaning and found the recipe tucked away in the pages of the August 1798 issue of *La Cuisine pour Dames.*

- 1 cup white sugar
- 2/3 cup water
- 2 cups pecan halves

Combine the sugars and water in a quart pot. Cook over medium heat until the syrup forms a ball in cold water. Add 2 cups pecan halves, quickly bring to a boil, remove from heat, and stir until syrup is slightly cloudy. Spoon onto waxed paper that has been laid over two sheets of newspaper (keeps pralines from breaking when cool by lifting with a spatula from the waxed paper). Makes 24 pralines.

Signature Recipe—Berthe Amoss

Marsha Diane Arnold—*Mak Kuchen*

Workin' in the kitchen with the smell of risin' bread circling around was a nice way to spend afternoons.

—From *The Bravest of Us All* by Marsha Diane Arnold

Marsha Diane Arnold

Birthday: July 7

Favorite place: Italy

Favorite foods: Fruit, any kind of homemade pie, and *mak kuchen*

Family:
    Spouse—Fred Arnold
    Son—Cal
    Daughter—Amy
Home: Born and raised in Kansas
    Childhood—Kingman, Kansas
    Now—Northern California

Marsha Diane Arnold grew up in farming country in Kansas. She left the farm after graduating from high school and entered Kansas State University, where she earned her undergraduate degree. Eager to leave the wheat fields behind, she and her husband Frederick Oak Arnold moved on to Northern California. Eventually two children were added to the family. Arnold, already a journalist, turned her thoughts to writing fiction for children. She is now a successful children's book author.

She sets her books in a variety of locations, but it is not a surprise that *The Bravest of Us All* takes us back to her childhood home in Kansas or that her Nanthaniel's "Great-paw" (in *The Chicken Salad Club*) might be reminiscent of her own Kansas grandparents.

"During my childhood, I spent many days in my Grandmother's farmhouse, *'with the smell of risin' bread circling around.'* Grandmother began her bread baking in the morning and placed the dough on the stove in the living room to rise. I loved those days I visited because I could smell that delicious dough rising, dough that would transform into cinnamon rolls, *gorovei* (coffee cake), *bona beroggi* (rolls filled with mashed, sweetened pinto beans), and my favorite, *mak kuchen* (poppy seed rolls)."

11

Perseverance

Marsha Diane Arnold crafted a tall-tale-like story, *The Pumpkin Runner,* from a true story involving the perseverance of Cliff Young, a sixty-one-year-old Australian potato farmer who trained on his brother's cattle ranch for a five-hundred-mile race from Melbourne to Sydney. Young was ridiculed—he was the oldest of eleven entrants, but he went on to win the race and took two days off the record. He shared his winnings with all the other runners.

Other books inspired by the biographies of people who persevered include the following:

Borden, Louise, and Mary Kay Kroeger. *Fly High! The Story of Bessie Coleman.* Illustrated by Teresa Flavin. Margaret K. Elderry, 2001. Coleman's perseverance and resourcefulness helped her become the first African American woman to earn a pilot's license despite her difficult childhood in Waxahachie, Texas.

Cohn, Diana. *Dream Carver.* Illustrated by Amy Cordova. Chronicle Books, 2002. Based on the life of renowned Oaxacan woodcarver Manuel Jimenez who became well-known in all of Mexico.

Lasky, Kathryn. *Marven of the Great North Woods.* Illustrated by Kevin Hawkes. Harcourt, 1997. Based on the experiences of the author's father, during the influenza epidemic of 1914, ten-year-old Marven survives in a lumber camp where he has been sent to escape the illness.

Ryan, Pam Muñoz. *When Marian Sang: True Recital of Marian Anderson.* Illustrated by Brian Selznick. Scholastic, 2002. Anderson's perseverance helps her to rise above the racism and finally reach the stage of the Metropolitan Opera at age fifty-seven.

Selected Books Written by Marsha Diane Arnold

The Bravest of Us All. Illustrated by Brad Sneed. (Dial, 2000)

Edward G. and the Beautiful Pink Hairbow. Illustrated by Karen Stormer Brooks. (Random House, 2002)

Heart of a Tiger. Illustrated by Jamichael Henterly. (Dial, 1995)

Hugs on the Wind. Coauthored by Vernise Elaine Pelzel. Illustrated by Elsa Warnick. (Abrams Books for Young Readers, 2006)

Prancing, Dancing Lily. Illustrated by John Manders. (Dial, 2004)

The Pumpkin Runner. Illustrated by Brad Sneed. (Dial, 1998)

Quick, Quack, Quick! Illustrated by Lisa McCue. (Random House, 1996)

Roar of a Snore. Illustrated by Pierre Pratt. (Dial, 2006)

The Tail of Little Skunk. Illustrator Michael Terry. (Random House, 2002)

On Sundays Marsha, her family, several of her father's seven brothers and sisters, and many of her twenty-eight cousins gathered at her Grandparent Krehbiel's farm. In addition to Marsha's favorite *mak kuchen,* the table was laden with fried chicken, mashed potatoes, coleslaw, Jell-O, freshly baked cinnamon rolls, coffee cakes, and pies.

Triple Fruit Pie

Among Marsha Diane Arnold's favorite foods are fruit and any kind of homemade pie. This recipe combines three fruits in a delicious triple fruit pie.

Pie Crust

- 2 2/3 cup all-purpose flour
- 1 cup Crisco vegetable shortening
- 1 teaspoon kosher or coarse salt
- 6 tablespoons ice water

1. Cut shortening into the flour and salt mixture with a pastry cutter until mixture resembles the texture of tiny split peas.

2. Add the ice water and combine with a fork. Quickly gather the dough into a ball and flatten into two 4-inch-wide disks. Wrap in plastic, and refrigerate at least 30 minutes.

3. Remove dough from refrigerator. If stiff and very cold, let stand until dough is cool but malleable.

4. Using a floured rolling pin, roll each dough disk on a lightly floured surface from the center out in each direction, forming 12-inch circle from each disk. Place one circle in bottom of pie pan. Put in filling as directed below and then place the top crust on the pie. Cut slits in the top to allow moisture and steam to escape.

Pie Filling

- 1/2 can each, cherry, peach, and blueberry pie filling

In the unbaked pie shell, place a ring of cherry pie filling in the outer portion of the pie crust. Make a second ring using the peach pie filling, and finally fill the center of the pie with the blueberry filling. Place a top crust on the pie (cutting slits for venting moisture and steam), brush with milk, and sprinkle with a light sprinkling of sugar. Bake in a moderate oven, 375 degrees F until crust is light brown.

Mak Kuchen (Poppy Seed Rolls)

Sweet Bread Dough Recipe

Bring to boil in large saucepan:

- 1 cup sour cream

Remove from heat and add the following ingredients:

- 2 tablespoons shortening
- 3 tablespoons sugar
- 1/8 teaspoon soda
- 1 teaspoon salt

Stir in until well blended. Cool to lukewarm

Add:

- 1 large egg unbeaten
- 1 package dry yeast

Stir until dissolved. Then sift into the mixture 2 1/2 cups flour.

Mix flour into the liquid ingredients with a spoon. When the dough begins to come away from the sides of the bowl, it is ready to knead. If more flour is needed to get to kneading stage, add up to 1/2 cup more flour. Once all the ingredients are well blended, turn the dough onto a lightly floured board. Knead to form a smooth ball. Cover the dough with a damp cloth and let stand for 5 minutes. Roll into a rectangle approximately 6 x 24 inches and 1/4 inch thick.

Poppy-Seed Filling

- 1 cup ground poppy seeds
- 1 cup sugar
- 1 cup cream
- 1/8 teaspoon salt

Mix well and cook slowly. Simmer until thick and sticky. Spread the mixture on the rolled-out dough and then roll up the dough into a long log—rolling from the long side of the rectangle, as for cinnamon rolls. Cut into 1-inch slices and put on greased baking sheet. Cover with a thin cloth. Let rise until it doubles in thickness. Just before baking, brush tops with egg yolk mixture (1 part yolk to 2 parts water). Bake at 350 degrees F for 25 or 30 minutes or until brown.

Signature Recipe (Poppy Seed Filling)—Marsha Diane Arnold

Tom Birdseye—Chunky Chocolate Chip Cookies

Tom Birdseye

Birthday: July 13

Favorite foods: Chocolate and … um, chocolate … and sushi, although not together.

Family:

    Spouse—Debbie

    Daughters—Kelsey (1985), Amy (1989)

Home:

    Childhood—Born in North Carolina; grew up in North Carolina and Kentucky

    Now—Oregon

"Too Bad," Amy said. "I thought you were just embarrassed about what happened yesterday. But if you're really sick, then these wouldn't help anyway." She smiled and pulled a plate of cookies from behind her back.

Chocolate chip cookies. Chunky chocolate chip cookies. Homemade chunky chocolate chip cookies.

"Uh …," I said, trying to keep from drooling. "Maybe just one wouldn't hurt."

—From *Attack of the Mutant Underwear* by Tom Birdseye

As a child growing up in North Carolina and Kentucky, Tom Birdseye never considered being a writer. He was more interested in exploring the out-of-doors. He was teaching in a fifth–grade classroom in Lincoln City, Oregon, when he began to write the story of Arlo Moore. By the time that story, *I'm Going to Be Famous,* was published, he was teaching in Sandpoint, Idaho. His dual career as a teacher and writer continued for another two years until he decided to devote his time to writing.

Tom earned an undergraduate degree in mass communications at Western Kentucky University. That same year—1974—he married his wife, Debbie Holsclaw. In 1977, he earned a second degree, this time in elementary education. For several years, he taught fifth-grade students, and bits and pieces of fifth-grade life show up regularly in his writing. Arlo Moore is a fifth-grader who aspires to break the world record for eating bananas. Eleven-year-old Tucker Renfro deals with the issues of divorce, sibling rivalry, and the unemployment of his parent in *Tucker*. Patrick, in *Just Call Me Stupid*, is another fifth-grader. Birdseye's later books have included older protagonists, retold folk stories, and even two nonfiction books written with his educator wife.

Tom Birdseye and his family now live in Oregon where Tom continues to write—and hike, canoe, and enjoy other outdoor activities.

Crunchy Chocolate S'mores

Crunchy foods help loose teeth loosen, and because chocolate is listed as a favorite food, perhaps these crunchy treats will help—or perhaps they will just feed a chocolate-craving tooth.

- 4 graham cracker squares
- 2 large marshmallows
- 1 (1.55 ounces) NESTLÉ CRUNCH Candy Bar

Toast each marshmallow over a bonfire or in a microwave (on high for 10–15 seconds). Place toasted marshmallow on one graham cracker square, top with half of the candy bar and another graham cracker square.

Selected Books Written by Tom Birdseye

Airmail to the Moon. Illustrated by Stephen Gammell. (Holiday, 1988)

Attack of the Mutant Underwear. (Holiday House, 2003)

The Eye of the Stone. (Holiday, 2000)

I'm Going to Be Famous. (Holiday House, 1986)

Just Call Me Stupid. (Holiday House, 1993)

Look Out, Jack! The Giant Is Back. Illustrated by Will Hillenbrand. (Holiday House, 2001)

Oh Yeah! Illustrated Ethan Long. (Holiday House, 2003)

Tarantula Shoes. (Holiday House, 1995)

A Tough Nut to Crack. (Holiday House, 2006)

Amy's Chunky Chocolate Chip Cookies

Cream together:

- 2/3 cup butter
- 2/3 cup vegetable shortening
- 1 cup white sugar
- 1 cup brown sugar
- 2 large eggs
- 2 teaspoon vanilla

Add into mixture:

- 4 cups sifted flour
- 1 teaspoon soda
- 1 teaspoon salt

Beat well and then fold in:

- 1 cup chopped nuts (optional)
- 12 ounces (or about 2 1/2 cups) chocolate chunks

Preheat oven to 375 degrees F. Drop by tablespoons onto lightly greased cookie sheet. Flatten with a spatula. Bake about 8–10 minutes until cookies are just beginning to brown and are still quite soft. Cool slightly and remove from pan onto paper towels to finish cooling.

Tooth Books

Airmail to the Moon features Ora Mae Cotton of Crabapple Orchard. Somebody stole her tooth, and when she finds out who she says, "I'm gonna open up a can of gotcha and send 'em airmail to the moon!" After pursuing a number of suspects, she discovers who the rascal really is … in a surprise ending. Not the usual lost tooth–tooth fairy story (although the tooth fairy does play a part), this humorous tale is set in the Appalachians. Most booklists about teeth include the usual tooth fairy books and those dealing with dental hygiene. This list combines some of those with others that contain interesting information about teeth.

Bate, Lucy. *Little Rabbit's Loose Tooth*. Illustrated by Diane deGroat. (Crown, 2006, reissue)

Beeler, Selby B. *Throw Your Tooth on the Roof: Tooth Traditions from around the World*. Illustrated by G. Brian Karas. (Houghton Mifflin, 1998)

Brill, Marlene Targ. *Tooth Tales from around the World*. Illustrated by Katya Krenina. (Charlesbridge, 1998)

Chandra, Deborah, and Comora, Madeleine. *George Washington's Teeth*. Illustrated by Brock Cole. (Farrar, Straus & Giroux, 2003)

Davis, Katie. *Mabel the Tooth Fairy and How She Got Her Job*. (Harcourt, 2003)

Olson, Mary W. *Nice Try, Tooth Fairy*. Illustrated by Katherine Tillotson. (Simon & Schuster, 2000)

Palatini, Margie. *Sweet Tooth*. Illustrated by Jack E. Davis. (Simon & Schuster, 2004)

Park, Barbara. *Junie B., First Grader Toothless Wonder*. Illustrated by Denise Brunkus. (Scholastic, 2003)

Reader's Digest. *Brush Your Teeth Please*. (Reader's Digest, 1993; Pop-Up edition)

Showers, Paul. *How Many Teeth?* (Let's-Read-and-Find-Out Science 1). Illustrated by True Kelley. (HarperTrophy, 1991)

Steig, William. *Doctor De Soto*. (Farrar, Straus & Giroux, 1990, reissue)

Jack and the Beanstalk

Those who know the story of Jack and the Beanstalk might be surprised at the goings on that followed Jack's exploits. In *Look Out Jack! The Giant Is Back* by Tom Birdseye, reader's find out that the giant's brother is interested in avenging his brother's death; so he plans to find Jack and make things right. In Raymond Brigg's tale, it's the giant's grandson who encounters one of Jack's relatives. Read these versions of Jack's story and of what happened later.

- Briggs, Raymond. *Jim and the Beanstalk*. (Putnam, 1997, reissue)
- Galdone, Paul. *Jack and the Beanstalk*. (Clarion, 1982)
- Kellogg, Steven. *Jack and the Beanstalk*. (HarperCollins, 1991)
- Stanley, Diane. *The Giant and the Beanstalk*. (HarperCollins, 2004)

Write your own version of Jack and the Beanstalk: various versions of Jack's tale have him rescuing a variety of objects from the giant—eggs from the golden hen, a golden harp, gold coins, a golden goose, and even a magic tablecloth that provides Jack and his mother with food whenever they need or want it. Whenever they spread the cloth and call for food, the table is set with a bountiful spread of good things to eat. The version you write might have Jack and his mother using their magic tablecloth to help them open a roadside food stand. We are sure that Jack's Three Bean Salad would sell well.

Jack's Three Bean Salad

- Chop one green pepper
- Chop one medium-sized onion
- Drain 1 medium can (15-oz) green beans
- Drain 1 medium can (15-oz) garbanzo beans
- Drain 1 medium can (15-oz) kidney beans

Mix pepper, onions, and all beans in the following vinegar dressing.

- 3/4 cup sugar
- 1 teaspoon salt
- 1/2 teaspoon black pepper
- 1/3 cup olive oil
- 2/3 cup white vinegar
- 1 teaspoon garlic powder

Marinate the bean mixture for several hours or overnight. Serve chilled.

Maribeth Boelts—Grilled Pork

Maribeth Boelts

Birthday: January 19

Favorite place: Cedar Falls, Iowa

Favorite foods: Banana cream pie, asparagus, barbeque ribs

Family:

Spouse—Darwin

Sons—Adam, Will

Daughter—Hannah

Home:

Childhood—Waterloo, Iowa

Now—Cedar Falls, Iowa

Thanksgiving Day—this shift's begun.
Ten Firefighters at Station 1.
Lou says, "I can cook today."
A list is made. They're on their way.

**—From *Firefighters' Thanksgiving*
by Maribeth Boelts**

Maribeth Boelts was born in Waterloo, Iowa, grew up there, and now lives nearby in Cedar Falls. During her childhood, she spent many days reading books in the Waterloo Public Library. She loved reading and writing. On school days, she and her friends often "cut through" the yard near the neighborhood fire station on their way to school. After school, she often stopped by the station to buy a pop. She says, "It was manned with friendly firefighters, and it was always open every day of the week." Not surprisingly Maribeth Boelts grew up and married a firefighter, as did her youngest sister.

After earning a degree in education from the University of Northern Iowa in nearby Cedar Falls, Maribeth began teaching. But in just three years, her love of writing took over, so she quit her job to became a full-time writer and mother. Her writing career has included newspaper work and writing for children. She wrote about many topics, most of the ideas coming from the children she has taught as a substitute teacher. In 1999, her "soft spot for firefighters" and her love of writing combined when she sold her first children's book about firefighters. Boelts says, *"The Firefighters' Thanksgiving* tells the story of a crew of firefighters who try to cook a Thanksgiving dinner, but due to many emergencies and fire calls, they are unable to get the job done. In the story, the neighborhood comes to the rescue, bringing the tired and hungry firefighters a full Thanksgiving spread."

Banana Banana Cream Pie

Ingredients:

- 1 cup whole milk
- 4 egg yolks
- 1 cup granulated sugar
- 5 tablespoons all-purpose flour
- 3 tablespoons butter, cut in small pieces
- 1/2 teaspoon ground cinnamon
- 1/2 teaspoon nutmeg
- 1 1/2 teaspoon vanilla extract
- 2 cups heavy cream (whipped and divided in two parts)
- 2 bananas, thinly sliced and tossed with 1 1/2 tablespoons lemon juice (about 1/2 lemon)
- 1/4 cup chopped walnuts
- 1 9-inch pie shell, baked

In a heavy saucepan (or in a microwave-safe large mixing bowl) bring the milk to the boiling point, when little bubbles form around the edge of the pan. Remove from heat.

In another bowl, beat the 4 egg yolks (best to use an electric mixer on medium speed) and gradually add 1 cup granulated sugar. Beat for 2 minutes until the mixture is thick and lemon-colored. Beat in 5 tablespoons of flour. With mixer on low speed, gradually add the hot milk.

Transfer mixture back to the heavy saucepan (or the microwave bowl) and bring the mixture to a boil again; let boil for about 1 minute, stirring often.

Remove the pan from heat and continue to beat with a spoon or a mixer until mixture is smooth.

Beat in 3 tablespoons butter (chunked into small pieces), a little at a time; then add the cinnamon, nutmeg, and vanilla extract. Let mixture cool.

While the egg mixture is cooling beat whipping cream until mixture is firm but not stiff. Then gently fold in half of the whipped cream into the egg mixture to lighten it, a little at a time.

Fold in the banana slices

Put entire mixture into a baked 9-inch pie shell.

Top the pie with the remaining half of the whipped cream. Optional: Sprinkle top of pie with chopped walnuts.

Refrigerate the pie until ready to serve.

Marybeth Boelts says, "At my husband's fire department, Waterloo Fire Rescue, there are several firefighters who have been given the title of "firehouse chef." One such firefighter gave me a recipe for his grilled pork. ... Nothing fussy about the recipe, but it is popular at the firehouse." The recipe is compliments of Rick, one of the firehouse chefs. Grill and serve in a festive serving dish.

Firehouse Grilled Pork

Feeds 8–10 firefighters

- 1 whole 8–9 pound pork loin
- Uncle Dougie's Grub Rub*

Wash and dry pork loin. Rub generously with Uncle Dougie's Grub Rub. Grill outside on a charcoal or gas grill over medium hot coals/heat (with the grill lid closed so the grill is oven-like; or place the loin on a grilling pan and bake in the oven at 300 degrees for approximately 1 1/2 hours.

*Uncle Dougie's Grub Rub is a seasoning available commercially from Uncle Dougie's and You Name It! Foods/Willowdale Enterprises in Barrington, Illinois. The seasoning is a combination of red peppers, black peppers, chile peppers, vinegar, sweet bell peppers, salt, onion, garlic, paprika, sugar, parsley, and other natural flavorings. Some would say that there is no substitute for Uncle Dougie's Grub Rub, but there are other brands of "grub-rub" and other hot seasonings that might be a suitable substitute depending on how spicy or hot you like your food.

Signature Recipe—Maribeth Boelts

Books by Maribeth Boelts

Big Daddy, Frog Wrestler. Illustrated by Benrei Huang. (Albert A. Whitman, 2000)

The Firefighters' Thanksgiving. Illustrated by Terry Widener. (Putnam's, 2004)

A Kid's Guide to Staying Safe on Bikes. (Powerkids Press, 1997)—one title in the Kids' Guide series.

Kids to the Rescue! First Aid Techniques for Kids. Text with Darwin Boelts. Illustrated by Marina Megale. (Parenting Press, 2003, revised)

Little Bunny's Pacifier Plan. Illustrated by Kathy Parkinson. (Albert A. Whitman, 1999)—one title in the Little Bunny Series.

Starlight Lullaby. Illustrated by Marisol Sarrazin. (Little Simon, 2006)

When It's the Last Day of School. Illustrated by Hanako Wakiyama. (Putnam's, 2003)

A Feast of Thanksgiving Books

Markes, Julie. *Thanks for Thanksgiving*. Illustrated by Doris Barrette. (HarperCollins, 2004)

Masurel, Claire. *Happy Thanksgiving, Emily!* (Books about Emily series). Illustrated by Susan Calitri. (Penguin, 2004)

Spinelli, Eileen. *Thanksgiving at the Tappletons'*. Illustrated by Megan Lloyd. (HarperCollins, 2003; reillustrated, originally published in 1982)

Spirn, Michele Sobel. *I Am the Turkey* (An I Can Read Book). Illustrated by Joy Allen. (HarperCollins, 2004)

Stanley, Diane. *Thanksgiving on Plymouth Plantation* (The Traveling-Time Twins Series). Illustrated by Holly Berry. (Joanne Cotler, 2004)

Booklist

Firefighter Books

- Demarest, Chris L. *Firefighters A to Z.* (Simon & Schuster, 2003)
- Ganci, Chris. *Chief: The Life of Peter J. Ganci, a New York City Firefighter.* (Scholastic, 2003)
- Hayward, Linda. *A DK Readers Jobs People Do: A Day in a Life of a Firefighter* (Level 1: Beginning to Read). (DK Publishing, 2001)

A BRIEF HISTORY OF FIREFIGHTING

Firefighting has a history dating back to the Egyptians, who used hand-operated wooden pumps to fight fires in the second century b.c.. The first paid firefighters in the United States were in Boston in 1680. Those fire departments used bucket brigades. People passed leather buckets filled with water, to be thrown on the fire, down a human chain. Benjamin Franklin—the founder of the first lending library, a signer of the Constitution, and an experimenter in the field of electricity—was also the person who founded the first volunteer fire department in the United States.

Roger Bradfield—Pickle Chiffon Pie

A long time ago there was a fat little king who ruled over the land as far as he could see in every direction. He was very wise, and his kingdom was a happy one. His wife, the Queen, was a very good cook and made him a pickle-chiffon pie every day. But every kingdom has problems. . . .

**—From *Pickle Chiffon Pie*
by Roger Bradfield**

Roger Bradfield

Birthday: September 22

Favorite place: Paris, France

Favorite foods: Ribs!

Family:

    Spouse—Joan

    Son—Reno

    Daughters—Venetia, Kari, Sue, Heidi

Home:

    Childhood—Minnesota

    Now—California

Jolly Roger Bradfield was born and raised in Minnesota. He studied art there too, at the Minneapolis School of Art in 1946, when he returned from serving in the U.S. Army during World War II. In 1948, he married Joan, and the next year the two of them went on to Paris where Roger studied art at the Academie Julian. A year later, they moved to London where Roger studied at the Heatherly School of Art. In London, he created humorous illustrations for *Punch* and *Good Housekeeping* magazines. After settling his family back in the United States in 1953, Bradfield opened a commercial art studio. He became known for his package design and for a comic strip, *Dooley's World,* that he drew. In the meantime, he also created a niche for himself as the author and illustrator of several successful children's books. In the 1960s, he wrote several books and then concentrated on his commercial art business, retiring in 1988. Since then he has traveled to Greece, Norway, Portugal, Italy, France, Spain, and Mexico to gather images and ideas for his paintings. A talented watercolorist, Bradfield paints a variety of subjects.

A self-portrait of Roger Bradfield.

INVENTING PICKLE-CHIFFON PIE

When asked how the title of Pickle-Chiffon Pie came about, here's how Robert Bradfield replied:

"Since the pie was such an important part of the story, I wanted it to be something special—not just apple pie or lemon. I put the question to my panel of five children, and after eliminating things like 'Mud' and 'Watermelon-Chiffon,' they finally came up with 'Pickle-chiffon pie.' That was it."

Pies, Pies, Pies!

Pickle-chiffon pie is unique, but delicious pies are featured in many other books. There are apple pies galore, and lemon pies and more.

Garland, Michael. *The President and Mom's Apple Pie* (Dutton, 2002)

Ichord, Loretta Frances. *Skillet Bread, Sourdough and Vinegar Pie*. (Millbrook, 2003)

Lear, Edward. *"A" Was Once an Apple Pie*. Illustrated by Suse MacDonald. (Orchard, 2005)

Lindsey, Kathleen D. *Sweet Potato Pie*. Illustrated by Charlotte Riley-Webb. (Lee & Low, 2003)

MacLachlan, Patricia, and Emily MacLachlan. *Once I Ate a Pie*. Illustrated by Katy Schneider. (Joanna Cotler, 2006)

Steinberg, David. *Grasshopper Pie: All Aboard Poetry Reader*. Illustrated by Adrian C. Sinnott. (Grosset & Dunlap, 2004)

Wong, Janet. *Apple Pie 4th of July*. Illustrated by Margaret Chodos-Irvine. (Harcourt, 2002)

RIBS

Roger Bradfield is not the only one who developed a love for ribs. William Taft, the twenty-seventh president of the United States, is featured in a fictional tale, *The President and Mom's Apple Pie* by Michael Garland, in which the president also enjoys ribs. When Taft arrives in a small town, he smells a delicious aroma. In his quest to find the source of the aroma, the three-hundred-pound president visits Tony's Italian Villa for spaghetti, then Big Ed's Barbecue for ribs, and Mrs. Wong's Hunan Palace. But Taft finally finds that the aroma is that of the cooling apple pie being baked by the narrator's mother. Now no one knows for sure if President Taft enjoyed ribs, but we do know that he enjoyed a lot of different foods and that he did get out and about the country while he was president, so Garland's story is based on probability but not actual facts. We know, too, that Taft had a gander for a pet and that shortly before he became president, spare ribs and "native pig" were among the cheapest meat available at 15 cents a pound.

Ribs—Country Style

One of Roger Bradfield's favorite foods is ribs. This recipe was developed to be cooked in a crock pot. It's the type of cooking that would allow Bradfield to spend his time drawing and painting.

Ingredients

- 2–3 pounds country-style boneless pork ribs
- 1 tablespoon vegetable oil
- 1 large onion, sliced thickly (about 1/4 inch thick)
- 1 bottle of your favorite barbeque sauce, or use recipe below

Trim the fat from ribs, and brown them in the oil with onion slices.

Place in a crock pot and pour your favorite barbeque sauce over the ribs. Or use this savory country sauce.

Country Sauce

- 1/3 cup low sodium soy sauce
- 1/2 cup tomato ketchup
- 1 tablespoon prepared mustard
- 3 tablespoon brown sugar
- 2 cloves garlic, minced
- Dash black pepper
- 2 tablespoon apple cider vinegar
- 1 teaspoon celery seed

Cook on low setting for 8 to 10 hours, or on high for 4 to 5 hours.

Serves 4 to 6.

Selected Books by Jolly Roger Bradfield

Benjamin Dilley's Lavender Lion. (Rand McNally, 1968)

Benjamin Dilley's Thirsty Camel. (Rand McNally, 1967)

The Flying Hockey Stick. (Rand McNally, 1966; Purple House Press, 2005)

Pickle-Chiffon Pie. (Rand McNally, 1967; Purple House Press, 2004)

There's an Elephant in the Bathtub. (Albert A. Whitman, 1964)

Pickle-Chiffon Pie

There are no pickles in the pie (just a few bits on the top), but it is a lovely shade of green.

Ingredients

Pie shell: Purchase or prepare a 9-inch graham cracker pie shell or 6 individual graham cracker pie shells.

- 2 envelopes Dream Whip® Whipped Topping Mix
- 3 cups cold milk
- 2 packages pistachio (4-serving size) pudding mix (or if pistachio flavor is not desired, use 2 packages of vanilla pudding and add several drops of green food coloring to make a pale-green pudding)
- Sweet pickle relish for garnish

Instructions

In a large mixing bowl, prepare whipped topping mix with 1 cup of the milk as directed on package. Set aside.

Prepare the pudding mixes, with a reduced amount of milk—2 cups. Beat at high speed for 2 minutes, scraping the bowl occasionally. Fold whipped topping mix into the prepared pudding mix. Spoon the whipped cream-pudding mix into pie shell or into individual pie shells and smooth. Garnish with one teaspoon of sweet pickle relish (for 9-inch pie shell) or 1/8 teaspoon (for individual pie shells). Chill at least 4 hours.

Pickles, Pickles, Pickles!

Barrett, Judi. *Pickles to Pittsburgh*. (Aladdin, 2000)

Bradfield, Jolly Roger. *Pickle-Chiffon Pie*. (Purple House Press, 2004)

Kennedy, Frances. *The Pickle Patch Bathtub*. Illustrations by Sheila Aldridge. (Tricycle Press, 2004)

Nolen, Jerdine. *Lauren McGill's Pickle Museum*. Illustrated by Debbie Tilley. (Silver Whistle, 2003)

Pearson, Mary. *Pickles in My Soup*. Illustrated by Tom Payne. (Children's Press, 2000)

Terban, Marvin. *In a Pickle And Other Funny Idioms*. (Clarion, 1983)

Marlene Targ Brill—Corn Bread

Marlene Targ Brill

Birthday: September 27

Favorite place: National Women's Art Museum in Washington, D.C.

Favorite foods: cheesecake

Family:

  Spouse—Richard Brill

  Daughter—Alison

Home:

  Childhood—Chicago, Illinois

  Now—Chicago suburb

"Who gets the corn bread?" asked little Milton.

"Any friend who may pass our way," answered his mother, smiling."

—From *Allan Jay and the Underground Railroad* by Marlene Targ Brill

Marlene Targ Brill has several favorite places—her cozy little office; the woods along the Continental Divide near both Colorado Springs and Banff; and the National Women's Art Museum in Washington. When Marlene Targ Brill was growing up in Chicago, she thought all great artists were "dead white men," mostly from Europe. When she first visited the National Women's Art Museum, she was overwhelmed with pride and emotion. The museum displayed every style of art from around the world and through the ages—all executed masterfully by women. Brill is an amateur artist and, for years, has taken watercolor classes. Learning about art is an important avocation for her. Brill also enjoys learning about other things as well—many of her books are built on research she has done to learn about a specific topic that interests her.

Jabicove Smazenky

Children in Poland, Czech Republic, Ukraine, and Mexico are often left snacks by the "tooth mouse." This tradition and others are found in Tooth Tales from around the World. *Jabicove smazenky (apple fritters) might have been a snack left for Czech children.*

Ingredients

- 6–8 apples (All-purpose apples such as Granny Smith, Rome Beauty, Fuji, and Jonagold, as well as many others, produce good results.)
- 2 cups powdered sugar
- 4 eggs, beaten
- 2 tablespoons melted butter
- 2/3 cup milk
- 2 tablespoons sugar
- 1/2 teaspoon salt
- 2 cups flour
- Oil or butter for frying

Core and slice the apples into 3/4-inch-thick slices. Pat the slices dry; sprinkle with powdered sugar. Put aside. Make a batter of the eggs, butter, milk, sugar, salt, and flour. Put a thick layer of oil or butter in a frying pan and heat over medium high until very hot. Dip each apple slice into the batter (coat completely) and add to the hot oil, turning once. Cook until fritters are golden brown. Drain and slightly cool the cooked fritters on a paper towel. Dust them with powdered sugar and serve warm.

(A similar sweet was wrapped in paper and left by the tooth mouse in exchange for a lost baby tooth.)

Signature Recipe—Marlene Targ Brill

Corn Bread

During the Civil War, corn bread was very popular—it was cheap and versatile. The differences between Northern and Southern corn bread were the type of corn meal used. Northerners used flint yellow, Southerners used Boone County white and flavoring. Another difference is that Northerners generally preferred sweets and added molasses to theirs; Southerners preferred salty foods and often fried the bread with cracklins (bacon fat).

This cornbread is a northern version. During the Civil War, the bread would have been baked in a hearth or over a fire.

- 1 1/2 cups corn meal
- 1 tablespoon sugar
- 1 teaspoon salt
- 1 teaspoon baking soda
- 2 eggs, well beaten
- 2 cups buttermilk
- 1 1/2 tablespoons melted butter

Put a 12-inch iron skillet to heat in a 450 degree F oven. Sift all the dry ingredients together and combine with eggs and buttermilk. Stir in the butter, keeping it smooth. Remove pan from the oven and pour batter into the hot, well-greased frying pan. Bake at 450 degrees F for 30 minutes.

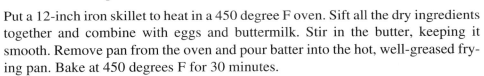

Our favorite family food while I was growing up was cheesecake. One favorite recipe, with lots of graham crackers for a crust and sprinkled on top, was handed down from my paternal grandmother. My Grandmother added raisins to her cheesecake. She made a cheesecake about every Sunday for our visits with her and my grandfather. The other favorite cheesecake recipe that was my mom's creation was made with cocoa powder, both in the crust and sprinkled on top. A holiday dinner wasn't complete without a sampling of this treat.

Today, my family doesn't share my desire for cheesecake. My daughter prefers healthier, or seemingly healthier, fare. A house favorite is pumpkin oatmeal cookies. We throw in everything, lots of nuts and dried fruits of all persuasions.

—Marlene Targ Brill

Pumpkin Oatmeal Cookies

Mix together:

- 2 cups cooked fresh or canned pumpkin
- 4 egg whites, lightly beaten

Cream into the pumpkin mixture:

- 2 cups brown sugar, packed
- 2 teaspoons baking soda
- 2 teaspoons cinnamon
- 1 teaspoon nutmeg
- 1 teaspoon cloves

Gradually add:

- 3 cups unbleached flour
- 6 cups rolled oats (oatmeal)
- 1 cup raisins (optional)
- 1 cup dried apricots (optional)
- 1 cup dried cherries (optional)
- 1 cup chopped walnuts (optional)

If mixture seems too dry, add a tablespoon or two of milk to make the dough the appropriate consistency. Drop by tablespoons onto a lightly greased cookie sheet, spaced two inches apart. Bake for 15 minutes or until the cookies begin to firm. Remove from oven and cool.

Selected Books Written by Marlene Targ Brill

Allen Jay and the Underground Railroad (On My Own History series). Illustrated by Janice Lee Porter. (Carolrhoda, 1993)

Barack Obama: Working to Make a Difference. (Lerner, 2006)

Bronco Charlie and the Pony Express (On My Own History series). Illustrated by Craig Orback. (Carolrhoda, 2004)

Doctors. (Lerner, 2005)

Margaret Knight: Girl Inventor. Illustrations by Joanne Friar. (Millbrook Press, 2001)

Marshall Major Taylor: Bicycle Superstar. (Twenty-First Century Books, 2007)

Minnesota. Maps and illustrations by Christopher Santoro. (Benchmark Books, 2004)

Tooth Tales from around the World. Illustrated by Katya Krenina. (Charlesbridge, 1998)

Veterans Day. Illustrations by Qi Z. Wang. (Carolrhoda Books, 2005)

More Tooth Books

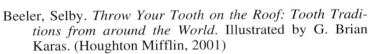

In addition to reading *Tooth Tales from around the World,* read these books about teeth.

Beeler, Selby. *Throw Your Tooth on the Roof: Tooth Traditions from around the World.* Illustrated by G. Brian Karas. (Houghton Mifflin, 2001)

Davis, Katie. *Mabel the Tooth Fairy and How She Got Her Job.* (Harcourt, 2003)

Keller, Laurie. *Open Wide: Tooth School Inside.* (Henry Holt, 2000)

Luppens, Michel. *What Do the Fairies Do with All Those Teeth?* Illustrated by Phillipe Beha. (Firefly, 1996)

Underground Railroad

When young Allen Jay—*Allen Jay and the Underground Railroad*—decided to help a young runaway, his mother was already preparing corn bread for a food basket. It was the middle of the day, and Allen wondered how his mother knew. Such things were not discussed, however, even among family members, lest someone would have to lie if asked directly or if a younger sibling (Milton, for example) would let some information slip to someone outside of the family. Read more about the Underground Railroad in the books that follow.

Hopkinson, Deborah. *Sweet Clara and the Freedom Quilt.* (Knopf, 1993)

Hopkinson, Deborah. *Under Quilt of Sky.* (Atheneum/Anne Schwartz Books, 2002)

Levine, Ellen. *If You Traveled on the Underground Railroad.* (Scholastic, 2003; reissue)

McGovern, Ann. *Wanted Dead or Alive: The True Story of Harriet Tubman.* (Scholastic, 1991; reissue)

Ringgold, Faith. *Aunt Harriet's Underground Railroad in the Sky.* (Knopf, 1992)

Schroeder, Alan. *Minty: A Story of Young Harriet Tubman.* Illustrated by Jerry Pinkney. Dial, 1996.

Tobin, Jacqueline. *Hidden in Plain View: A Secret Story of Quilts and the Underground Railroad.* (Anchor Publications, 2000)

Vaughan, Marcia. *The Secret to Freedom.* (Lee & Low Books, 2001)

Winter, Jeanette. *Follow the Drinking Gourd.* (Knopf, 1988)

Craig Brown—Potato Salad

After everyone was done eating potato salad, Jell-O, hot dogs, and all the other food, the watermelon was cut and S'mores were made over the open fire.

—Craig Brown

Craig McFarland Brown

Birthday: September 4

Favorite place: Any place in the country near a barn or on a farm

Favorite foods: great salads, blueberry pie

Family:

Son—Cory

Daughter—Heather (married to Michael)

Home:

Childhood—Fairfield, Iowa

Now—Colorado Springs, Colorado

Craig Brown was born and raised in Iowa. His books are most often reflective of his Iowa roots. As a boy, he loved exploring the countryside on his bike and enjoyed solitary days in the nearby fields. He also enjoyed the get-togethers held in her grandmother's backyard. Says Craig, "As a young boy growing up in a small farming community with my mother, sister, and grandmother, many of our summers were spent at my grandmother's house—less than a block from where I lived with my mother and sister. The exciting part for me was when we would have bonfires in the backyard of my grandmother's house. All the neighbors within a block or two would bring dishes to pass, but it was my grandmother's chocolate bars that everyone waited for with eager anticipation.

"Adults sat in the spacious backyard while the kids ran about the neighborhood playing hide-and-seek, horseshoes, and croquet.

"The evening was wonderful and added to the magical quality of an eight-year-old's grandmother and her backyard."

Brown left Iowa to attend art school in Wisconsin and soon developed an interest in stippling—the use of dots to create the lines and shapes within a picture. For over a decade he worked in advertising while developing his illustrative portfolio. Finally a trip to New York and a workshop with Uri Schulevitz helped him secure a contract for his first children's book. He was asked to illustrate a text by another author. It took it several more years to earn a contract where he would both write and illustrate the book. His first book, *Patchwork Farmer,* was his first full-fledged entry into the world of children's books. One of his recent books, *Barn Raising,* features an Iowa Amish community and its efforts to raise a neighbor's barn after a fire.

After *Barn Raising* was published, Brown turned his research westward as he became interested in the mail-carrying mules that still deliver mail to the south rim of the Grand Canyon to the residents on the Havasupai Indian Reservation. The story of the trek in and out of Supai is the subject of his next book.

When the neighbors gathered in Brown's grandmother's backyard the food always included potato salad. This is a favorite recipe for potato salad Iowa style.

Iowa Style Potato Salad

Hard boil six eggs. Peel and slice the eggs. Reserve 6–8 slices for garnish. Chop the remaining eggs and set aside.

Peel 5 pounds red-skinned potatoes and cut into 3/4-inch pieces.

Boil potatoes in salted water until they are just tender (about 12 minutes).

Have ready and set side:

- 1/4 cup juices from jar of sweet pickles

While the potatoes are cooking, whisk together the following ingredients:

- 1 cup mayonnaise
- 1/2 cup buttermilk
- 5 teaspoons Dijon mustard
- 1 teaspoon sugar
- 3/4 teaspoon ground black pepper
- 3/4 cup chopped red onion
- 3/4 cup chopped celery
- 1/2 cup chopped sweet pickles

As soon as the potatoes are tender, drain them and transfer to large bowl. Add the chopped eggs. Drizzle pickle juices over potatoes and eggs and toss gently.

Cool just enough to allow the potatoes to firm up. Pour mayonnaise mixture over potatoes and eggs. Toss gently to blend. Season to taste with salt. Adding the mayonnaise mixture while the potatoes are still warm will allow the sauce to soak into the potatoes and will result in a more savory taste. Place in a serving bowl, and garnish with the sliced eggs. Sprinkle with paprika (optional). Add a few sprigs of parsley. Cover and put in refrigerator to chill. (Can be made 8 hours ahead.)

Makes 10–12 servings.

POTATOES IN AMERICA

Potatoes have only been popular in western U.S. culture for a few hundred years. The Incas in Peru are the first known culture to use potatoes in their diet. Inca potatoes had purple skins and yellow insides. The Incas grew them, ate them, and revered them. In the early 1500s, European explorers discovered the food, and soon the potato was a staple on Spanish ships of exploration. However, the general population did not embrace the potato so readily. It was suspected of carrying all types of diseases and of causing deformities and other conditions. As early as 1589, Sir Walter Raleigh, known for his expeditions to the Americas, planted potatoes on his estate near Cork, Ireland. Slowly the potato came to be accepted all over Europe and in the Western Hemisphere. Ireland embraced the potato so completely that when the crop became diseased, it caused such a serious famine that half of Ireland's population fled to the United States or Australia between the years of 1845 and 1849. By 1872, potato production in the United States had become associated with the state of Idaho. Today McDonald's makes billions each year selling French-fried potatoes, and potato chips are America's favorite snack.

Booklist

Selected Books Written and/or Illustrated by Craig Brown

Barn Raising. (Greenwillow, 2002)

How to Raise a Raisin? Text by Pam Muñoz Ryan. (Charlesbridge, 2003)

My Barn. (Greenwillow, 1991)

Patchwork Farmer. (Greenwillow, 1989)

Potatoes, Potatoes, Everywhere

Coy, John. *Two Old Potatoes and Me*. Illustrated by Carolyn Fisher. (Knopf, 2003). A father and his daughter plant two potatoes hoping that new ones will grow.

Jones, Charlotte Foltz. *Mistakes That Worked*. Illustrated by John O'Brien. (Doubleday, 1994). Includes story of George Crum and his invention of the potato chip.

Lied, Kate. *Potato: A Tale from the Great Depression*. Illustrated by Lisa Campbell Ernst. (National Geographic, 1997; 2002 paperback)

Stowell, Penelope. *The Greatest Potatoes*. Illustrated by Sharon Watts. (Jump at the Sun, 2005). Tells how George Crum invented potato chips.

Tang, Greg. *Math Potatoes: Mind-Stretching Brain Food*. Illustrated by Harry Briggs. (Scholastic, 2005)

Taylor, Gaylia. *George Crum and the Saratoga Chip*. Illustrated by Frank Morrison. (Lee & Low, 2006)

More Farm Books

In addition to reading Craig Brown's books, read these books about farms and farm animals.

Aliki. *Milk: From Cow to Carton*. (HarperTrophy, 1992)

Bell, Rachel. *Cows*. (Heinemann, 2000)

Gibbons, Gail. *Farming*. (Holiday, 1988)

Gibbons, Gail. *Milk Makers*. (Atheneum, 1985)

Gibbons, Gail. *Pigs*. (Holiday House, 2000)

Rendon, Marcie R., and Cheryl Walsh Bellville. *Farmer's Market: Families Working Together*. (CarolRhoda, 2001)

Thomas, Eric. *A Farm through Time*. (DK Publishing, 2001; 2007)

Don Brown—Chopped Liver

My mom ..., despite her roots that stretched back to County Cork, learned to master several Jewish dishes like brisket and chopped liver for my father.

—Don Brown

For twenty-five years, Don Brown has been making his living by drawing. In his childhood, he copied the cartoon work of famous cartoonists, including Shel Silverstein. His other childhood activities were no different from other boys at the time: sports, television, teasing girls, and aggravating his parents. After high school, he headed off to St. Lawrence University, where he earned a history degree. He then became a movie theater manager, a professional clam digger, and a waiter. Although still interested in history, it had not prepared him for a career.

A chance meeting with an art director took him into the world of magazine and advertising illustration. Brown had no formal training and little knowledge of the publishing world, but he persisted and overcame those handicaps. In 1980, he began working as a freelance illustrator. Meanwhile, he married and became the father to two daughters.

In the mid-1980s, he contributed some articles to a children's history magazine, *Cobblestone*. He wanted to read stories to his daughters about strong heroic women. It was difficult to find stories that fit that description so he set out to write one. His first biographical book, *Ruth Law Thrills a Nation,* was published in 1993. That marked his entrance into the world of children's books. Since then, he has written about heroic women as well as some men who have made a mark in history—some well known and others less so. Many of his books have been recognized with awards and included on numerous lists of recommended titles.

Kid Blink Beats THE WORLD is set in the late 1800s where the newsboys live in the tenements and try to contribute to their family's meager existence by selling newspapers. While the more affluent residents of New York would have savored New York cheesecake, those who lived in the tenements would have been fortunate if they would have had cinnamon bread sticks.

Cinnamon Bread Sticks

- 3/4 bag or about 16 slices of leftover (stale) bread
- 2 sticks butter, melted
- 1 cup sugar
- 1 tablespoon cinnamon

Cut bread into slices (about 1/2 inch wide) and place on a baking sheet. Brush melted butter (melted lard would have been used in the poorest of households) over bread. Mix sugar and cinnamon and sprinkle over bread. Bake 15 minutes at 250 degrees F. Turn strips over and brush butter and sprinkle sugar and cinnamon mixture on the second side. Bake another 15 minutes and then turn over twice more (every 15 minutes). Bake a total of 1 hour.

Mary Anning

Mary Anning (1799–1847) was raised in the Lyme Regis area on the southern shores of Great Britain. The cliffs at Lyme Regis are known for being rich in spectacular fossils from the seas of the Jurassic period. Mary's father, Richard, was an occasional fossil collector. When his early death left the family in poverty, his wife Mary began to collect fossils, sell them, and support her family with the income. In the mid-1800s, the daughter Mary, whose eye was very keen, took charge of the fossil business. Although her work made very important contributions to paleontology in its early days as a scientific discipline, recognition of her life's work was limited until recently.

Books about Mary Anning

Atkins, Jeannine. *Mary Anning and the Sea Dragon.* Illustrated by Michael Dooling. (Farrar, Straus & Giroux, 1999)

Brown, Don. *Rare Treasure: Mary Anning and Her Remarkable Discoveries.* (Houghton Mifflin, 1999)

Goodhue, Thomas. *Curious Bones: Mary Anning and the Birth of Paleontology.* (Morgan Reynolds, 2002)

Walker, Sally M. *Mary Anning: Fossil Hunter* (On My Own Biographies). Illustrated by Phyllis V. Saroff. (Carolrhoda, 2000)

"I'm finishing a novel about the 1890s and Manhattan's Lower East Side, a brimming, boiling stew pot of different immigrant cultures. The protagonist is a boy of Irish and Jewish parents who tries to make his way through the poverty and violence of the densely crowed streets. To earn money, he falls in with a notorious gangster and embarks on an adventure among the Lower East Side's angels, odd balls, schemers, and mugs.

"His blended heritage is one that I have personal knowledge [of], being a child of Irish and Jewish lines as well. From my own experience, I know cultures can intersect oddly in one family, and over the years, I've collected stories of other mixed families."

—Don Brown

Brown's Irish mother mastered several Jewish dishes like brisket and chopped liver. However, she made some changes. For example, when she prepared chopped liver, she substituted mayonnaise for schmaltz—chicken fat. When that change was revealed to traditionalists, the change left them "open-mouthed." Brown's favorite, however, was his mother's "latkes, glorious fried potato pancakes served with applesauce."

Chopped Liver

- 1/2 pound chicken livers
- Kosher salt
- 2 tablespoons vegetable oil
- 2 medium-sized onions, chopped, and sautéed
- 1 egg (hard-boiled)
- 3–4 teaspoons mayonnaise (or rendered chicken fat [schmaltz])
- salt and pepper

Chopped Liver Sandwiches

Line a broiler pan with foil. Place 1/2 pound chicken livers on the pan. Sprinkle lightly with kosher salt. Place the pan (with the liver) on the oven rack about 3 inches from the heat. Broil 3 minutes or until the top is light brown. Turn the livers over and broil 3 minutes more or until cooked through and color is no longer pink; cut to check. Cool livers slightly.

Heat 2 tablespoons vegetable oil in a heavy skillet, on medium heat. Add 2 medium-sized onions, chopped, and sauté. Stir often and cook for 15–20 minutes or until golden brown.

Use a fork to mash the chicken livers and one hard-boiled egg (or, if you wish to have the mixture smoother and less coarse, use a food processor), mixing all together with 3–4 tablespoons mayonnaise (if you are a traditionalist, use rendered chicken fat [schmaltz]). Salt and pepper (use freshly ground black pepper) to taste.

Chopped liver can be kept, covered, 2 days in refrigerator. Serve cold, on rye bread, either open face or as sandwich with a top and bottom piece of bread.

Selected Books Written by Don Brown

Across a Dark and Wild Sea. (Roaring Brook, 2002)

Alice Ramsey's Grand Adventure. (Houghton Mifflin, 1997)

American Boy: The Adventures of Mark Twain. (Houghton Mifflin, 2003)

Bright Path: Young Jim Thorpe. (Roaring Brook Press, 2006)

Far beyond the Garden Gate: Alexandra David-Neel's Journey to Lhasa. (Houghton Mifflin, 2002)

The Good Lion. Adapted from Beryl Markham's autobiography. (Houghton Mifflin, 2005)

Kid Blink Beats THE WORLD. (Roaring Brook, 2004)

Mack Made Movies. (Roaring Brook, 2003)

Odd Boy Out: Young Albert Einstein. (Houghton Mifflin, 2004)

One Giant Leap: The Story of Neil Armstrong. (Houghton Mifflin, 2001)

Rare Treasure: Mary Anning and Her Remarkable Discoveries. (Houghton Mifflin, 1999)

Ruth Law Thrills a Nation. (Houghton Mifflin, 1993)

Uncommon Traveler: Mary Kingsley in Africa. (Houghton, 2000)

A Voice from the Wilderness: The Story of Anna Howard Shaw. (Houghton Mifflin, 2001)

Joseph Bruchac—Blueberry Pancakes

Bill's cook always prided himself on making the lightest flapjacks in creation. They were so light that a hummingbird's tongue would have weighed less than a stack of 'em piled two foot high.

—From "Bill Greenfield's Breakfast"
in *Hoops Snakes, Hide Behinds and Side-Hill Winders: Tall Tales from the Adirondacks* by Joseph Bruchac (The Crossing Press, 1991)

Joseph Bruchac

Birthday: October 16

Favorite place: The house where I was raised by my grandparents (where I still live) and the ninety-acre wood around it (which are placed in a conservation easement)

Favorite foods: Blueberry Pancakes

Family:

Spouse—Carol

Sons—James and Jesse

Home:

Childhood—Greenfield Center, New York

Now—Greenfield Center, New York

Joseph Bruchac was born and raised in Greenfield Center, New York. His ethnic background includes English and Slovak blood, but it is his Abenaki ancestry that his maternal grandparents, who raised him in the Adirondack mountain foothills, nurtured. His Abenaki grandfather, Jesse Bowman, worked as a lumberjack in the Adirondack mountains; the little town of Greenfield Center was known for its part in the American tall tale tradition. In fact, says Bruchac, "Greenfield Center bears the name of a famous 'liar' Bill Greenfield." Bruchac's grandfather also ran a little general store where "neighbors would gather around the potbellied stove and swap yarns. Food figured in a good many of those stories."

Bruchac earned an undergraduate degree from Cornell University and advanced degrees (including a Ph.D.) from Syracuse University and from the Union Institute of Ohio. He and his younger sister, Margaret, along with Joseph's two sons, James and Jesse, are involved in many projects that seek to preserve all aspects of the Abenaki culture—including language, music, traditions.

With his wife, Carol, Bruchac founded the Greenfield Review Literary Center and the *Greenfield Review Press*. Bruchac's more than seventy books include an autobiographical account, *Bowman's Store: A Journey to Myself*. This autobiography integrates Native American myths and legends with accounts of events that shaped his boyhood. Bruchac's story illuminates much about the history of the Abenaki people.

A full-time writer and storyteller , Bruchac tells traditional tales of the Adirondacks and the Native peoples of the Northeastern Woodlands at conferences and at schools and libraries throughout the United States and in Europe.

Bill Greenfield—a Tall-Tale Logger

Joseph Bruchac tells the story "Bill Greenfield's Breakfast" in *Hoop Snakes, Hide Behinds and Side-Hill Winders: Tall Tales from the Adirondacks*. Bill Greenfield prided himself in having a cook who knew his business and who was proud of his work. On this particular day, the cook was up thirty-six hours before dawn and cooked up an enormous breakfast meal. And even though the cook's flapjacks were so light that "a stack of flapjacks two feet high would have weighed less than a hummingbird's tongue," they weren't light enough for the loggers, who complained that they were overly heavy on that particular day. The next morning, the cook decided to rectify the situation, and he mixed and remixed the batter until the flapjacks were so light that each time he put one of the flapjacks on the platter the flapjack just floated up and out of the cookhouse window. The loggers got to taste the fluffy light flapjacks only after old Greenfield used up ten boxes of shells during his efforts to shoot down the flapjacks. After picking out the buckshot, the loggers enjoyed the finest and lightest flapjacks that they had ever tasted.

Carol's Extra-Light but Not Gravity Resistant Pancakes

Joseph Bruchac's wife Carol has a recipe for blueberry pancakes made with blueberries picked from the Bruchac's very own bushes. Carol's pancakes might not float in the air, but they are extra-light.

- 1 egg
- 2 tablespoons Canola oil
- 1 cup of buckwheat pancake mix (such as Hansford, Ployes, or Maple Farm)
- 1/4 cup half and half or milk
- 2 tablespoons maple syrup
- 3/4 to 1 cup water, depending on how thick you want your pancakes
- 3 handfuls of home grown blueberries, fresh or frozen

Mix all ingredients. Cook on a pre-heated greased grill. Makes 18-20 pancakes.

Signature Recipe—Carol Bruchac

THE HISTORY OF PANCAKES

A pancake is a thin, flat cake, made of batter and baked on a griddle or fried in a pan. As early as the Song dynasty in China (fourth century B.C.), people were eating pancakes. One of the first, a "spring pancake" was a thin pancake made of ground rice and filled with vegetables and meat.

The pancake has a very long history and was featured in cookbooks as far back as 1439. During medieval times, pancakes appeared in the Near East; later they showed up in Europe. Over the next few hundred years, the pancake evolved in various forms. Old English pancakes were mixed with ale. German pancakes were leavened with eggs, served very thin, and topped with jam or jelly. During the sixteenth and seventeenth centuries, the pancake became a very popular item with both the rich and the poor in Holland.

Other cultures have enjoyed variations— crisp lentil pancakes (India), buckwheat blini (Russia), delicate crepes (France), tortillas (Mexico), and pancakes made of corn or potatoes. The Dutch had *pannekoeken,* made with wheat flour, with the batter poured over sliced baked apples or cooked bacon and baked in the oven. The pancakes are served with a thick pancake syrup not unlike molasses syrup.

During the 1920s and early 1930s, a restaurant proprietor, Monsieur Joseph, created the French crepes Suzette—a very thin rolled-up pancake. He provided the crepes to a theater troupe in London when the script called for the actors to eat crepes during a specific scene. Eventually diners at the Savoy Hotel in London feasted on the French Crepe. Pancakes became so popular that on Shrove Tuesday, the day before Lent begins, the English used all their supplies of eggs, milk, butter, and other fats, along with sugars and spices, to make stacks and stacks of pancakes. This helped them rid their kitchen of items forbidden during the observance of Lent. In some English localities, Shrove Tuesday was even referred to as Pancake Day.

In the late 1930s, Henri Charpentier, a French chef, brought the recipe for his crepe Suzette with him when he emigrated to the United States. He is credited with popularizing the French pancake in America. At first they were served with butter, sugar, and citrus juice or liqueur. But Americans soon were using maple-flavored syrup and filling them with savory fruits or even chocolate chips. Today pancakes are served in many varieties, including the common buttermilk pancakes, called flapjacks, buttercakes, griddle cakes. Tortillas, crepe Suzettes, and the Dutch version of apple *pannekocken* are popular in many homes (and restaurants).

Apple Pannekoeken

Joseph Bruchac grew up in Upstate New York among the Abenakis and many French residents. In a more southern part of the state, what is now known as New York City was settled by the Dutch. A traditional pancake served by the Dutch is the apple pannekoeken. *Here is a recipe.*

- 1 Jonathan or Granny Smith apple, sliced
- 2 tablespoons butter
- A short cup flour (about 7/8 of a cup)
- 5 eggs
- 1 cup skim milk
- 1 tablespoon vanilla
- Dash of salt
- Fruit for topping: sliced bananas, kiwi, strawberries, blueberries, peaches, mangoes, or whatever is in season.

Preheat oven to 420 degrees F. Prepare 4 small 8-inch ramekins, or one large pie pan by lightly buttering the bottom of the pans. Sauté apples in a buttered skillet until soft, and spread the soft apples on the bottom of the pans. Mix until well blended the eggs, flour, milk, vanilla, and salt. Pour the blended mixture over the apples and back in the oven for 25–30 minutes or until lightly browned. Remove from over and slide the *pannekoeken* onto a serving plate. Sprinkle with powdered sugar, top with fresh fruits, and sprinkle again with powdered sugar. Makes 3–4 servings.

Selected Books Written by Joseph Bruchac

Hidden Roots. (Scholastic, 2004)

Hoops Snakes, Hide Behinds and Side-Hill Winders: Tall Tales from the Adirondacks. Illustrated by Tom Trujillo. (The Crossing Press, 1991, out of print)

Jim Thorpe's Bright Path. Illustrated by S. D. Nelson. (Lee & Low, 2004)

Many Nations: An Alphabet of Native America. Illustrated by Robert F. Goetzl. (Scholastic, 2004)

Navajo Long Walk: The Tragic Story of a Proud People's Forced March from Their Homeland. Illustrated by Shonto W. Begay. (National Geographic Society, 2002)

Pocahontas. (Harcourt, 2003)

Rachel Carson: Preserving a Sense of Wonder. Illustrated by Thomas Locker. (Fulcrum, 2004)

Sacajawea: The Story of Bird Woman and the Lewis and Clark Expedition. (Scholastic, 2001)

Turtle's Race with Beaver. With James Bruchac. Illustrated by Arianne Dewey and Jose Aruego. (Dial, 2003)

Betsy Byars—Chocolate Mayonnaise Cake

Betsy Byars

Birthday: August 28

Favorite place: the beach

Favorite foods: popcorn

Family:

Spouse—Ed Byars

Son—Guy

Daughters—Laurie Myers, Betsy Duffey, and Nan Byars (Daughters Laurie and Betsy are both writers, and each have collaborated with Betsy Byars in producing a couple of story collections.)

Home:

Childhood—Charlotte, North Carolina

Now—on an airstrip in Seneca, South Carolina

"Later I'm going to make my famous mayonnaise cake—it's the best thing you ever ate—you can't even taste the mayonnaise—and take it over. I'm going to put candles on it and silver Decorettes—the works."

—From *The Pinballs* by Betsy Byars

Betsy Byars's writing career began when she and her husband, Edward, were living in Illinois while Ed attended graduate school. At first it was articles; then she began to write books for children. When her children went off to school, Betsy would sit down and write.

For many years, the Byars family lived in West Virginia. Edward taught at West Virginia University and Betsy wrote. Later the family moved to Clemson, South Carolina. Betsy's own experiences and the experiences of her children became seeds for stories. During all of these years, Betsy and her husband Edward spent summers flying. While still living in Illinois, they became interested in soaring—high-class soaring—and over a period of thirty-five years they continued their flying adventures. At first Betsy flew with her husband; but in 1984 she obtained her own pilot's license. Now Edward has retired and the couple has moved to Seneca, South Carolina. The top floor of the house is Betsy's office. The bottom level of their home is a hangar, and the two of them can taxi out and fly off right from their home.

Popcorn Balls

One of Betsy Byars's favorite foods is popcorn. Here's a popcorn ball recipe that might please others who share her love of popcorn.

Prepare 5 quarts popped corn. (The amount of unpopped corn you will need varies as different corn yields various amounts depending on how well it pops. You can usually count on 1 cup of unpopped corn producing 5 cups of popped corn, or maybe more.)

Put popped corn in a large pan and set aside.

Boil together without stirring until thermometer registers 260 degree F on a candy thermometer

- 1 1/2 cups water
- 1/2 cup white corn syrup
- 2 cups sugar

When the mixture reaches 260 degrees F, add:

- 1/3 teaspoon salt
- 1/3 teaspoon white vinegar
- 1 tablespoon vanilla (substitute other flavoring for 1 teaspoon of the vanilla if desired)

Let boil to 264 degrees F.

Gradually pour the syrup onto the popcorn, using a spoon all of the time to turn corn that it may be evenly coated. Shape into balls (the size of baseballs), and let stand in a cold place until brittle.

Optional: if you want colored popcorn balls add a few drops of food coloring to the water.

"One of my daughters came home from a sleepover with the news that they had made the best cake in the entire world. 'Do you have plenty of mayonnaise?' she asked. I didn't have much hope for the results, but the cake was great, very moist as you might imagine. For years nobody ever made a chocolate cake without checking the supply of mayo. When Carlie is going to make a birthday cake in *The Pinballs,* there's really only one recipe worthy of the occasion."

—Betsy Byars

Chocolate Mayonnaise Cake

Sift together and set aside (dry ingredients):

- 2 cups all purpose flour
- 1/2 cup cocoa
- 1 1/2 teaspoons baking soda
- 1/4 teaspoon salt

Cream together:

- 1 cup sugar
- 3/4 cup mayonnaise
- 1 cup water
- 1 teaspoon vanilla

Add dry ingredients to the creamed mixture; stir until well blended. Pour batter into greased and floured layer cake pans (or a 9 x 13 inch pan). Bake at 350 degrees F for about 25 minutes. Test with a toothpick; if the toothpick comes out clean, the cake is done. Can also test by touching the top of the cake lightly; when it springs back to the touch, it is done.

Signature Recipe—Betsy Byars

Selected Books Written by Betsy Byars

Black Tower: A Herculeah Jones Mystery. (Viking Juvenile, 2006)

Boo's Dinosaur. Illustrated by Erik Brooks. (Henry Holt, 2006)

The Golly Sisters Go West: (I Can Read Book Series, Level 3). Illustrated by Sue Truesdell. (HarperCollins, 1999; reprint)

Keeper of the Doves. (Putnam, 2002)

King of Murder: A Herculeah Jones Mystery. (Viking Juvenile, 2006)

Little Horse on His Own. Illustrated by David M. McPhail. (Henry Holt, 2004)

Me Tarzan. Illustrated by Bill Cigliano. (HarperCollins, 2000)

My Dog, My Hero. Text by Betsy Byars, Laurie Myers, and Betsy Duffey. Illustrated by Loren Long (Henry Holt, 2000)

The Pinballs. (HarperCollins, 1987, paperback)

The SOS File. Text by Betsy Byars, Laurie Myers, and Betsy Duffey. Illustrated by Arthur Howard. (Henry Holt, 2004)

The Summer of the Swans. (Viking, 1970)

Foster Children

In Betsy Byars's *The Pinballs,* Carlie feels like she is bounced around like a pinball. She has no say in what happens—and here she is stuck in a foster home with Harvey and Thomas J; but all three set out to take control of their own world. Other characters have other experiences as children in foster situations.

Blackwood, Gary L. *Shakespeare Stealer.* (Puffin, 2000, paperback)

Byng, Georgia. *Molly Moon Stops the World.* (HarperCollins, 2004)

Byng, Georgia. *Molly Moon's Incredible Book of Hypnotism.* (HarperCollins, 2003)

Hobbs, Will. *Maze.* (HarperCollins, 1999, paperback)

Levine, Gail Carson. *Dave at Night.* (HarperCollins, 2001, paperback)

Pelzer, Dave. *The Lost Boy: A Foster Child's Search for the Love of a Family.* (Health Communications, 2004); the second book in an autobiographical trilogy: *A Man Named Dave* (Plume, 2000, Book 3) and *A Child Called "It": One Child's Courage to Survive* (Health Communications, 1995—Book 1)

Snicket, Lemony. *The Grim Grotto: Book the Eleventh* (A Series of Unfortunate Events). Illustrated by Brett Helquist (HarperCollins, 2004); a book in a series about the plight of the three Baudelaire orphans.

Steatfeild, Noel. *Dancing Shoes.* (Bantam Doubleday Dell, 1994; reprint)

Stephanie Calmenson—Apple Cake

Stephanie Calmenson with her chocolate- dappled dachshund, Harry, at their favorite apple stand. Photo by Ronnie J Schultz © 2005

© 2005, Ronnie J. Schultz

Stephanie Calmenson

Birthday: November 28

Favorite place: Any beach

Favorite foods: Apples. I like cold, crisp apples or anything made with apples: Apple pie, apple sauce, apple strudel, apple crisp, apple stuffing, apple pancakes ... You get the idea.

Family:

> **Spouse—Mark Goldman**
>
> **Dad—Kermit Calmenson, His 90th birthday—January 28, 2007.**
>
> **Pet—Harry, a two-year-old long-haired, chocolate-dappled dachshund. Harry stars in *May I Pet Your Dog*. Harry's favorite food is ... *practically everything*! (especially apples).**

Home:

> **Childhood—Brooklyn, New York**
>
> **Now—Manhattan, New York**
>
> **on an airstrip in Seneca, South Carolina**

The Panda Palace opened
At six one night.
All the tables were ready,
The room was just right.
As the diners arrived,
They were graciously greeted.
Mr. Panda himself
Helped each one get seated.

—From *Dinner at the Panda Palace* by Stephanie Calmenson

Growing up in Brooklyn, New York, Stephanie Calmenson wrote pen pal letters to a friend on the other side of the world and sent friends and family letters from camp. She wrote to companies and magazines to let them know what she thought of their publication or product. She wrote and wrote. She earned an education degree and taught early childhood grades in the New York Public Schools. In 1976, forced out of teaching by citywide budget cuts, she joined Doubleday and Company. It was during her work at Doubleday that she embarked on a graduate program in education. During a children's literature course, she discovered her love for picture books, and during a course in writing for children, she began a kind of writing different from that of her childhood days. She began to write stories.

Stephanie's very first story was accepted for publication, and she has been writing children's books ever since. She has more than 100 books in publication—most written under her own name—but she has coauthored several anthologies with her friend Joanna Cole and has authored still other books using a pseudonym, Lyn Calder.

57

Calmenson has written books featuring pandas, a vain principal, dogs, bunnies, and other animals, always addressing childhood issues, and almost always with humor. She has retold folklore, created quirky versions of old favorites, and collected riddles and tales that amuse young readers.

One of her first books came about when Calmenson overhead a child diner telling his mother that he was going to ask for a "table for two." The idea for a counting book came to mind and soon Calmenson had the start for one of her best-known books, *Dinner at the Panda Palace*.

Animals, looking forward to eating a sundry of food, came into the palace, and when the restaurant was filled with elephants, hyenas, penguins, bears, and other animals numbering fifty-five in all, a lone mouse arrived. Was there room? Mr. Panda invited her in and sat her down and served her cheese because "No matter how many,/No matter how few./There'll always be room/At the palace for you." In a second book, *Birthday at the Panda Palace,* Mr. Panda invites the mouse back for a celebration of Mouse's birthday and gives Mouse a surprise gift.

Other favorites include the vain school principal Mr. Bundy, who appears in a modern-day spoof on Hans Christian Andersen's *The Emperor's New Clothes*. The popularity of that book spawned a companion title, *The Frog Principal,* this one a parody on the Grimm's tale of "The Frog Prince." When the magician, Marty Q. Marvel, visits the school and entertains the students with his magic act, they all get more than they bargained for when Mr. Bundy is accidentally turned into a frog. But Mr. Bundy does not let his life as a frog interfere with his duties as a principal.

Selected Books Written by Stephanie Calmenson

Birthday at the Panda Palace. Illustrated by Doug Cushman. (HarperCollins, 2007)

Dinner at the Panda Palace. Illustrated by Nadine Bernard Westcott. (HarperCollins, 1991)

The Frog Principal. Illustrated by Denise Brunkus. (Scholastic, 2001)

Good for You!: Toddler Rhymes for Toddler Times. Illustrated by Melissa Sweet. (HarperCollins, 2001)

Kindergarten Kids: Riddles, Rebuses, Wiggles, Giggles and More! Illustrated by Melissa Sweet. (HarperCollins, 2005)

Perfect Puppy. Illustrated by Thomas F. Yezerski. (Clarion, 2001)

The Principal's New Clothes. Illustrated by Denise Brunkus. (Scholastic, 1989)

Rosie, A Visiting Dog's Story. Photographs by Justin Sutcliffe. (Clarion Books, 1994)

Shaggy, Waggy Dogs (and Others). Photographs by Justin Sutcliffe. (Clarion Books, 1998)

The Teeny, Tiny Teacher. Illustrated by Denis Roche. (Scholastic, 1998)

Welcome, Baby! Baby Rhymes for Baby Times. Illustrated by Melissa Sweet. (HarperCollins, 2002)

Apple Streusel Muffins

Preheat oven to 425 degrees F. Grease 12 muffin cups.

Sift together, in a large bowl:

- 2 cups flour
- 1/2 cup sugar
- 3 teaspoons baking powder
- 1 teaspoon salt

With a pastry blender, cut in, until mixture is crumbly

- 1/2 cup solid stick butter or margarine

Reserve 1/2 cup of the mixture for the streusel topping.

Into the main portion of the butter and flour mixture, stir in:

- 2 cups peeled and chopped apples
- 1/2 teaspoon grated lemon rind
- 1 beaten egg
- 2/3 cup sour milk (if you don't have sour milk, add 1 teaspoon lemon or vinegar to the sweet milk and let stand until it curdles)
- Stir lightly until mixture is moist.
- Spoon batter into 12 greased muffin cups.

Streusel Topping:

- Topping mixture (reserved from process above)
- 1/4 cup chopped walnuts
- 2 tablespoons brown sugar
- 1/2 teaspoon grated lemon rind
- Mix and sprinkle over batter in each muffin cup.

Bake in a 425 degree F oven for 20 minutes or until a toothpick comes out clean when inserted in the center. Serve warm.

Dinner at the Panda Palace is a book about self-esteem, hospitality and … food. Elephant eats peanut butter and jelly sandwiches, the penguins eat fish; lions and hyenas eat meat; giraffes eat leaves; pigs eat corn; bears eat bread and honey; hen and chicks eat seeds; peacocks eat snails; monkeys eat bananas; and the mouse eats cheese. Author Stephanie Calmenson says, "I like all of these foods, including snails. But the recipe I am going to share is a recipe made with apples because 'I LOVE apples.' The recipe is for a delicious cake my husband Mark bakes." Perhaps, just perhaps, this cake will show up in *Birthday at Panda Palace* as the birthday cake for Mouse. Check Doug Cushman's illustrations to see what kind of cake he makes for Mouse.

Mark's Apple Cake

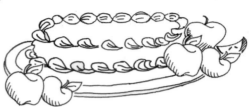

- 1 1/2 cups vegetable oil
- 2 cups sugar
- 3 eggs
- 3 cups flour
- 1 teaspoon each of salt, cinnamon, and baking soda
- 1 teaspoon vanilla
- 3 large red delicious apples peeled, cored and thickly sliced (3–4 cups)
- 1 cup chopped walnuts
- 1 cup raisins optional

Preheat oven to 350 degrees F.

Beat oil and sugar in electric mixer while assembling dry ingredients. Add eggs and vanilla to oil and sugar mixture and beat until creamy. Sift together dry ingredients and stir into batter. Turn mixture into buttered and floured 9-inch angel food pan. Bake 1 hour and 15 minutes or until done (when a toothpick comes out dry). "Frost" with low-fat whipped topping and, if desired, pipe a decorative border of whipped topping around the edge; or serve with a scoop of vanilla or cinnamon ice cream.

Signature Recipe—Stephanie Calmenson

Booklist

Apples, Apples, Apples!

There are many varieties of apples. One variety, the red delicious, originated in Iowa when a seedling was found in 1895; another seedling found almost a century earlier in Ontario (1796) by John McIntosh was the beginning of the McIntosh apple. The Stayman apple came from a Kansas Winesap apple in 1966. The history of various varieties of apples can be an interesting research journey. Historians believe that seeds and apple trees were brought to American (from England) as early as 1629 by John Endicott, one of the early governors of Massachusetts Bay Colony. John Chapman, known as Johnny Appleseed, is often credited for taking the seeds west (as far as the Ohio River valley), although pioneers and Native Americans certainly took seeds and planted them as they moved into new areas and went farther west. Read these books about the history and production of apples.

Cheripko, Jan. *Brother Bartholomew and the Apple Grove.* Illustrated by Kestutis Kasparavicius. (Boyds Mills Press, 2004)

Gibbons, Gail. *Apples.* (Holiday House, 2000)

Gibbons, Gail. *The Seasons of Arnold's Apple Tree.* (Voyager, 1988)

Hall, Zoe. *The Apple Pie Tree.* Illustrated by Shari Halpern. (Blue Sky Press, 1996)

Keller, Kristin Thoennes. *From Apples to Applesauce.* (First Fact Books, 2005)

Maestro, Betsy. *How Do Apples Grow?* Illustrated by Giulio Maestro. (HarperCollins, 1993)

Mayr, Diane. *Out and About at the Apple Orchard* (Field Trips). Illustrated by Anne McMullen. (Picture Window Books, 2002)

Wong, Janet. *Apple Pie Fourth of July.* Illustrated by Margaret Chodos-Irvine. (Harcourt, 2002)

Zagwyn, Deborah Turney. *Apple Batter.* (Tricycle, 1999)

Elisa Carbone—Polenta

Photo Credit: Sharon Natoli

One of the fondest memories from my childhood is of my grandfather, Nonno Mario, standing at the stove, stirring a big pot of polenta (cornmeal mush) with a sawed off wooden broom stick.

—Elisa Carbone

Elisa Carbone

Birthday: January 2

Favorite place: Mountains of West Virginia

Favorite foods: Fried polenta

Family:

    Spouse—Jim Casbarian

    Son— Daniel

    Daughter—Rachel

Home:

    Childhood—Virginia

    Now—Maryland and West Virginia

Elisa Carbone's grandfather, Nonno Mario, stirred big pots of polenta with a sawed off broomstick—Elisa says, "that was the way his mother used to stir the polenta back in Italy when he was growing up." Both of Carbone's grandparents emigrated from Italy. More than forty of Elisa Carbone's cousins still live in a tiny northern Italian town of Castelletto d'Orba, a town where Elisa has stayed, sometimes for several months at a time. When Elisa's grandparents came to the United States they brought with them their memories of a favorite food—polenta.

"[While my grandfather was making the polenta,] my grandmother, Nonna Marcella, would have been at the counter chopping onions, parsley, tomatoes and chicken for the chicken cacciatore [we would later eat], served over steaming plates of golden polenta. And whenever my grandparents spent the night, they would make sure there was leftover polenta for breakfast. Fried in butter until it was crispy, with maple syrup on top, it was *heavenly*.

"Nonno Mario and Nanna Marcella both grew up poor, barefoot, and hungry in Italy around the turn of the century. They ate polenta every day—and not much else. (They had no chicken cacciatore to put on top, but sometimes they had a little cheese or a spoonful of tomato sauce.) I could tell that when they introduced me and my brothers and sister to polenta, that they were proud of this food that had kept them alive and healthy through those difficult times.

"When I began researching my novel. *Stealing Freedom,* I was fascinated to learn that slaves in nineteenth-century America also subsisted on polenta, except that it was called corn-meal mush. A typical topping, if they were lucky enough to have a garden, was steamed greens. They also sometimes fried it, in fatback instead of butter. In fact, in the opening scene of *Stealing Freedom,* Ann Maria Weems and her brother, Addison, are sneaking up the hill to feed slabs of fried cornmeal mush to the chained slave catcher dogs. This is something they did in order to make friends with the fierce dogs, just in case they ever needed to try to escape."

> *"Let's just do it quick so we can get back." The smell of the fried cornmeal mush in her apron made her stomach grumble for its own supper. She broke the slab of mush in two and gave half to Addison....*

> *Ann ran the last few steps to the fence. One hound lunged at her, the other at Addison beside her. She thrust the cornmeal mush toward the sharp teeth and glowing eyes.* (From *Stealing Freedom*)

"When I researched the lives of the Jamestown settlers for my novel *Blood on the River: James Town 1607,* I again found cornmeal mush being used as a staple food. The Algonquian Indians—the tribe of Chief Powhatan and his daughter Pocahontas—provided corn to the settlers in Jamestown. Over and over again, this corn saved the settlers from starvation. The Indians added water to the ground corn, cooked it in clay pots, and called it *hominy.* Often fish, venison, or oysters were added to make a stew. Hominy is a little different from polenta because the corn is processed with lye and not as finely ground, but it is the same idea.

"Polenta, cornmeal mush, hominy—it has kept people from going hungry for thousand of years. And it is about he best thing I've ever tasted, especially when you put it in the fridge overnight, slice it, fry it in butter and put some maple syrup on top."

Elisa Carbone's first piece of fiction was published in 1992, and she has continued to write ever since. Her historical fiction titles have dealt with feral children, women in the West, slavery, the settling of Jamestown, and the civil war. She has turned her historical research into novels and picture books.

Selected Books Written by Elisa Carbone

Blood on the River: Jamestown 1607. (Viking, 2006)

Last Dance on Holladay Street. (Random House, 2005)

Night Running: How James Escaped with the Help of His Faithful Dog. Illustrated by E. B. Lewis. (Knopf, 2007)

The Pack. (Viking, 2003)

Sarah and the Naked Truth. (Cloonfad Press, 2006)

Starting School with an Enemy. (Cloonfad Press, 2005)

Stealing Freedom. (EMC/Paradigm, 2003)

Storm Warriors. (Knopf, 2001)

Corn, Corn, Corn!

More than seven thousand years ago, people in central Mexico cultivated a wild grass, teosinte. The kernels on the cobs were small and widely spaced and individually covered by their own floral parts (similar to oats and barley). The cob readily broke into small fragments. Native Americans continued to cultivate the grain for thousands of years. About one thousand years ago, the crop spread throughout North and South America, first in the southwestern United States and then to the eastern woodlands and present-day North American, as well as, south to the Peruvian coast. The Tainos on the Northern Antilles Islands called the crop *mahis* (maize)—"source of life."

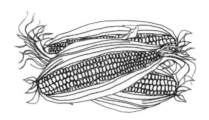

When Europeans arrived in the Americas, they were introduced to maize by the Native Americans. English and German settlers referred to the crop as "corn"—their generic term for an edible grass crop. They distinguished it from other grains by calling it "Indian corn." Maize or corn was an important food among the Native Americans. They already had numerous ways to prepare it that they shared with the settlers. Corn was made into bread, porridge, soup, fried corn cakes, and pudding. Corn soon became a staple for the Pilgrims and other settlers as well.

Today the most common types of corn are

- Flint corn (Indian corn that has a range of colors from white to red)
- Dent corn (field corn, used primarily as livestock feed and for industrial purposes)
- Sweet corn (people food—on the cob, frozen, or canned)
- Popcorn (a type of flint corn)

Corn is used as food and for many industrial products and processes, too.

Corn!

Aliki. *Corn Is Maize*. (HarperTrophy, 1987)

Fussell, Betty. *The Story of Corn*. (University of New Mexico Press, 2004; for older readers)

Rhoads, Dorothy. *The Corn Grows Ripe*. (Puffin, 1993)

Chicken Cacciatore

In Italian *cacciatore* means "hunter" and is term used for simmering. Cacciatore is chicken simmered in a well-seasoned tomato sauce, "hunters style."

Cut up 2 1/2 to 3 pounds of boneless chicken into 1-inch pieces. Set aside.

Then in a large skillet, over medium heat, cook:

- 2 medium sized onions, chopped in 1-inch or smaller pieces
- 2 cloves of garlic, minced
- 2 tablespoons cooking oil

When the onions are tender, remove the onions and hold. Add more oil to the skillet if needed, and in the same skillet brown the chicken pieces for about 15 minutes.

Add the onions back into the skillet and then add:

- 1 (8 ounces) can tomatoes, undrained
- 1 medium green pepper, cut into 1-inch pieces
- 1 (2½-ounce) jar sliced mushrooms, drained
- 1 or 2 bay leaves
- 2 teaspoon dried oregano or basil
- 1/2 teaspoon dried rosemary, crushed
- 1 teaspoon salt
- 1/4 teaspoon pepper

Cover and simmer for 30 minutes. Stir in wine and cook uncovered over low heat for about 15 minutes longer or until chicken is tender, turning occasionally. Skin off fat and discard bay leaves. Transfer chicken and sauce to serving dish. Serve with hot cooked pasta. Makes 4 servings.

WHAT IS POLENTA?

Cornmeal can be ground coarse, medium, or fine. Finely ground cornmeal is most often used for making cornbread and other baked goods. The medium or coarsely ground cornmeal is used for polenta (or cornmeal mush). Cornbread and other baked goods are made with regular cornmeal.

Polenta, a northern Italian dish, is best known as golden-yellow cornmeal mush, usually eaten hot, flavored with butter and cheese, or topped with a sauce. Often polenta is prepared, cooled until firm, then sliced and pan-fried to a golden brown.

Polenta or Cornmeal Mush

- 1 pound or slightly more of coarsely ground cornmeal (consistency of fine-to medium-grained sand, not flour)
- 2 quarts boiling water (have more handy)
- A heaping teaspoon of salt

Use a 5-quart cooking pot and put in the water and salt. When the water comes to a boil, gradually add the corn meal in a stream—the water should not stop boiling. Stir constantly with a wooden spoon to keep lumps from forming. As the mush thickens, continue stirring, for about a half hour. The more you stir, the better the polenta will be—when it is finished cooking it should have the consistency of firm mashed potatoes. Add additional boiling water if necessary. The polenta is done when it peels easily off the sides of the pot.

Eat fresh as a side dish to stews or meat dishes, or pat into a loaf shape and cool until the polenta is firm. Slice and fry, until golden brown, in butter or bacon fat. Serve hot with maple syrup.

Nancy Carlson—Cupcakes with Pink Frosting

Nancy Carlson

Birthday: October 10

Favorite place: Boundary waters in Minnesota and Canada

Favorite foods: Cookies, cookies, and more cookies. I also love pasta of all kinds.

Family:

Spouse—Barry McCool

Sons— Patrick McCool (1985), Michael McCool (1988)

Daughter—Kelly McCool (1983)

Home:

Childhood— Edina, Minnesota

Now—Bloomington, Minnesota

I should have a recipe for cupcakes with pink frosting because I draw cupcakes with pink frosting in many of my books. Cupcakes represent "Life Is Fun."

—Nancy Carlson

After Nancy graduated from Minneapolis College of Art, she began her first job: dusting children's books and helping customers in the Walker Art Center's gift shop. Her fascination with the children's books resulted in her decision to submit some of her sketches to a local publisher. She spent a year or longer contacting publishers and working on two books authored by other authors before she was offered a contract to create her own book. In 1982, *Harriet's Recital* was published by CarolRhoda. Four more books about Harriet were published that same year. Nancy has created more than thirty-five books, many of them starring Louanne, Harriet, or Loudmouth.

Her books are often described as optimistic and upbeat. Warm and fuzzy animal characters—dogs, cats, pigs, and even frogs—along with her young child characters struggle with a variety of childhood problems and fears. Childhood fears are resolved, and problems are solved with reasoning and good humor. Carlson's cartoon-like style complements the energy-filled stories.

Cookies, Cookies, Cookies!

One of Nancy Carlson's favorite foods is cookies—cookies, cookies, and more cookies. People did not always eat cookies. Cookies as a food originated in Rome sometime around the third century B.C., and they were called *bis coctum* meaning twice baked. The *bis coctum* had no sugar added and was more like what the English might call a biscuit and what those in the United States would call a cracker.

Bis coctum is the origin of the word "biscuit." The small, sweet cakes, similar to our present-day cookies, probably originated in the geographic region of India or Persia around the seventh century. That may have been because that's where sugar was first cultivated. The *bis coctum* became a way to allow cereal grains to be stored over a long period of time. Because it was a convenient food, it became part of the diet of sailors and soldiers. Later, explorers who discovered various spices on their travels during the sixteenth and seventh centuries helped transform the cookie from a convenience food to a sophisticated snack. When the *bis coctum* arrived in Holland, the Dutch added sugar and called their creations *koekje,* meaning "little cake." Later the Dutch brought their *koekje* to America, and in the eighteenth century, the word became "cookie."

By the end of the eighteenth century, cookie factories were common in England and France, and later in America.

100 Days of School

On the hundredth day of school, celebrate by asking each student to bring 100 items: 100 buttons, 100 toothpicks, and so forth. Perhaps someone will bake 100 soft black walnut molasses cookies. In addition to Carlson's *Henry's 100 Days of Kindergarten,* read these titles:

Kasza, Keiko. *The Wolf's Chicken Stew.* (Putnam, 1987)

Medearis, Angela. *The 100th Day of School.* Illustrated by Joan Holub. (Scholastic, 1996)

Rockwell, Anne. *100 School Days.* (HarperCollins, 2002)

Slate, Joseph. *Miss Bindergarten Celebrates the 100th Day of Kindergarten.* Illustrated by Ashley Wolff. (Penquin Putnam, 1998)

Wells, Rosemary. *Emily's First 100 Days of School.* (Hyperion, 2000)

Black Walnut Molasses Cookies

Make your own cookies using this age-old tested recipe. This recipe yields 100 cookies for 100 days or 100 children. (You'll need a big mixing bowl for this.)

Cream together:

- 2 teaspoons pure vanilla extract
- 1 teaspoon black walnut extract
- 3 3/4 cups (7 1/2 sticks) butter, at room temperature
- 3 cups dark brown sugar, firmly packed
- 3 large eggs
- 3/4 cups molasses

Add these spices and blend thoroughly:

- 3 tablespoons baking soda
- 3/4 teaspoon salt
- 2 1/4 teaspoons ground ginger
- 1 tablespoon ground cinnamon
- 1 1/2 teaspoons ground cloves

Gradually add:

- 6 cups all-purpose flour
- 2 cups chopped black walnuts

Continue blending the wet ingredients with the flour and walnuts. Beat with an electric mixer for 2 minutes, scraping the sides of the bowl a few times.

Divide the dough in half. Wrap each portion of dough in waxed paper and chill for 1 hour. Preheat oven to 350 degrees F with the rack in the center position. Roll the chilled dough into 1-inch balls and place 2 inches apart on a lightly greased and floured baking sheet or a baking sheet lined with baking parchment. Bake until the tops are set, 12 to 15 minutes. Cool on wire racks. Makes about 100 soft black walnut molasses cookies.

"Life Is Fun" Cupcakes with Pink Fluffy Icing

Beat until light and fluffy:

- 1 cup (2 sticks) unsalted butter, softened
- 1 1/2 cup granulated sugar

Add one at a time, beating after each addition:

- 3 eggs

Add and beat:

- 1/4 cup applesauce
- 2 teaspoons vanilla extract

Add and beat:

- 2 teaspoons baking powder
- 1/2 teaspoon salt

Alternately add and beat on low until blended:

- 3 cups flour
- 1 cup milk

Gently stir in

- 1/4 cup confetti sprinkles.

Preheat oven to 350 degrees F. Line 24 muffin tins with paper liners or butter and flour the tins; set aside. Make the batter as directed above.

Spoon the batter into the prepared muffin tins, 3/4 full.

Bake until the tops of the cupcakes are springy when lightly pressed with fingertip but not quite golden, 20 to 22 minutes. Cool 15 minutes in the muffin tin on a wire rack.

Pink Fluffy Icing

- 2 cups confectioners' sugar
- 1/4 cup butter, softened
- 3 tablespoons cream
- 1 teaspoon vanilla extract
- 1 teaspoon red food color

Beat ingredients together until fluffy. Frost each cupcake, swirling the frosting on the top.

Selected Books Written and Illustrated by Nancy Carlson

First Grade, Here I Come. (Viking Juvenile, 2006)

Get Up and Go. (Viking Juvenile, 2006)

Harriet and George's Christmas Treat. (Carolrhoda, 2001)

Henry's 100 Days of Kindergarten. (Viking Juvenile, 2005)

Hooray for Grandparents' Day. (Viking, 2000)

How about a Hug? (Viking, 2001)

I Don't Like to Read. (Viking, 2007)

It's Not My Fault. (Carolrhoda, 2003)

Look Out Kindergarten, Here I Come. (Viking Juvenile, 1999)

Louanne Pig in Making the Team. (CarolRhoda, 2006)

Louanne Pig in the Perfect Family. (Nancy's Neighborhood Series) (CarolRhoda, 2004)

Loudmouth George Earns His Allowance. (Nancy's Neighborhood Series) (CarolRhoda, 2007)

My Best Friend Moved Away. (Viking, 2001)

My Family Is Forever. (Viking, 2004)

Smile a Lot! (Carolrhoda, 2002)

There's a Big, Beautiful World Out There! (Viking, 2002)

Think Big! (Nancy Carlson's Neighborhood) (CarolRhoda, 2005)

Penny Colman—Concoction (Vegetable Stew)

Penny Colman

Birthday: September 2

Favorite place: Organ Pipe Cactus National Monument in the Sonoran Desert, Barnegat Bay, and the Jersey Shore

Favorite foods: apples, milk, mushrooms, broccoli, blueberries, turkey, soups, and stews

Family:

    Sons—Jonathan (married to Katrin; daughter Sophie), David (married to Crystal), Stephen (married to Sarah)

Home:

    Childhood—Born in Denver, Colorado, but grew up in North Warren, Pennsylvania

    Now—Englewood, New Jersey

Shortly after I wrote Rosie the Riveter: Women Working on the Home Front in World War II, *I started creating a concoction that uses lots of vegetables and delights everyone who eats it.*

"What do you call this?" people would ask me.

"Just a concoction," I'd reply. And that was its name until one eater dubbed it:

"Penny Colman's Delicious, Delightful Concoction."

—Penny Colman

Penny Colman is known for her many books focusing on the role of females in history. Her own history begins in Denver, Colorado, where she grew up in a household with three brothers, Vin, Kip, and Jon—the household was noisy. It wasn't until she was seventeen that her sister Cam was born. Since Colman's father, Norman Morgan, was a psychiatrist and for a time worked at a mental institution, the family lived on the institution grounds.

Colman went to college, earned undergraduate and graduate degrees, and became a mother to three boys: first Jonathan, and eleven months later, identical twin sons, David and Stephen. While living in Oklahoma, Colman did some postgraduate work. She says, "For many years, I had large vegetable gardens.... The kindergarten teacher at the nearby school would bring her class on a field trip to my garden. The children would pick lettuce and spinach and pull up some carrots and take them back to school to make a salad."

Penny wrote about another garden in *Girls: A History of Growing Up Female in America,* in which she described the role of the colonial girl in "poking seeds into the ground, chasing away crows, and picking Indian corn, peas, beans, and spinach." In *Rosie the Riveter: Women Working on the Home Front in World War II,* Coleman wrote about the nearly twenty million victory gardens in America—gardens that were producing a third of all vegetables grown in the country.

FUNERAL CUSTOMS

When Penny Colman researched *Corpses, Coffins, and Crypts; A History of Burial,* she found that over the years many customs changed, but one that has seemed to stay is the tradition of taking food to grieving families. "Food," says Colman, "has been a part of burial rituals in all times and cultures." This pie is often served at post-funeral meals.

Funeral Pie

Prepare or purchase pastry for a two-crust nine-inch pie. Set aside.

In a saucepan, bring to boil, reduce heat and simmer for five minutes.

- 2 cups raisins
- 1 cup orange juice
- 1 cup water
- 1 tablespoon lemon juice

Combine the following ingredients and then add to the raisin mixture and cook until mixture thickens (stir as the mixture cooks):

- 1 1/2 cups sugar
- 2 tablespoons cornstarch
- 1 teaspoon allspice
- 1 cup chopped walnuts or other nuts
- 1 tablespoon lemon juice

Line a pie pan with a pastry crust and pour in filling. Cover with the second pie crust and flute or seal the edges by crimping with your fingers or with the tines of a fork. Brush the top of the pie with a bit of milk and sprinkle a tablespoon of sugar onto the top crust. Bake in a preheated oven (425 degrees F) 20 to 25 minutes or until crust is golden brown and filling is bubbly. Let cool before serving. Serve with ice cream or with whipped cream.

Penny Colman's Delicious Delightful Concoction

The Concoction

Penny Colman loves to cook, "especially," she says, "with fresh garden vegetables." With those vegetables, she concocted this recipe, which one of her friends eventually named for her.

Amounts below are suggested amounts only—the concoction can be varied with more or less of any of the ingredients.

- 1 onion
- 1 clove garlic
- 1 package (1–2 pounds) of ground turkey (amount may vary depending on how many you intend to feed)
- Seasonings: salt, rosemary, dill, Worcestershire sauce, Tabasco sauce
- 2 broccoli stems
- 2 carrots
- 2 stems of celery
- 1 cup mushrooms
- 1 16-ounce can of crushed tomatoes
- 1 ear of corn (scrap the kernels from the cob) or 1 can (10 ounces) corn
- 1 handful of fresh spinach
- Wondra or flour

1. Chop one onion and one glove of garlic.

2. Using one tablespoon of olive oil in a large pot, brown the chopped onion and garlic.

3. Add and brown one package of ground turkey. Season to taste using salt, rosemary, dill, Worcestershire sauce, and Tabasco sauce. Use a spoon to chop up and stir the turkey meat. After it is thoroughly brown, remove any liquid.

4. Peel the stem of two broccoli stems and chop (stem only, save the flowerets for later), chop two carrots and two stems of celery.

5. Clean and slice a cup of mushrooms.

6. In a frying pan, brown the carrots. Once the carrots are partially cooked, add the celery, and a bit later add the broccoli and mushrooms.

7. Then add the browned carrot mixture to the turkey mixture in the pot. Add broccoli flowerets and a handful of chopped green beans.

(Continued)

8. Add enough water to submerge the meat and vegetables. Add a large can of crushed tomatoes and simmer for about an hour.

9. Taste the broth and add more seasonings to taste. Cut the kernels from an ear of corn, or add a small can of corn. Simmer about 15 minutes more.

10. Wash a handful of fresh spinach and slice into strips. Stir the spinach strips into the concoction.

11. Thicken the broth with Wondra or two tablespoons of flour dissolved in a 1/4 cup cold water.

Serve with tortilla chips. Some will make a bed of chips and spoon the concoction on top of the chips. Others will ladle the concoction into a bowl and break chips on top of the concoction or use the chips as a spoon with which to eat the thickened concoction.

Signature Recipe—Penny Colman

 Booklist

Selected Books Written by Penny Colman

Adventurous Women: Eight True Stories about Women Who Made a Difference. (Henry Holt, 2006)

Corpses, Coffins, and Crypts: A History of Burial. (Henry Holt, 1997)

Girls: A History of Growing Up Female in America. (Scholastic, 2000)

Rosie the Riveter: Women Working on the Home Front in World War II. (Crown, 1995)

Strike! The Bitter Struggle of American Workers from Colonial Times to the Present. (Millbrook Press, 1995)

Toilets, Bathtubs, Sinks, and Sewers: A History of the Bathroom. (Atheneum, 1994)

Where the Action Was: Women War Correspondents in World War II. (Crown, 2002)

Diane deGroat—Sugar Cookies

[Gilbert takes cookies to his school's Valentine's Day party.] They are heart shaped sugar cookies that his mother had baked. Upon each is written, in icing, "Happy Valentine's Day!" The cookies serve as a peace offering after he had sent nasty Valentines to some of his classmates.

—Diane deGroat (speaking of *Roses Are Pink, Your Feet Really Stink*)

Diane deGroat

Birthday: May 24

Favorite place: My backyard

Favorite foods: Anything with sugar

Family:

Daughter: Amanda

Home:

Childhood—Belleville, New Jersey

Now—Amherst, Massachusetts

Diane deGroat spent her first years after graduating from Pratt Institute in 1969 working for a book publisher, where she learned all aspects of publishing: layout, book design, and so forth. Eventually she realized that freelance illustrators seemed to be able to set their own work hours, sleep late if they wished, and work at home. That type of life appealed to her, so in 1972 she began her own career as a full-time freelance artist. Now she has written many books and has illustrated more than 115—picture books and novels.

Volunteering in a school library allowed her to hang around a lot of children and helped her come up with ideas for her middle grade series about spunky Annie Pitts. deGroat's Amherst, Massachusetts, home includes a custom studio where she illustrates and writes her books. Although she writes her picture books in longhand and then types the text into a computer, she writes her Annie Pitts books directly on the computer. Usually when she is creating a picture book, she writes the text without considering the illustrations. After the text is completed, she deals with the illustrations. Illustrating a picture book normally takes about three months, but she once completed a book in six weeks.

Selected Books Written and Illustrated by Diane deGroat

Annie Pitts, On Ice. (North-South, 2004)

Brand-New Pencils, Brand-New Books. (HarperCollins, 2005)

Goodnight, Sleep Tight, Don't Let the Bedbugs Bite! (Chronicle/SeaStar, 2002)

Jingle Bells, Homework Smells. (HarperCollins, 2000)

Liar, Liar, Pants on Fire. (Chronicle/SeaStar, 2003)

Lola Hides the Eggs. (HarperCollins, 2004)

Lola's Trick or Treat. (HarperCollins, 2005)

Love, Lola. (Chronicle/SeaStar, 2002)

No More Pencils, No More Books, No More Teacher's Dirty Looks. (HarperCollins, 2006)

Roses Are Pink, Your Feet Really Stink. (HarperCollins, 1996)

We Gather Together, Now Please Get Lost! (Chronicle/SeaStar, 2001)

French Raspberry Dessert

A "red" dessert is very festive for Valentine's Day and other special days, such as July 4th or winter holidays.

Mix:

- 2 packets of graham crackers, crushed
- 1/2 cups melted butter
- 2 tablespoons sugar

Press mixture into a 9 x13 inch baking pan and bake in a 350-degree F oven for 8 minutes. Remove from oven and set aside to cool.

Prepare:

2 packages of Dream Whip as directed on package or use two containers of Cool Whip; set aside.

Mix together

- 1 1/2 cups powdered sugar
- 1 8-ounce package cream cheese (room temperature)

Blend together:

The whipped cream and the cream cheese mixture. Spread mixture over the graham cracker crust. Then cover the whipped cream/cream cheese layer with 2 cans raspberry pie filling (or cherry pie filling—then it would be French Cherry Dessert).

Chill until ready to serve.

There are several legends about the origin of Valentine's Day; its traditions are explained in *Hearts, Cupids, and Red Roses: The Story of the Valentine Symbols* by Edna Barth (Clarion, 2001). Eventually, February 14 emerged as St. Valentine's Day, a day celebrated by sending poems and simple gifts such as flowers. School children exchange Valentine's Day cards with sentiments of love and friendship. Social gatherings and balls are also often part of the festivities.

In the United States, Miss Esther Howland is given credit for sending the first valentine cards. Commercial valentines were introduced in the 1800s, and now the date is very commercialized. The town of Loveland, Colorado, does a large post office business around February 14. The concepts of friendship and doing nice things for others are a good idea any time of the year.

Valentine Books

Bond, Felicia. *The Day It Rained Hearts*. (Laura Geringer, 2001)

Brown, Marc. *Arthur's Valentine*. (Little, Brown, 1988)

Bunting, Eve. *Valentine Bears*. Illustrated by Jan Brett. (Clarion, 1984)

Devlin, Wende. *Cranberry Valentine*. Illustrated by Harry Devlin. (Simon & Schuster, 1986)

Hopkins, Lee Bennett. *Good Morning to You, Valentine: Poems for Valentine's Day*. Illustrated by Tomie dePaola (Boyds Mill Press, 1993)

Kneen, Maggie. *The Very Special Valentine*. Illustrated by Christine Tagg. (Chronicle, 2004)

Park, Barbara. *Junie B. Jones and the Mushy Gushy Valentine*. Illustrated by Denise Brunkus. (Random House, 1999)

Prelutsky, Jack. *It's Valentine's Day*. Illustrated by Yossi Abolafia (HarperTrophy, 1996)

Roberts, Bethany. *Valentine Mice*. Illustrated by Doug Cushman. (Houghton Mifflin, 2001)

Sharmat, Marjorie Weinman. *Nate the Great and the Mushy Valentine*. (Delacorte, 1994)

Spinelli, Eileen. *Somebody Loves You, Mr. Hatch*. Illustrated by Paul Yalowitz. (Simon & Schuster, 1991)

Diane's Favorite Sugar Cookies

"This," says Diane deGroat, "is my favorite recipe for sugar cookies. [It] makes a lot of cookies!" She suggests that you can cut the recipe in half and still have plenty.

In a mixing bowl cream:

- 1 cup butter
- 2 cups sugar

Beat in:

- 2 eggs

Add:

- 2 tablespoons lemon juice
- 1 tablespoon milk
- 1 teaspoon vanilla
- 1 teaspoon lemon rind

Sift together in another bowl:

- 5 cups flour
- 4 teaspoons baking powder
- 1/2 teaspoons salt

Add flour mixture to creamed mixture slowly. Batter will be thick. Chill overnight.

The next day, preheat the oven to 350 degrees F. Roll half of the dough to 1/4 inch thick. Use heart-shaped (or any shape) cookie cutter to cut cookies. Place on an ungreased baking sheet. Sprinkle with sugar (unless you plan to frost them).

Bake for 10–12 minutes. The cookies shouldn't get brown, except around the edge. Remove from baking pan and cool on a rack. If not topped with sugar, frost with your favorite frosting, and decorate as you wish.

Signature Recipe—Diane deGroat

Norah Dooley—Rice

Norah Dooley shares stories about her neighbors and her old neighborhood in Central Square, Cambridge—a neighborhood that has been described as a block like the United Nations.

Norah Dooley

Birthday: July 17

Favorite place: on the beach, by a river, by a pond, feet in a stream looking up through trees or in a city at night outside or in a café, with a double espresso, watching people

Favorite foods: rice—of all descriptions but especially brown rice, basmati rice, wild rice, and arborio

Family:

Spouse—Robert

Daughters: Four daughters

Home:

Childhood—Belleville, New Jersey

Now—Amherst, Massachusetts

Norah Dooley has worked as a waitress, a cab driver, a machine operator, a breakfast cook, a bicycle courier, a burglar alarm monitor, and a substitute teacher—her favorite job. Her first chosen career was painting; now it is storytelling. In 1990, Dooley studied at Lesley College with some of the best storytellers in the area. The following year, a bedtime story she had first told her young daughters became her first book, *Everybody Cooks Rice.* Here is what Norah says about the book:

It was late. Bedtime was long past and our daughters wanted yet another story before sleep. I was out of folk tales, fairy tales, and on the spot stories with the girls as the main characters and I was tired.

"Look," I said. "All the big kids on the block have had their dinners and gone to sleep and you should too."

"Well, oh yeah?" countered my eldest, nearly five years old. "What did they have to eat for dinner?" I remembered a recent block party when everybody brought some variation of rice and beans. 'What if?' I wondered, what if everybody was cooking rice tonight? As I took the girls on a virtual tour of our neighbor's kitchen, the idea for my first picture book, *Everybody Cooks Rice*, was born. I started my journey as "a mom with a good idea" and became a published writer.

—Norah Dooley

Dooley's neighbors come from more than eleven countries and represent European, Asian, Arab, and African cultures. Her first book was soon followed with three other books featuring bread, soup, and noodles.

Dooley spent her early years in New York City on Staten Island, in a rural area where the next-door neighbor raised hundreds of chickens. She and her sister and brother played in the woods—Robin Hood, World War II, and Knights of the Round Table were all games they enjoyed. At age thirteen, the family moved to the Boston area. She eventually earned a fine arts degree from Tufts University and a graduate degree in Creative Arts in Learning from Lesley College. She paints, tells stories, sings, plays fiddle and pennywhistle, and calls contra dances.

Norah Dooley lives in Massachusetts with her husband, Robert, and their four daughters. She continues to visit dozens of schools every year, telling her stories, and introducing young readers and their reading-cooking adults to the families and recipes of her neighbors.

RICE

Rice is grown all over the world. In *Everybody Cooks Rice,* nine types of rice dishes are featured—rice and black-eyed peas from Barbados, biryani from India, *nucc cham* from Vietnam, and from Italy— *risi e bisi.* But there are at least 120,000 strains of rice, and just as many ways to prepare it. Rice originated in the fourth century in Asia (northern Thailand), where it was a species of grass. Around the eight or ninth century, the plant had made its way to Europe; by the seventeenth century, it had been introduced in the United States. Hawaii was growing and exporting rice in the nineteenth century. In 1887, Hawaii exported thirteen million pounds.

Eventually, the rice production declined in Hawaii. But despite the decline of growers in Hawaii, Americans consume an average of 22 pounds of rice a year—and the amount seems to be increasing. Worldwide, most of the rice is eaten in the country where it grows. Less than 5 percent of rice is imported or exported to other countries. Of the rice that is exported, Thailand leads the export market with more than 32 percent of the market. Overall, Asian countries grow and consume more than 90 percent of the rice grown in the world. Chinese rice growers favor the long grain rice, while the Japanese like the more sticky rice and thus used more short grain rice.

Books Written by Norah Dooley

Everybody Bakes Bread. Illustrated by Peter J. Thornton. (CarolRhoda, 1997)

Everybody Brings Noodles. Illustrated by Peter J. Thornton. (CarolRhoda, 2002)

Everybody Cooks Rice. Illustrated by Peter J. Thornton. (CarolRhoda, 1991)

Everybody Serves Soup. Illustrated by Peter J. Thornton. (CarolRhoda, 2000)

Chicken with Pineapple and Rice (Polynesian)

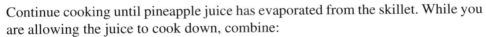

Heat in a large skillet:

- 4 tablespoons peanut oil
- 8 boneless skinless chicken breasts

Cook chicken 3–4 minutes on each side. Add juice from 2 cans (8-ounce) pineapple chunks just before chicken is finished cooking.

Continue cooking until pineapple juice has evaporated from the skillet. While you are allowing the juice to cook down, combine:

- Pineapple chunks from the 2 (8-ounce) cans pineapple chunks
- 2 cups apricot pineapple marmalade
- 4 tablespoons soy sauce

Cook until the sauce is a glaze. While the chicken is cooking, prepare

- 2 cups of rice (we prefer to mix long-grain white and brown); prepare as directed and drain.

Remove the chicken from the heat and serve on top of the rice.

Bread, Bread, Bread!

Norah Dooley also wrote *Everybody Bakes Bread*. Read *Everybody Bakes Bread*, share some other bread books, and invite parents or grandparents to share their bread-baking traditions and recipes.

Badt, Karin Lulsa. *Pass the Bread!* (Children's Press, 1995)

Carle, Eric. *Walter the Baker.* (Simon & Schuster, 1995)

dePaola, Tomie. *Tony's Bread.* (Putnam, 1996)

Ichord, Loretta Frances. *Skillet Bread, Sourdough, and Vinegar Pie: Cooking in Pioneer Days.* Illustrated by Jan Davey Ellis. (Millbrook, 2001)

Keller, Kristin Thoennes. *From Wheat to Bread.* (First Facts Books, 2004)

Kleven, Elisa. *Sun Bread.* (Dutton, 2001)

Morris, Ann. *Bread, Bread, Bread.* Photos by Ken Heyman. (HarperTrophy, 1993)

Paulsen, Gary. *The Tortilla Factory.* Illustrated by Ruth Wright Paulsen. (Harcourt, 1995)

Raspberry-Peach Rice Parfait

- 1 1/2 cup instant rice
- 1 cup fresh raspberries
- 1 cup canned or fresh peaches (sliced and cut into small pieces)
- 1 1/2 cups water
- 16 ounces vanilla yogurt
- 1 cup (more or less) of whipped cream

Bring water to a boil in a small saucepan. Stir in rice, cover, and then remove from heat. Let sit for approximately 5 minutes, until all water is absorbed.

After rice is cooled, stir in vanilla yogurt. Chill for 30 minutes.

Mix all of the peaches and 1/2 cup of the fresh raspberries, reserving a 1/2 cup raspberries for garnish. Chill.

Just before serving, layer yogurt and rice mixture and the peaches in parfait glasses or dessert dishes. Top with a dollop of whipped cream and garnish with raspberries.

Makes 8 servings.

Lois Ehlert—Vegetable Soup

Photo Credit: Lillian Schultz

The first book I both illustrated and wrote was Growing Vegetable Soup. *It was about my garden. I also like to cook.*

—Lois Ehlert

Lois Ehlert began her career in children's books by illustrating stories written by other writers. Even after she began to write her own books, she continued to illustrate books by other authors. Among those books are *Chicka Chicka Boom Boom* by Bill Martin, Jr., and John Archambault (Simon & Schuster, 1989). However, the books in the booklist on page 88 are all written *and* illustrated by Lois Ehlert.

Lois Ehlert

Birthday: November 9

Home:

   Childhood—Beaver Dam, Wisconsin

   Now—Milwaukee, Wisconsin

When Lois Ehlert was creating the illustrations for *Eating the Alphabet: Fruits and Vegetables from A to Z,* she went to her grocery store and purchased fruits and vegetables by the alphabet. On one trip, she would purchase apples, apricots, artichokes; on the next, it would be broccoli, bananas, and other" "B" fruits and vegetables. By the time she got to the "P" page, she was buying potatoes, parsnips, peas, pumpkins, and peppers on the way to the "Y" page with yams and the "Z" page with zucchini. She used the fresh fruits and vegetables as models for her paintings. Then she would photocopy the paintings and use the photocopies to maneuver and create the prototype for each of her alphabet letter collages. Once the composition for each letter was finalized she went back to her paintings and created the final collage.

Lois Ehlert was born and raised in Wisconsin. Her parents encouraged her art activities by giving her wood and scraps of cloth from their projects and a place for her to create. After high school, she entered Layton School of Art. Her first job after art school was as a graphic designer and children's book illustrator. But when she realized that as an illustrator she did not have much control over the color process, she began concentrating on graphic design work. Eventually the techniques used to produce picture books were improved, and Ehlert decided to return to illustrating. While still working as a freelance graphic designer, she created *Growing Vegetable Soup,* a book that combines pictures and words to show the steps involved in growing a vegetable garden.

Ehlert uses collages to create her simple, bold art and sometimes uses actual objects, and cutouts of objects cut from paper. She generally prefers to paint her own paper so that she has just the right color or texture. Many of her books come from bits and pieces in her life. Several of her books focus on growing fruits and vegetables—she has had a garden most of her life. Her book *Hands* is a tribute to her father, who created woodworking projects with his hands and tools. *Nuts to You* came about after a squirrel sneaked into her house through a window. In *Snowballs,* there is one illustration showing a clothesline hung with mittens. She knitted the mittens on either end of the string, and then used them as part of the collage elements. *Hands: Growing Up to Be an Artist,* a thinly veiled account of Ehlert's life, tells the story of a young girl who, encouraged by a father who built with wood and a mother who sewed, grows up to become an artist.

Ehlert lives in Milwaukee where she uses the studio in her home to make art. She has a huge drawing board with large windows nearby. Cabinets and work surfaces are on both sides of the windows. The cabinets hold a multitude of markers, pens, pencils, paints, and colored papers. On top of the cabinets are jars full of brushes, paints, and scissors; a tape dispenser, rubber cement; and a telephone—so she can keep on talking while she works. At the end of the week, the calendar on her desk is spotted with ink and paint splotches.

Selected Books Written and Illustrated by Lois Ehlert

Circus. (HarperCollins, 1992)

Color Farm. (HarperCollins, 1990)

Color Zoo. (HarperCollins, 1989)

Eating the Alphabet: Fruits and Vegetables from A to Z. (Harcourt, 1989)

Feathers for Lunch. (Harcourt, 1990)

Growing Vegetable Soup. (Harcourt, 1987)

Hands: Growing Up to Be an Artist. (Originally published in 1997; rev. Harcourt, 2004)

Leaf Man. (Harcourt, 2005)

Market Day: A Story Told with Folk Art. (Harcourt, 2000)

Nuts to You! (Harcourt, 1993)

Pie in the Sky. (Harcourt, 2004)

Planting a Rainbow. (Harcourt, 1988)

Red Leaf, Yellow Leaf. (Harcourt, 1990)

Snowballs. (Harcourt, 1995)

Top Cat. (Harcourt, 1997)

Under My Nose (autobiography), photographs by Carlo Ontal. (Richard C. Owen, 1996)

Waiting for Wings. (Harcourt, 2001)

Cherry Pie in the Sky

In Pie in the Sky, *Ehlert says, "you will see birds pecking at cherries—and even a raccoon! So, human beings aren't the only ones who eat cherries. I think they are the only ones who make cherry pie, however."* At the end of the book, Ehlert includes a recipe for cherry pie. Here is our version of the best cherry pie in the Midwest.

Ingredients

- 3 cups pitted cherries (tart pie cherries)
  2 tablespoons cornstarch
- 1/4 cup water
- 1/2 cup sugar
- 1/8 teaspoon almond extract
- 2–3 drops red food coloring
- Chopped walnuts (optional)

Set oven to 425 degrees F. Line an 8-inch pan with pie crust. Mix sugar, starch, and water together. In a medium saucepan, heat until the mixture begins to thicken and change from milky in color to clear. Add red food coloring and then add cherries to the sugar mixture and mix gently—do not stir so much that the cherries begin to break or dissolve. Stir in extract. Remove the pan from heat, and cool slightly before pouring it into the pie crust. Cover with the top crust, sealing the edges. Cut slits. Brush the top with milk and sprinkle with sugar. Bake at 425 degrees F for 10 minutes. Reduce heat to 400 degrees F and bake until crust is done, about 30 to 40 minutes.

Serve with ice cream.

One crust variation: Instead of a top crust, sprinkle the top of the cherry filling with crushed walnuts. When serving, garnish ice cream or whipped cream with a sprinkling of crushed walnuts.

Pies

A cherry pie is featured in Ehlert's *Pie in the Sky,* but you'll find apple pies, berry pies, chiffon pies, and even alligator pies in stories by other authors and illustrators. Enjoy any kind of pie and share a story.

Bradfield, Jolly Roger. *Pickle-Chiffon Pie.* (Purple House Press, 2004)

Cazet, Denys. *The Perfect Pumpkin Pie.* (Atheneum/Richard Jackson, 2005)

Jackson, Alison. *I Know an Old Lady Who Swallowed a Pie.* Illustrated by Judith Byron Schachner. (Dutton, 1997)

Lee, Dennis. *Alligator Pie.* (Gardners Books, 2001)

Lindsey, Kathleen D. *Sweet Potato Pie.* Illustrated by Charlotte Riley-Webb. (Lee & Low, 2003)

Moulton, Mark Kimball. *Miss Fiona's Stupendous Pumpkin Pies.* Illustrated by Karen Hillard Crouch. (Ideal's Children's Books, 2004)

Priceman, Marjorie. *How to Make an Apple Pie and See the World.* (Dragonfly Books, 1996)

Spirin, Gennady. *A Apple Pie.* (Philomel, 2005)

Beef Vegetable Soup

In Ehlert's Growing Vegetable Soup, *she includes a recipe for vegetable soup. You might want to use that one or the one that follows, or perhaps you will invent a recipe of your own—with beef or chicken stock and adding the vegetables you like.*

Brown in a skillet:

- 1 pound stew beef, cut into bite-size pieces with 2 tablespoons oil
- Place the browned beef and the following ingredients into a large soup pot:
- 2 packages (10 ounces each) frozen mixed vegetables (or fresh vegetables, cleaned and cut up in small chunks)
- 2 cups beef broth
- 1/4 teaspoon salt, or to taste
- 1/4 teaspoon pepper, or to taste
- 1 1/2 cups water
- 2 medium potatoes, cubed

Bring soup mixture to a boil, reduce heat, and simmer for 1 1/2 hours. Serve with a dollop of sour cream (if desired) and a garnish of cilantro.

Makes 2 quarts.

Jill Esbaum—Cinnamon Rolls

Photo Credit: Mark's Place

Jill Esbaum

Birthday: November 1

Favorite place: family farm, near Dixon, Iowa

Favorite food: cinnamon rolls, of course

Home:

  Childhood—Bluegrass, Iowa

  Now—Dixon, Iowa

The smell of Granny's cinnamon rolls lured me back to the kitchen.

—Jill Esbaum

I am fortunate to have grown up near my maternal grandparents. In retirement, Grandpa was the perfect example of a small town Mr. Fix-it, always tinkering in his old garage on somebody else's radio, lawn mower, or washing machine. Grandma was a whiz in the kitchen. She was one of those people who never flinched when unexpected company dropped by just before mealtime, and she always had a special treat at hand for hungry grandkids. In my first book, *Stink Soup,* the character of Granny is very much like my own grandmother, from her countrified speech patterns to her soft heart. At one point in the story, I wrote, "The smell of Granny's cinnamon rolls lured me back to the kitchen." Even now, a whiff of yeasty cinnamon rolls transports me to Grandma's kitchen, and I can close my eyes and see every detail of the room.

—Jill Esbaum

Growing up in a small Iowa town, Jill Esbaum enjoyed reading comics (*Archie* and *Mad Magazine*) and anything else she could get her hands on—from *Black Beauty* to the Nancy Drew mysteries. She lived a block from her elementary school and next door to her best friend. It was an idyllic childhood. In the summer her family camped and fished, and she played softball. In the winter, fierce snowball fights took place with the neighborhood boys (a group that included her brother). And Jill told stories to anyone who would listen or who she thought might listen.

In many ways, Jill never left that idyll. She and her family operate a farm in Iowa—it's located on a quiet dusty gravel road and is home to fields of corn and soybeans, and hundreds of pigs.

When she began reading books to her two sons and one daughter, she realized how much she missed telling stories. She enrolled in a community college writing course and began telling stories again—this time on paper (or the computer). Now everyday she wakes up knowing that she is doing something she loves doing—writing for young readers.

Jill and her husband Dana have two grown sons, Tyler and Brett, and an almost-grown daughter, Kerri. Jill is a writing instructor and a softball coach, and she is active in church and school events, as well as an active member of the Iowa Chapter of the Society of Children's Book Writers and Illustrators. She still enjoys the memories of her grandmother's cinnamon rolls.

TOMATOES

In Stink Soup, Annabelle offers to help her grandmother make tomato juice during a visit to her grandmother's home after a big tomato harvest, even though she didn't like tomatoes. In fact, she did not look forward to eating anything made with the many tomatoes. But there was a mountain of tomatoes, and of course that meant a lot of tomatoes for cooking and preparing family meals, too. Here's a recipe for salsa that we have found even non-tomato lovers enjoy. Often those who grow tomatoes also raise peppers and onions, but if not, store-bought items can be substituted for home-grown produce.

Although most people consider the tomato a vegetable, it is really a fruit. Tomatoes are grown for their edible fruit. The fruit is usually red to red-orange, but it can also be pink, yellow, green, white, or striped. Tomatoes vary in size from less than one inch to bigger than tennis ball size. We generally think of fruits as something we like, and vegetables as something we have to eat to stay healthy. Tomatoes have a little bit of both. This cake incorporates fruits and nuts—including tomatoes.

Salsa

Ingredients

- 5 large ripe tomatoes, diced and chopped
- 1/4 cup tomato juice
- 2 ripe bell peppers, diced and chopped
- 1/4 cup thinly sliced green onion, chopped
- 1/4 cup chopped fresh parsley or cilantro
- 2 tablespoons lemon or lime juice
- 1/8 teaspoon pepper
- 1 clove garlic, minced
- 1/4 teaspoon salt, or to taste

Combine tomatoes and tomato juice with other ingredients; cover and chill at least 4 hours. Serve with tortilla chips. Makes about 4 cups.

Fruits and Nuts Cake

Ingredients

- 4 ounces (1/2 stick) soft butter or margarine
- 1 cup sugar
- 2 eggs
- 1 teaspoon baking soda
- 1 1/2 cups pureed tomatoes (or a 10-ounce can tomato soup)
- 2 cups sifted all-purpose flour
- 1 teaspoon ground cinnamon
- 1/2 teaspoon ground cloves
- 1/4 teaspoon nutmeg
- 1/2 cup chopped dried apricots
- 1/2 cup chopped dried cherries
- 1/2 cup golden raisins
- 1 large apple, chopped
- 1 cup chopped walnuts or pecans

Preparation:

In a small bowl, stir baking soda into tomatoes and set aside.

Cream together the butter, sugar, and eggs.

Then add tomato mixture into the creamed ingredients. Gradually add flour and the remaining fruits, nuts, and spices. Mix thoroughly. Pour into greased and floured 9 x 5–inch loaf pans (should be enough batter for two loaves). Bake at 325 degrees F for about 50 to 55 minutes or until a toothpick comes out clean when inserted in center. Wrap loaves in foil and refrigerate until ready to serve with a dollop of whipped cream or a scoop of ice cream.

Mississippi Travels

Esbaum's second book, *Steeeeemboat a Comin'*, is a story set in 1867. The fictional account uses verse (and some great vocabulary—"galoots" and "roustabouts") to describe the excitement brought to tranquil towns on the Mississippi as the steamboat moves along the river, stopping now and again. Share Esbaum's book and then enjoy other books about Clemons and the Mark Twain era.

Anderson, William. *River Boy: The Story of Mark Twain.* (HarperCollins, 2003)

Brown, Don. *American Boy: The Adventures of Mark Twain.* (Houghton Mifflin, 2003)

Granny's Cinnamon Rolls

- 4 to 5 cups all-purpose flour, divided
- 1 box (9 ounces) Jiffy brand one-layer white cake mix
- 2 packages (1/4 ounce each) quick-rise yeast
- 1 teaspoon salt
- 1 cup warm water (120–130 degrees)
- 2 tablespoons butter or margarine
- 1/2 cup sugar
- 1 tablespoon cinnamon

In a large mixing bowl, combine 3 cups flour, cake mix, yeast, salt, and warm water. Mix until smooth. Add enough of the remaining flour to form a soft dough. Turn out onto a lightly floured surface. Knead until smooth, about 6–8 minutes. Roll dough into a 9 x 18–inch rectangle. Spread with butter and sprinkle with sugar and cinnamon. Roll dough jelly-roll style, starting with the long end. Slice the roll at 1-inch intervals; place rolls flat on a greased cookie sheets. Cover and let rise in a warm place until doubled, about 15 minutes. Bake at 350 degrees F for 15–18 minutes. Frost, if desired, with your favorite butter cream icing. Yields 18 rolls.

Signature Recipe—Jill Esbaum

Books Written by Jill Esbaum

Estelle Takes a Bath. Illustrated by Mary Newell DePalma. (Henry Holt, 2006)

Ste-e-e-e-eamboat a-Comin'! Illustrated by Adam Rex. (Farrar, Straus & Giroux, 2005)

Stink Soup. Illustrated by Roger Roth. (Farrar, Straus & Giroux, 2004)

Jean Fritz—Hoe Cakes

When George finished his three small hoecakes and his three cups of tea, he was still hungry. And if he was hungry, he thought, what about Washington?

—From *George Washington's Breakfast* by Jean Fritz

Jean Fritz's biographical tales emerge from the pages of American history and have become a touchstone for writers. Her stories about John Hancock, Paul Revere, and other Revolutionary War heroes help introduce readers to the people behind important historical events.

In 1981, interviewer Elaine Edelman from *Publishers Weekly* (July 24, 1981, p. 77) asked Fritz why she never wrote about women. Her response was that she "was not a sociologist." But in 1992, she did begin to write about some of the important women in history. She wrote about George Washington's mother, Harriet Beecher Stowe, and Elizabeth Stanton. Food has seldom been a topic in Fritz's books, but in *George Washington's Breakfast* she and her character, a young boy named George, go on a quest to find out what George Washington ate for breakfast. One of her first books, *The Cabin Faced West,* came about because Fritz discovered that a family story of George Washington eating at the home of her great-great-grandmother, Ann Hamilton, was documented in a diary entry in which Washington mentions that he had "bated" one night at the Hamiltons.

Fritz's research often took her to the sites involved in the story. When her husband, Michael, was living, the family often set off together to explore and discover.

Selected Books Written by Jean Fritz

The Cabin Faced West. Illustrated by Feodor Rojankovsky. (Putnam, 1998; reprint)

George Washington's Breakfast. (Putnam, 1998)

Harriet Beecher Stowe and the Beecher Preachers. (Putnam, 1994)

Leonardo's Horse. Illustrated by Hudson Talbott. (Putnam, 2001)

The Lost Colony of Roanoke. Illustrated by Hudson Talbott. (Putnam, 2004)

Who's Saying What in Jamestown, Thomas Savage? Illustrated by Sally Wern Comport. (Putnam, 2007)

Will You Sign Here, John Hancock? Illustrated by Trina Schart Hyman. (Putnam, 1976; reprint)

You Want Women to Vote, Lizzie Stanton? Illustrated by DyAnne DiSalvo-Ryan. (Putnam, 1995)

Coconut Sorbet

One of Jean Fritz's favorite foods is coconut sorbet, a dish that she says is "not easily obtained." However, if you have an ice cream maker, it is easy to make.

Combine:

- 14 ounces of coconut milk
- 3 to 5 tablespoons sugar
- 1/4 teaspoon vanilla extract
- pinch of salt

Mix all the ingredients well in a large bowl. Freeze in an ice cream maker, following the instructions that came with the icemaker.

Elizabeth Cady Stanton and the Right to Vote

In *You Want Women to Vote, Lizzie Stanton?* Fritz wrote about Elizabeth Cady Stanton and her efforts for women's suffrage. Stanton's contemporaries, many of whom worked in the suffrage movement as well, included Lucretia Mott, Lucy Stone, Susan B. Anthony, Anna Howard Shaw, Amelia Bloomer, Frances Willard, and Elizabeth Blackwell. Read about other suffragists in the following books.

Blackwell, Alice Stone. *Lucy Stone: Pioneer of Woman's Rights.* (University Press of Virginia, 2001)

Corey, Shana. *You Forgot Your Skirt, Amelia Bloomer*! *A Very Improper Story.* Illustrated by Chesley McLaren. (Scholastic, 2000)

Davis, Lucile. *Elizabeth Cady Stanton: A Photo-Illustrated Biography* (Photo-Illustrated Biographies) (Capstone Press, 1998)

Davis, Lucile. *Lucretia Mott: A Photo-Illustrated Biography* (Photo-Illustrated Biographies). (Capstone Press, 1998)

Davis, Lucile. *Susan B. Anthony: A Photo-Illustrated Biography* (Photo-Illustrated Biographies) (Capstone Press, 1998)

Kurtz, Jane. *Bicycle Madness.* Illustrated by Beth Peck (about Frances Willard). (Henry Holt, 2003)

Lickteig, Mary J. *Amelia Bloomer: A Photo-Illustrated Biography* (Photo-Illustrated Biographies). (Capstone Press, 1998)

McCully, Emily Arnold. *The Ballot Box Battle.* (Knopf, 1996)

Sterling, Dorothy. *Lucretia Mott.* (The Feminist Press at CUNY, 1999)

Woolridge, Connie Nordhielm. *When Esther Morris Headed West: Women, Wyoming, and the Right to Vote.* Illustrated by Jacqueline Rogers. (Holiday House, 2001)

ORIGIN OF HOE CAKES

Traditionally hoe cakes were made of cornmeal and resembled a pancake. The name came from the fact that slaves and early colonists cooked the cakes on the blade of a hoe over an open fire. Soldiers sometimes used the blade of their sword. Eventually cooks began to put wheat flour and sugar in the batter, but those cakes would more accurately called cornbread or journey cake (sometimes Johnny cake).

Hoe cakes were eaten at breakfast, as George Washington did, or were served as an accompaniment to a main course at the evening meal. When the cakes were cooked on hoes or hot stones, the cakes were made of a very stiff dough.

Hoe Cakes

Combine these dry ingredients and set aside:

- 2 cups fine stone-ground cornmeal
- 2 teaspoons baking powder, preferably single-acting
- 1 teaspoon salt

In another bowl mix together, until smooth:

- 2 large eggs, lightly beaten
- 2 cups whole milk or buttermilk

Stir the egg and milk mixture quickly into the dry ingredients. Beat as little as possible.

Heat a griddle or cast-iron skillet over medium heat. Once it is hot, brush lightly with shortening. Pour or scoop about two tablespoons of batter onto the griddle, for each hoe cake. Do not crowd the cakes or put them so close that they touch one another.

When the bottoms are browned and air holes appear on the tops (about 3 1/2 minutes) turn the cakes and cook until the second side is browned, another 3–4 minutes.

Once removed from the griddle, keep warm in a 150 degree F oven while the rest of the hoe cakes are cooked. Serve warm with or without butter. Makes about a dozen hoe cakes.

Wendy Anderson Halperin—Dazzling Bread

Photo Credit: Sharron L. McElmeel

I heard on the radio today: Art is making the ordinary into something SPECTACULAR ... or something DAZZLING which may be why I have always made this bread. The very ordinary ingredients: Flour, butter, salt, sugar, and yeast.

—Wendy Anderson Halperin

Wendy Anderson Halperin grew up among the cornfields of Illinois among a family of four children. The children played by Lake Michigan where they sometimes gathered rocks to paint and decorate, at the kitchen table. After her school days in Illinois, she studied art in New York and in California, married and had three children, and became a full-time author and illustrator. She now works between her summer and winter homes—both in Michigan. Her three children are grown and are off on their own. She shares her life with John Mooy—a storyteller and educator. And when she has time, she makes delicious, dazzling bread.

Wendy Anderson Halperin

Birthday: April 10

Favorite place: At my drawing board, listening to a book on tape, finishing some art

Favorite foods: A hearty salad with fresh, crunchy stuff; sometimes fruity, and sometimes with nuts. And homemade bread.

Family:

Spouse: John (storyteller with a kind soul)

Son: Joel (very independent and has my smile)

Daughter: Kale (an artists' artist); Lane (brings joy to the world by dancing)

Home:

Childhood—Illinois

Now—Michigan

Selected Books Written and Illustrated by Wendy Anderson Halperin

Aylesworth, Jim. *Full Belly Bowl*. Illustrated by Wendy Anderson Halperin. (Atheneum, 1999)

Burnett, Frances Hodgson. *The Racketty-Packetty House: 100th Anniversary Edition*. Illustrated by Wendy Anderson Halperin. (Simon & Schuster, 2006)

Cates, Karin. *Secret Remedy Book: A Story of Comfort and Love*. Illustrated by Wendy Anderson Halperin. (Orchard, 2003)

Halperin, Wendy. *Love Is....* Adapted from the King James Bible. Illustrated by Wendy Anderson Halperin. (Simon & Schuster, 2001)

Lindbergh, Reeve. *The Visit*. Illustrated by Wendy Anderson Halperin. (Dial, 2005)

Rylant, Cynthia. *Let's Go Home: The Wonderful Things about a House*. Illustrated by Wendy Halperin. (Simon & Schuster, 2002)

Seeger, Pete. *Turn! Turn! Turn!* Illustrated by Wendy Anderson Halperin. (Simon & Schuster, 2003)

Spurr, Elizabeth. *The Peterkins' Christmas*. Illustrated by Wendy Anderson Halperin. (Atheneum, 2004)

Spurr, Elizabeth. *The Peterkins' Thanksgiving*. Illustrated by Wendy Anderson Halperin. (Atheneum, 2005)

Wood, Doug. *Nothing to Do*. Illustrated by Wendy Anderson Halperin. (Dutton, 2006)

Yolen, Jane. *Soft House*. Illustrated by Wendy Anderson Halperin. (Candlewick, 2005)

 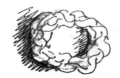

D A Z Z L i N G

B R C A D

I heard on the radio today: Art is making the ordinary into something SPECTACULAR.... OR something DAZZLING, which may be why I have always made this bread.

The very ordinary ingredients: Flour, butter, salt, sugar + yeast. This is the recipe for 2 braided loaves. I usually double it and make round ones and straight ones.

Bag of Flour , ½ stick of butter, 2 tablespoons, 1 teaspoon, sugar salt (unbleached)

and 2 Packages of Fleishmans powdered yeast.

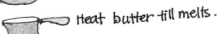

In a big bowl put 2 cups of flour, 2 packages of, yeast 2 Tbsp. sugar, 1 tsp. salt

Heat butter till melts. run tap water untill it is it's Hottest. HOT WATER

Take ↑ OFF stove, and put 2 cups of hot water into butter then pour mixture over FLOUR MIXTURE. Stir (wooden spoon)

Then beat mixture at low speed ½ minute scraping sides. Then Beat at HIGH speed for 3 MINUTES. Then..... More Add Flour... by hand ... to make a moderatly stiff dough.

Flour

sprinkle Flour onto counter

Flour

Knead the FLOUR (ALOT) 10 minutes. You can tell You're Done when the dough isn't sticky. Add handfull of flour whenever the dough starts sticking to the counter.

Clean the bowl, Dry it. Then put some oil in it about a teaspoon... and rub all the inside of the bowl. You don't want the bread to stick to the sides.

Put Bread in bowl.

Put a dish towel under hot water. (wring out)

Put Towel over Bread and let it rest for about 1½ hour. Until it DouBles in size!

Then PUNCH it down!

Take it out of the bowl and make This shape.

Then take a knife and cut it in to TWO.

Take and cut that into 3 pieces (set other one a side)

roll into a snake
roll other into a snake
roll other into a snake

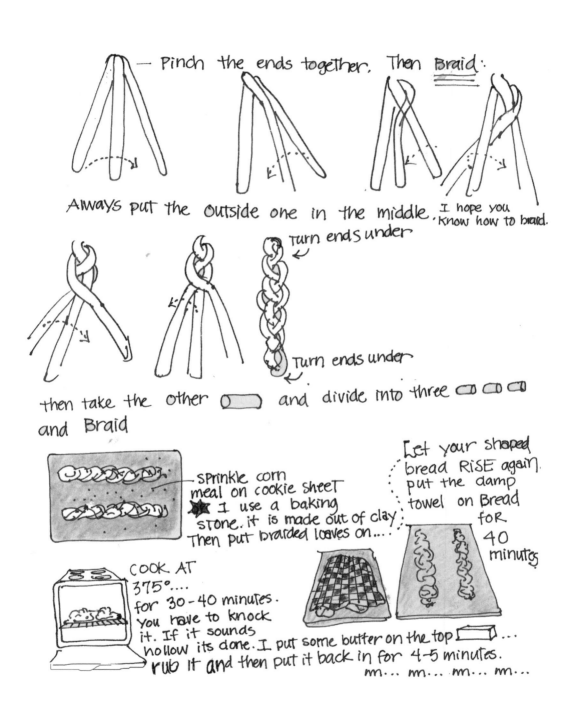

— Pinch the ends together. Then Braid:

Always put the outside one in the middle. I hope you know how to braid.

turn ends under

Turn ends under

then take the other and divide into three

and Braid

sprinkle corn meal on cookie sheet ★ I use a baking stone. it is made out of clay. Then put braided loaves on....

Let your shaped bread RISE again. put the damp towel on Bread for 40 minutes

COOK AT 375°.... for 30-40 minutes. You have to knock it. If it sounds hollow its done. I put some butter on the top rub It and then put it back in for 4-5 minutes.

m... m... m... m...

Will Hillenbrand—Blueberry and Nut Salad

Photo Credit: Altman

In Please Say Please, Penguin has a party and invites nine animal friends, but they need some lessons about polite dinner behavior. Penguin tries to share some painless etiquette tips for each situation. Giraffe, for example, can't totally suppress her burp, but she does manage to cover her mouth and minimize the volume. Giraffe's sneeze that blows the salad here and there is another problem that will need some attention.

—About *Please Say Please!*: *Penguin's Guide to Manners*

Will Hillenbrand's work is characterized by his multifaceted style and his inspired use of color and light. Although he uses a variety of media, he consistently turns to oil paints as a media, using it in most of his illustrations. In *Wicked Jack,* Hillenbrand created his illustrations with oil paints, oil pastels, graphite, and a smudge of coal. Other books enjoy their own distinctive edge: highbrow eggheads, spiky-haired Jack, and details that showcase specific settings from Giorgio's Italy to Ali Baba's Baghdad and Sam Sundays mansion along with Jack's tumbledown cottage. Hillenbrand's lively use of oil is often combined with watercolor, in addition to the oil pastels and graphite use. This layering gives his colors a quality that seems to intensify each color.

Will Hillenbrand

Will Hillenbrand's first efforts at illustrating were with crayons when he was a child. He listened to stories told in his father's barbershop and on his grandmother's farm—and he would illustrate them. In high school, he set his crayons aside and experimented with other mediums—oil paints, acrylics, oil pastels, watercolor—every medium available to him. Following high school, Hillenbrand entered the Art Academy of Cincinnati and after graduation worked in advertising, even though he had already fallen in love with picture books. He filled his office with marionettes, toys, and folk-art animals. Just as early in his childhood he was inspired by the family stories that swirled around him, his inspiration now comes from his wife and son.

Blueberry Blueberry Pie

Check the ingredients—you'll need sugar, cornstarch, salt, lemon juice, three cups of blueberries, butter, whipping cream, vanilla, and powered sugar.

Bake a prepared pie shell and set aside to cool.

Prepare the filling by combining:
- 3/4 cup sugar
- 2 1/2 tablespoon cornstarch
- 1 teaspoon salt

Blend in:
- 2/3 cup water
- 1 cup blueberries.

Bring to a boil and cook, stirring constantly until the mixture is very thick. It will take approximately 15 to 20 minutes.

Stir in:
- 2 tablespoons butter
- 1 1/2 tablespoons lemon juice.

Cool to nearly room temperature, and then gently stir in 2 more cups of blueberries. Refrigerate and allow to chill thoroughly.

While the filling is chilling, either whip 1 cup of whipping cream or use 16 ounces of your favorite purchased whipped topping. Mix in 2 tablespoons of powdered sugar and 1/2 teaspoon vanilla (if not using purchased topping).

Once the pie crust has cooled and the filling has chilled, spread half of the whipped cream over the baked 9-inch pie shell. Layer in the blueberry filling and top with the remaining whipped cream. Garnish with a few fresh blueberries.

BLUEBERRIES—WILD AND CULTIVATED

When Europeans arrived in North America, they found two types of blueberries growing wild, the highbush and lowbush varieties. Botanists estimate that the berries had been growing in North American since around A.D. 700. The lowbush variety of blueberries still grow wild in the state of Maine and in eastern Canada. Those wild berries are harvested and used mostly for baking and in processed foods. Blueberries are now also cultivated (domesticated and raised as a crop; usually highbush variety) throughout the United States. More than 40 percent of the blueberries grown in the United States come from Michigan and Indiana, although states in New England (particularly Maine and Connecticut) and Oregon and Washington are also known for blueberry production. Blueberries can be found in the United States and Canada primarily from April until October. July is the month that blueberries are in peak production in these states. Blueberries are grown in the southern states as well. In Georgia, North Carolina, Mississippi, Louisiana, and Florida, the berries are generally harvested before the summer months.

Blueberry and Nut Salad

- 1 cup fresh blueberries
- 1/2 cup pineapple chunks, or sliced strawberries, banana, or raspberries (your preference)
- 1/2 cup walnut or almonds pieces
- 3 cups torn romaine lettuce
- 1/4 cup of lemon honey dressing (see below)

Toss together all ingredients except the dressing. Refrigerate to keep lettuce crisp. When ready to serve, toss again with chilled dressing.

Lemon Honey Dressing

- 1 cup lemon juice
- 1/2 cup oil
- 1/2 cup honey

Combine ingredients in a quart jar with a tight fitting lid. Shake well. Cover and refrigerate to blend flavors. Shake well before serving.

Blueberries in Books

Low, Alice. *Blueberry Mouse*. Illustrated by David Michael Friend. (Mondo Books, 2004)

McCloskey, Robert. *Blueberries for Sal*. (Viking, 1948)

Paterson, John and Katherine. *Blueberries for the Queen*. Illustrated by Susan Jeffers. (HarperCollins, 2004)

Selected Books Illustrated by Will Hillenbrand

Adler, David A. Andy Russell Series. Illustrations by Will Hillenbrand. (Harcourt, 2005 and other dates)

Cuyler, Margery. *The Bumpy Little Pumpkin*. Illustrations by Will Hillenbrand. (Scholastic, 2005)

Cuyler, Margery. *Please Say Please!: Penguin's Guide to Manners*. Illustrations by Will Hillenbrand. (Scholastic, 2004)

Hillenbrand, Jane. *What a Treasure!* Illustrated by Will Hillenbrand. (Holiday House, 2006)

Hillenbrand, Will. *Cock-a-Doodle Christmas*. Illustrated by Will Hillenbrand. (Marshall Cavendish, 2007)

Hillenbrand, Will. *My Book Box*. Illustrated by Will Hillenbrand. (Harcourt, 2006)

Kimmel, Eric. *The Tale of Ali Baba and the Forty Thieves*. Illustrations by Will Hillenbrand. (Holiday House, 1996)

Kutner, Merrily. *Down on the Farm*. Illustrations by Will Hillenbrand. (Holiday House, 2004)

Livingston, Myra Cohn. *Calendar*. Illustrated by Will Hillenbrand. (Holiday House, 2007)

Root, Phyllis. *Kiss the Cow*. Illustrated by Will Hillenbrand. (Candlewick, 2003)

St. George, Judith. *The Journey of the One and Only Declaration of Independence*. Illustrations by Will Hillenbrand. (Penguin Putnam, 2005)

Wilson, Karma. *Grandma's Whopper Birthday Cake*. Illustrations by Will Hillenbrand. (Margaret K. McElderry, 2006)

Wooldridge, Connie Nordhielm. *Wicked Jack*. Illustrations by Will Hillenbrand. (Holiday House, 1995)

Yolen, Jane. *This Little Piggy: Lap Songs, Finger Plays, Clapping Games and Pantomine Rhymes*. With music arrangements by Adam Stemple. Illustrations by Will Hillenbrand. (Candlewick, 2006)

Deborah Hopkinson—Baking Powder Biscuits

Deborah Hopkinson

Birthday: February 4

Family:

    Sisters—Janice Fairbrother and Bonnie Johnson

    Spouse—Andrew Thomas

    Son—Dimitri Thomas

    Daughter—Rebekah Hopkinson

Home:

    Childhood—Massachusetts

    Now—Oregon

I love biscuits—especially homemade baking powder biscuits.

—Deborah Hopkinson

Says Deborah Hopkinson, "I love biscuits—especially homemade baking powder biscuits. One of my fondest childhood memories is of my father, Russ Hopkinson, making biscuits. My mom did most of the cooking (and could bake a mean chocolate cake!), but my dad had his specialties, too. A devoted fly fisherman, he loved to cook up a mess of brookies (translation: brook trout) from his favorite pond in Maine. And he also made biscuits.

"I've included recipes in several of my picture books. There's an authentic Fannie Farmer recipe in *Fannie in the Kitchen,* for instance, and a recipe for sourdough in The Klondike Kid series. For the Prairie Skies series, set in Kansas following the Kansas-Nebraska Act of 1854, I decided to make use of my dad's biscuit recipe. Book Three of the trilogy is titled *Our Kansas Home,* and in it, Charlie Keller's mother makes biscuits, a staple of pioneer life.

"In the story, Charlie's mother offers the biscuits to some men who are looking for her abolitionist husband. Since the family is also hiding, a runaway enslaved girl named Lizzie, it's a tense moment. While Charlie and Lizzie wait breathlessly inside the cabin, Momma sits outside and says to the men, 'Now gentlemen, I baked extra biscuits this morning. But since my husband's not here, you're welcome to them. And if I do say so myself, I make excellent biscuits.'

"I think my dad was pleased to see his name and his recipe in this book, and I often turn to it myself, especially when I can't find the old index card I scribbled it on years ago."

Russ Hopkinson's Baking Powder Biscuits (adapted)

- 2 cups flour
- 1 tablespoon baking powder
- 1/4 teaspoon salt
- 1 tablespoon sugar
- 1/4 cup shortening (old timers would have used bacon drippings or lard but Crisco, butter, or margarine can be substituted)
- 1 cup milk

Quickly combine the ingredients in a large bowl. Spoon the batter in an ungreased muffin tin, dividing equally among the cups. Fill about two-thirds full as the batter will rise when baking. Bake at 450 degrees F for about 12 minutes or until golden brown. Makes twelve biscuits. Serve with butter and jam, or as strawberry shortcake.

BISCUITS

In some countries, biscuits are more like unleavened crackers, but the puffy leavened breads that are common in the United States are called "soda biscuits" or "baking soda biscuits." Recipes for soda biscuits are found in many nineteenth-century cookbooks. Often those traveling in wagon trains baked biscuits in a portable iron pot that sat up from the fire on three small feet allowing air to flow under the bottom. The lid was lipped, making it easy to pile heated rocks on top for more even temperatures. It was reliable but had no scientific temperature controls.

In some southern regions of the United States, baking soda is called "Sody Sallyratus" (soda and sallyratus—"sal" meaning salt and "acrate" meaning to mix with air). Without baking soda, biscuits would be hard and flat. It is the baking soda—sody sallyratus—that causes the dough to rise, forming fluffy biscuits. According to Milledge Staley,* President Dwight D. Eisenhower's steward during Eisenhower's Army days, one of Eisenhower's favorite foods to eat was dried beef (probably in a cream sauce) on baking powder biscuits.

*As quoted in the Victor Valley (California) *Daily Press* in an article "Hail to the Chief" by Stuart Kellogg. No date.

1897 Baking Soda Buttermilk Biscuits (rolled and cut)

Recipe

- 2 cups flour
- 1/2 teaspoons baking soda
- 1/2 teaspoons salt
- 4 tablespoons shortening
- 3/4 cups buttermilk

In a large mixing bowl, sift together flour, soda, salt. Cut in shortening until mixture resembles corn meal. Make a well in the center of the flour mixture and add buttermilk all at once. Stir into a soft dough. Knead on a floured surface for one minute. Roll into a half-inch thickness. Cut with a floured biscuit cutter or a jar top. Place on ungreased cookie sheet or iron skillet. Bake at 450 degrees F for 10 to 12 minutes or until light brown. Serve warm with butter and jelly (or apple butter).

 Booklist

Baseball

Deborah Hopkinson's *Girl Wonder: A Baseball Story in Nine Innings* is a fictional tale based on the life of Alta Weiss, who at age seventeen was the first female to pitch baseball for a semipro all-male team, the Vermilion Independents. Her story complements the stories of several other girls and women who have made their own mark in the world of baseball.

Adler, David A. *Mama Played Baseball.* Illustrated by Chris O'Leary. (Harcourt, 2003)

Corey, Shana. *Players in Pigtails.* Illustrated by Rebecca Gibbon. (Scholastic, 2003)

Hubbard, Crystal. *Catching the Moon: The Story of a Young Girl's Baseball Dream.* Illustrated by Randy Duburke. (Lee & Low, 2005)

Moss, Marissa. *Mighty Jackie: The Strike-Out Queen.* Illustrated by C. F. Payne. (Simon & Schuster/Paula Wiseman, 2004)

Patrick, Jean L. *Girl Who Struck Out Babe Ruth.* Illustrated by Jeni Reeves. (Lerner, 2000)

Rappaport, Doreen, and Lydall Callan. *Dirt on Their Skirts.* Illustrated by E. B. Lewis. (Dial, 2000)

Fannie Farmer's Raised Waffles

When Deborah Hopkinson wrote about Fannie Farmer in Fannie in the Kitchen: The Whole Story from Soup to Nuts of How Fannie Farmer Invented Recipes with Precise Measurements, *she included an authentic Fanny Farmer recipe for her "Famous Griddle Cakes." Here's another Fannie Farmer recipe.*

Ingredients

- 1/2 cup warm water
- 1 package dry yeast
- 2 cups warm milk
- 1/2 cup (1 stick) melted butter
- 1 teaspoon salt
- 1/2 teaspoon sugar
- 2 cups all-purpose flour
- 2 eggs, beaten
- 1/4 teaspoon baking soda

First Day:

Step 1: In a large bowl (ingredients will double in size), pour the 1/2 cup warm water and sprinkle in the yeast from the packet. Stir and let stand for five minutes.

Step 2: Add the warm melted butter, salt, and sugar.

Step 3: Sift flour into the mixture and beat until no lumps remain and the batter is smooth. Use a hand rotary beater or a whisk.

Step 4: Cover with a tight cover (plastic wrap works well) and let sit overnight at room temperature.

Second Day:

Step 5: Preheat waffle iron.

Step 6: While the waffle iron is preheating, blend in the eggs and baking soda into the mixture. Stir until well mixed. Batter should be very thin.

Step 7: Cook batter and serve immediately with syrups or toppings of your choice. Great as an accompaniment to eggs and bacon or sausage.

Selected Titles by Deborah Hopkinson

Apples to Oregon: Being the (Slightly) True Narrative of How a Brave Pioneer Father Brought Apples, Peaches, Pears, Plums, Grapes, and Cherries (and Children) across the Plains. Illustrated by Nancy Carpenter. (Atheneum, 2003)

Fannie in the Kitchen: The Whole Story From Soup to Nuts of How Fannie Farmer Invented Recipes with Precise Measurements. Illustrated by Nancy Carpenter. (Atheneum, 2001)

From Slave to Soldier: Based on a True Civil War Story. Illustrated by Brian Floca. (Atheneum, 2005)

Girl Wonder: A Baseball Story in Nine Innings. Illustrated by Terry Widener. (Atheneum, 2003)

Into the Firestorm: A Novel of San Francisco, 1906 (Knopf, 2006)

Our Kansas Home. Illustrated by Patrick Faricy. (Aladdin, 2003)

A Packet of Seeds. Illustrated by Bethanne Andersen. (Greenwillow, 2004)

Prairie Skies: Cabin in the Snow. Illustrated by Patrick Faricy. (Aladdin, 2002)

Prairie Skies: Pioneer Summer. Illustrated by Patrick Faricy. (Aladdin, 2002)

Saving Strawberry Farm. Illustrated by Rachel Isadora. (Greenwillow, 2005)

Shutting out the Sky: Life in the Tenements of New York, 1880–1915. (Orchard Books, 2003)

Susan B. Anthony, Fighter for Women's Rights. (Simon & Schuster, 2005)

Sweet Clara and the Freedom Quilt. Illustrated by James Ransome. (Knopf, 1993)

Sweet Land of Liberty. Illustrated by Leonard Jenkins. (Peachtree, 2007)

Up Before Daybreak: Cotton and People in American. Illustrated with photographs. (Scholastic Nonfiction, 2006)

Under the Quilt of Night. Illustrated by James Ransome. (Atheneum, 2000)

Photo Credit: Karl Meyer

It was not until I was an adult and, while on my way through Maryland, [that I] had my first taste of southern fried chicken. I thought I'd died and gone to heaven.

—Carol Otis Hurst

Carol Otis Hurst

Carol Otis Hurst

Birthday: October 13

Favorite place: In my living room on a cold winter's night with good company, good food, and a fire in the fireplace.

Favorite foods: Anything I haven't tried before.

Family: I was one of seven children. I married young and divorced young. Learned later. I have two wonderful daughters, Jill and Rebecca. Jill is a labor union organizer. Rebecca is a webmaster. Rebecca has two boys, Keith and Jesse, and they are practically perfect.

Daughters—Jill and Rebecca (mother of grandsons, Keith and Jesse)

Home:

Childhood—Springfield and then Westfield, Massachusetts

Now—Have lived in Tennessee, Ohio, and Minnesota but belong in Massachusetts.

Carol Otis Hurst is a storyteller and a writer. For years she told her stories before hundreds of children and adults, resisting the requests to write those stories down. But eventually she put some of her stories on paper, and in 2001 a fictionalized biography of her father was published. *Rocks in His Head* is a tale that gives readers a sense of the past and a vision for the future. More of Hurst's stories followed as books, fueled by the many stories she heard as a child and those she found and told as an adult. Here, Carol talks about another of her books.

"*You Come to Yokum* is set on Yokum Pond in Becket, Massachusetts in 1919 and is based on the stories in and about the inn that my grandparents ran there at the time.

"Winnie, a shy woman easily moved to tears, is the cook at the inn. The narrator's father, Fred, is wary of Winnie and, when she frequently bursts into tears, says to his wife, 'Grace, see to Winnie,' and leaves the room.

"Hence [in the book]: "*Although Winnie is a good cook, she has never cooked for a crowd before and is understandably nervous about doing so.*

"*Aunt Winnie tried out a different supper on us each night, doubling, tripling, and quadrupling her recipes. My father watched Aunt Winnie, and Aunt Winnie watched us taste the food. If the new recipe was bad, and we pushed the food around on our plates a bit, or made even the slightest face, Aunt Winnie would burst into tears and rush from the room.*

Dad would sigh and say, 'Grace, see to Winnie.'

After she got Aunt Winnie calmed down, Mother would help her remove that food and rustle up some leftovers from a more successful meal.

"One of Winnie's most successful dishes is fried chicken. And although Winnie really was my great-aunt and she really was a good cook, my own mother was not any great shakes in the kitchen. Although she made something she called fried chicken, it was not until I was an adult and, while on my way through Maryland [that I] had my first taste of southern fried chicken. I thought I'd died and gone to heaven."

Books Written by Carol Otis Hurst

In Plain Sight. (Houghton Mifflin/Walter Lorraine Books, 2002)

A Killing in Plymouth Colony. With Rebecca Otis. (Houghton Mifflin/Walter Lorraine Books, 2003)

Rocks in His Head. Illustrated by James Stevenson. (Greenwillow, 2001)

Terrible Storm. Illustrated by S. D. Schindler. (Greenwillow, 2007)

Through the Lock. (Houghton Mifflin/Walter Lorraine Books, 2001)

Torchlight. (Houghton Mifflin, 2006)

The Wrong One. (Houghton Mifflin/Walter Lorraine Books, 2003)

You Come to Yokum. Illustrated by Kay Life (Houghton Mifflin/Walter Lorraine Books, 2005)

Carol's Favorite Fried Chicken

Marinate 8 chicken thighs or drumsticks overnight in:

- 1 cup dry red wine
- 1/4 cup red wine vinegar
- 3 minced garlic cloves
- 1 tablespoon Dijon style mustard
- Remove chicken from marinate

Whisk together 1 egg and 1/2 cup of the marinade.

In another bowl, stir together:

- 1 cup flour
- 1 teaspoon salt
- 1/4 teaspoon dried thyme.

Dip chicken in egg mixture and then roll in the flour mixture. Repeat dipping and dredging.

Let chicken stand for fifteen minutes.

Heat one inch of vegetable oil in skillet to 375 degrees F. Fry chicken in batches one minute on each side. Then reduce oil heat to 300. Fry chicken uncovered for 25 minutes. Drain on paper towels.

Signature Recipe—Carol Otis Hurst

Family Stories

The roots of most of Carol Otis Hurst's books are incidents or tales from her family. Many authors write accounts based on family stories or the family stories of their friends. These stories can be great models to help other writers look into their family history, to look for stories to gather—stories that might become their own version of a tale to be told.

Cooney, Barbara. *Hattie and the Wild Waves.* (Viking, 1990)

dePaola, Tomie. *Nana Upstairs & Nana Downstairs.* (Putnam 1987; 1998)

Felipe Herrera, Juan. *Grandma and Me at the Flea/Los Meros Meros Remateros.* Illustrated by Anita De Lucio-Brock. (Children's Book Press, 2002)

Houston, Gloria. *My Great Aunt Arizona.* Illustrated by Susan Condie Lamb. (HarperCollins, 1992)

Houston, Gloria. *The Year of the Perfect Christmas Tree.* Illustrated by Barbara Cooney. (Dial, 1988)

Howard, Elizabeth Fitzgerald. *Papa Tells Chita a Story.* Illustrated by Floyd Cooper. (Simon & Schuster, 1995)

Lasky, Kathryn. *Marven of the Great North Woods.* Illustrated by Kevin Hawkes. (Harcourt, Brace, 1997)

Look, Lenore. *Love as Strong as Ginger.* Illustrated by Stephen T Johnson. (Atheneum, 1999)

Martin, Jacqueline Briggs. *The Finest Horse in Town.* Illustrated by Susan Gaber. (Purple House Press, 2003)

Mathers, Petra. *Kisses from Rosa.* (Knopf, 1995)

Pak, Soyung. *A Place To Grow.* Illustrated by Marcelino Truong. (Levine/Scholastic, 2002)

Paterson, John, and Katherine Paterson. *Blueberries for the Queen.* Illustrated by Susan Jeffers. (HarperCollins, 2004)

Pinkney, Gloria Jean. *Back Home.* Illustrated by Jerry Pinkney. (Dial, 1992)

Rylant, Cynthia. *Christmas in the Country.* Illustrated by Diane Goode. (Blue Sky, Scholastic, 2002)

Rylant, Cynthia. *The Relatives Came.* Illustrated by Stephen Gammel. (Bradbury Press, 1985)

Rylant, Cynthia. *When I Was Young in the Mountains.* Illustrated by Diane Goode. (Dutton, 1982)

Say, Allen. *Grandfather's Journey.* (Houghton Mifflin, 1993)

Say, Allen. *Tea with Milk.* (Houghton Mifflin, 1999)

Warhola, James. *Uncle Andy's: A Faabbbulous visit with Andy Warhol.* (Putnam, 2003)

Yolen, Jane. *Owl Moon.* Illustrated by John Schoenherr. (Philomel, 1987)

Peanut Brittle

Carol Otis Hurst grew up in the 1930s and 1940s. According to food historians, peanut brittle is probably a nineteenth-century American invention. It became a very popular treat during the Depression in the 1930s. Many children enjoyed a piece of this hard candy that was easy to make. Here is an old-fashioned recipe used in the 1930s and a more contemporary one that uses a microwave to cook the confection.

Peanut Brittle—1930s Style

- 2 cups of granulated sugar
- 2 cups of raw peanuts
- 1 teaspoon of salt

Sprinkle the sugar over the bottom of a cast iron frying pan and heat slowly until the sugar melts and turns light brown (300 degrees F). Handle carefully and protect yourself from splattering.

As the sugar heats, spread the peanuts on a buttered marble pastry board or a buttered cookie sheet and sprinkle with salt. When the sugar has reached the proper consistency and temperature, immediately pour over the peanuts.

When cool, break into pieces.

Peanut Brittle

- 1 1/2 cup raw peanuts with or without skins
- 1 cup sugar
- 1/2 cup white corn syrup
- 1/8 teaspoon salt
- 1 teaspoon butter
- 1 teaspoon vanilla
- 1 teaspoon baking soda

Using a 2-quart microwaveable container, stir together the nuts, sugar, syrup, and salt. Microwave on high for 4 minutes. Remove and stir. Return to microwave to cook for 2 minutes. Removed from microwave and quickly stir in baking soda. Immediately pour onto a lightly buttered baking sheet and spread thin. The mixture will not cover the entire baking sheet. When cool, break into small pieces and store in an airtight container.

Johanna Hurwitz—Blueberry Soup

I poured a cup of blueberry soup for one of the ladies.... As I moved toward the second woman, who was holding her cup out, I tripped on a rock.

**—From *A Llama in the Family*
by Johanna Hurwitz**

I grew up in New York City where all food came from the supermarket. However, I was lucky that I got to spend a week or two each summer visiting with cousins who lived in the country. When I stayed with them I ate tomatoes and carrots that grew in their own small garden, saw corn growing in nearby fields, went to a chicken farm where my aunt bought fresh eggs, and then I watched with horror and fascination as a chicken was slaughtered for our dinner. That's how I learned about the real sources of food. One of the activities I enjoyed during these summer vacations was going berry picking. If I was visiting in late June/early July, we went to fields where we could pick fresh strawberries. A late July/early August visit meant the chance to pick blueberries.

Then I grew up and became a parent. My husband and I were raising our son and daughter in New York City too. But every August we rented a house in Vermont so our children could experience country life. And once again, I found myself picking wild berries. This time the fruits were raspberries and blackberries. Eating fresh berries is always delicious, but when I discovered that I had more berries than we could consume, I began making jam. It was the start of a thirty-five year tradition. Nowadays I make about three dozen jars of jam each summer that are given as gifts to friends over the year. Of course, I save some for my family. We love to spread these berry preserves on a slice of toast or an English muffin in the middle of the winter. It is like having a mouthful of summer on a cold and snowy day.

123

Besides jam, one can also make pies, cobblers, cakes, muffins, quick breads and many other treats from fresh berries. I once went on a llama trek in Vermont where the guide served a cold home-made blueberry soup. I loved the soup and begged for the recipe. I also wrote a book about a boy whose mother leads llama treks.

—Johanna Hurwitz

Tenement Living

Dear Emma continues the tale of the friendship between Dossi and Emma that began in *Faraway Summer*. A strong component of this story involves Dossi's family in the New York tenements and the events surrounding the Triangle Shirt-waist Factory fire in the early 1900s. Learn more about this period of time by reading these books:

Auch, Mary Jane. *Ashes of Roses*. (Henry Holt, 2002), fiction

Broyles, Janell. *The Triangle Shirtwaist Factory Fire of 1911* (Tragic Fires Throughout History). (Rosen, 2004)

Hopkinson, Deborah. *Shutting Out the Sky: Life in the Tenements of New York, 1880–1924*. (Orchard Books, 2003)

Houle, Michelle M. *Triangle Shirtwaist Factory Fire: Flames of Labor Reform*. (American Disasters). (Enslow, 2002)

Landau, Elaine. *The Triangle Shirtwaist Factory Fire*. (Cornerstones of Freedom. Second Series). (Scholastic, 2005)

Littlefield, Holly. *Fire at the Triangle Factory*. Illustrated by Mary O'Keefe Young. (Carolrhoda On My Own Book). (Carolrhoda, 1995)

Schaefer, Adam R. *The Triangle Shirtwaist Factory Fire*. (Landmark Events in American History). (World Almanac Library, 2003)

Von Drehle, David. *Triangle: The Fire That Changed America*. (Atlantic Monthly Press, 2003)

MOLASSES OR SUGAR—IN THE TENEMENTS

During the 1880s and into the early 1900s (the era of the tenements), molasses was the most popular sweetener in the United States because it was much cheaper than refined sugar. After the end of World War I, refined sugar prices dropped drastically resulting in many consumers using white sugar in place of molasses. But during World War II, molasses helped sweeten foods as white sugar was rationed. Molasses now costs approximately twice as much as white sugar.

Tenement Baked Beans

Beans sweetened with molasses were popular in early American history. Those who desired to reduce the gaseous nature of beans routinely drained the "soaking water" from the beans and added fresh water for cooking. That seemed to reduce the flatulence resulting from the beans.

In a large pot, soak navy or pea beans overnight in 6 cups of water. Drain the "soaking water" from the beans. Return the beans to the pot and add another 6 cups of water and 1/2 teaspoon of baking soda.

Bring water and beans to a boil and simmer on low for 10 minutes. Drain (save the liquid).

Preheat the oven to 300 degrees F, and then in an ungreased bean pot or large casserole dish, combine beans with:

- 1/2 pound bacon (cooked and diced) or bits of leftover ham
- 1 small onion, chopped
- 1/3 cup molasses
- 1 teaspoon salt
- 5 tablespoons firmly packed brown sugar
- 1 teaspoon ground mustard
- 1/2 teaspoon pepper
- 1 cup of the liquid reserved from the cooked beans

Once well blended, cover bean pot or casserole dish.

Bake, covered, for 2 1/2 to 3 hours. Add remaining liquid (from bean cooking) and stir again. Bake another 1 1/2 hours or until beans are tender. Uncover the last 30 minutes of baking. Remove from oven and serve. Serves 8.

Selected Books Written by Johanna Hurwitz

Dear Emma. Illustrated by Barbara Garrison. (HarperCollins, 2002), sequel to *Faraway Summer* (HarperCollins, 1998)

Elisa Michaels, Bigger & Better. Illustrated by Debbie Tilley. (HarperCollins, 2003)

Ethan at Home. Illustrated by Brian Floca. (Candlewick Press, 2003)

Fourth Grade Fuss. Illustrated by Andy Hammond. (HarperCollins, 2004)

Helen Keller: Courage in the Dark. Illustrated by Neverne Covington. Step into Reading Series: Step 4 (Random House, 1997, 2003)

A Llama in the Family. Illustrated by Mark Graham. (HarperCollins, 1994)

A Llama in the Library. Illustrated by Mark Graham. (HarperCollins, 1999)

Blueberry Soup

In Hurwitz's book, A Llama in the Family, *the mother serves blueberry soup. This recipe is the one that Hurwitz obtained from the guide after her own Llama trek in Vermont.*

- 5 cups blueberries
- 4 cups water
- 4 whole cloves
- 2 inch cinnamon stick

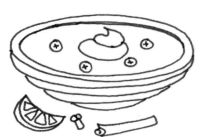

Bring to boil.

Add 2/3 cup honey or maple syrup.

Simmer for 30 to 50 minutes.

Put into food mill or mixer. Add juice of one lemon and one tablespoon blueberry vinegar (recipe follows). Strain through a sieve.

Chill. Serve chilled with a dollop of plain or vanilla yogurt on each portion.

Signature Recipe—Johanna Hurwitz

Blueberry Vinegar

Blueberry vinegar is available in specialty groceries, but if you cannot locate a commercial source, consider making you own. You'll need:

- 1 cup fresh blueberries
- 2 cups white vinegar
- 2 tablespoons sugar

Sterilize a 1-quart glass jar and place the blueberries in the jar. Into a non-aluminum saucepan, combine the vinegar and sugar. Cover and place the sauce pan over high heat. Bring the mixture to a boil. After the mixture reaches the boiling point, remove from heat, and pour vinegar mixture over blueberries. Cover and let stand at room temperature.

Let the blueberry mixture stand for 3 days and then strain the mixture through several layers of damp cheesecloth. Discard the blueberries and put the blueberry vinegar into decorative jars sealed with a cork or another type of airtight lid. This recipe makes 2 cups of blueberry vinegar.

Jennifer R. Jacobson—S'mores Bars

Photo Credit: Jake Jacobson

Jennifer Richard Jacobson

Birthday: June 3

Favorite place: On top of a mountain

Favorite food: S'mores, Pesto

Family:

    Spouse—Jake

    Son—Erik

    Daughter—Holly

Home:

    Childhood—Peterborough, New Hampshire

    Now—Cumberland, Maine

Starlit nights, warm, sparkling campfires, and friends or family—that's what my favorite food, s'mores means to me.

— Jennifer R. Jacobson

Jennifer Jacobson shares a memory that helped to inspire her book, *Winnie Dancing on Her Own*: "As a young girl camping with my family, I was the patient one. No huffing and puffing on flaming marshmallows for me! No black ash would be found in my chocolate and graham cracker sandwich. I set out to toast the ideal marshmallow—a golden, toffee brown—by placing my hands as close to the coals as I could bear. Those chocolaty clouds of melted perfection were always worth the wait.

"I spent many summers at a camp in Vermont where s'mores were always part of the fun. So it's no wonder that these treats made their way into not only one of my Winnie books, but two! In *Winnie Dancing on Her Own*, Winnie makes s'mores for her friends during a slumber party. The girls are snuggled up in Winnie's city apartment—no campfire here—so she makes her s'mores in the microwave. She didn't have the freshiest of ingredients:

'Here are some graham crackers,' said Mr. Fletcher.

'They've gone soft,' said Winnie.

'And some marshmallows...'

'They're hard as rocks,' said Winnie.

"But suddenly Winnie understands. Her father has bought chocolate bars. And when these three ingredients are heated together, they never fail to make a 'gooey, delicious snack.' "

"In *Truly Winnie*, a story that takes place at summer camp, Winnie and her friends make s'mores in the more traditional way. Is Winnie as patient a marshmallow cooker as I was? I'm not sure. I guess I'll leave that up to the reader to decide."

Selected Books Written by Jennifer R. Jacobson

Andy Shane and the Very Bossy Dolores Starbuckle. Illustrated by Abby Carter. (Candlewick, 2005)

Moon Sandwich Mom. Illustrated by Benrei Huang. (Albert Whitman, 1999)

A Net of Stars. Illustrated by Greg Shed. (Dial, 1998)

Stained. (Atheneum/Richard Jackson Books, 2005), YA

Truly Winnie. Illustrated by Alissa Imre Geis. (Houghton Mifflin, 2003)

Winnie Dancing on Her Own. Illustrated by Alissa Imre Geis. (Houghton Mifflin, 2001)

Jennifer Jacobson

Writing poetry and keeping journals were both regular parts of Jennifer's growing up in New Hampshire before she won a high school essay contest, and headed off to college. Eventually Jennifer earned a graduate degree from Harvard School of Education. For a number of years she taught, was a curriculum director, and worked in other ways in the field of education, putting her learned strategies into action. Now she is a frequent author-in-residence in many schools and an educational consultant who works with teachers throughout the United States.

During a year of teaching first graders in Yarmouth, Maine, Jennifer wrote her first novel—unfortunately the novel was not publishable. Once her children were born, she turned her creative energy to writing picture books. Her children are not in her books, but her daughter's newfound bravery did inspire a story line in *A Net of Stars*. Her son's desire for a mother "who is fun" resulted in a book titled *Moon Sandwich Mom*. She now writes picture books and novels for elementary readers and for young adults.

S'mores

$\widehat{Recipe}$

Most campers know the routine: toast a marshmallow, and then smash it between two graham crackers and a piece of chocolate bar and you have a s'more. We're not sure when the first s'more came about, as there were several "sandwich cookies" created before s'mores were first documented. However, the 1927 Girl Scout handbook had this recipe for "Some Mores"—the name was only shortened to s'mores later—perhaps in the 1940s.

Ingredients

- 8 long sticks (such as kebob skewers, for toasting the marshmallows)
- 16 graham crackers
- 8 bars plain chocolate (any of the good plain brands, broken in two—Hershey candybars work well)
- 16 large marshmallows

Toast two marshmallows over the coals to a crisp gooey state and then put them between two graham crackers with 2 halves of a chocolate bar to make a sandwich. The heat of the marshmallow between the halves of chocolate bar will melt the chocolate a bit. Though it tastes like "some more," one is really enough.

GRAHAM CRACKERS AND SYLVESTER GRAHAM

Sylvester Graham's name has become a household word, since young children teethed while munching on the munchable crackers named for Graham. Sylvester Graham was a nineteenth-century minister who believed strongly in Christianity, temperance, and vegetarianism. He believed that those who did not eat meat would not have a desire to drink alcohol. That theory was never verified, but his theory of wholesome living did catch on. In several large cities, during the 1830s through 1850s Graham boardinghouses sprung up to serve others who desired to follow the healthy living style espoused by Graham. One of the foods he promoted was the "digestive biscuit" made from "unbolted" flour. The flour was un-sifted and coarsely ground wheat with a high fiber content. The flour and a popular biscuit made from the flour was associated with Graham's name and long after his death at age fifty-one, his "graham crackers" have lived on—at least on the North American side of the Atlantic Ocean. Those in other parts of the world, including England, do not have Graham crackers and would have to substitute another whole wheat cracker/biscuit.

Inventions such as Graham crackers that have been named after a person are called eponyms. Other eponyms include the Sousaphone (John Phillip Sousa), the dahlia flower (botanist Anders Dahl), Alzheimer's disease (neuropathologist Alois Alzheimer, and the Ferris Wheel (George Washington Gale Ferris—an American engineer).

S'mores Bars

In Truly Winnie, *Jennifer wrote, "That night, all of the girls were sitting around the campfire, eating s'mores—one of Winnie's favorite foods." When it was time for a book launch party for* Winnie, *Jennifer Jacobson wanted serve something special so she made these s'more bars.*

- 2 cups graham cracker crumbs
- 1/3 cup sugar
- 1/2 cup butter, melted
- 1 pound milk chocolate
- 4 cups mini-marshmallows—or use large marshmallows cut into small chunks.

Combine crumbs, butter, and sugar. Reserve 1 cup of the mixture. Press the remainder of the mixture into the bottom of a 13 x 9–inch baking dish. Bake the crust in a preheated 350 degree F oven for 12 minutes, or until it is golden. Let cool. In a double-boiler (or set a metal pan over a saucepan of simmering water), melt the chocolate, stirring as it melts. Pour the melted chocolate over the crust and spread it evenly. Sprinkle the mini-marshmallows, pressing them lightly, and top with the reserved crumb mixture. Broil the desert under a preheated broiler for about 2 inches from the heat for 30 seconds or until the marshmallows are golden. Remove from the oven and let cool. Cut into 24 squares.

Signature Recipe—Jennifer Jacobson

Helen Ketteman—Old Time Jam Cake

Helen Ketteman

Birthday: July 1

Favorite place: Home!

Favorite foods: Chocolate (I love Mexican and Thai food!)

Family:

Spouse—Charles H. Ketteman

Sons—William Gregory Ketteman and Mark David Ketteman

Home:

Childhood—Harlem, Georgia

Now—Florida

Helen Ketteman was born in Augusta, Georgia, and grew up in Harlem, Georgia, the daughter of a physician and a teacher. She earned an undergraduate degree from Georgia State University, married, and settled in Dallas, Texas, for a time. She says her Southern upbringing has had a definite effect on her writing. She is a master of the tall tale and a well-known storyteller. Of her childhood she says: "I have to admit I have a sweet tooth. I grew up in the South, where everybody had a fresh homemade cake in the pantry just in case someone dropped by to visit. Heaven forbid guests drop in unexpectedly and you get caught without anything delectable to feed them! So I grew up learning to make cakes from scratch. [I have written] a story called *The Great Cake Bake*. It's about a rambunctious lady who's wild about contests and very competitive. She hears about a cake-baking contest on the Fourth of July, and of course, she plans on winning. Her zeal to make the biggest and most spectacular cake, however, causes all sorts of trouble."

Old Time Jam Cake

Helen Ketteman made many cakes during her growing up years, but this is one of her favorites.

Ingredients

- 4 eggs separated
- 1 teaspoon soda
- 1 cup white sugar
- 1 cup brown sugar
- 1 cup butter (soft enough to beat but not melted)
- 1 1/2 teaspoon cinnamon
- 1 1/2 teaspoon cloves
- 1 1/2 teaspoon allspice
- 1 teaspoon cocoa
- 1 cup blackberry jam
- 1 cup raisins
- 3 cups flour
- 1 cup buttermilk

Beat egg yolks. Put in soda, sugars, and butter. Add cinnamon, cloves, allspice, nutmeg, and cocoa. Beat egg whites and add in. Add jam and raisins to mixture. Add flour and buttermilk alternately. Preheat oven to 350 degrees F. Bake in pan until done (around 30 minutes; test with toothpick). Cool and frost as desired.

Signature Recipe—Helen Ketteman

CHILI—MEXICAN, TEXAN, AND OTHER VARIETIES, WITH OR WITHOUT BEANS

Traditionally, chili combines ground or coarsely chopped beef (or other meat), dried red chili powder, onion, garlic, some liquid, and sometimes *comino* (cumin), oregano, beef suet, tomato, and masa (finely ground corn meal) to thicken. Historically, Texas-style chili has no beans; Southerners and Midwesterners generally add beans. These days some Texans are adding beans to their chili as well.

Chili falls clearly within Hispanic food traditions. Peppers and masa trace their use to Mexico. In 1842, when Sequoyah and a contingent of Cherokees from the Cherokee Nation visited the Rio Grande valley seeking survivors of the 1839 Texan-Cherokee War, the travelers were fed a fiery concoction of chunks of meat boiled with peppers.

Food historians believed that chili originated in Texas-Mexico border towns and spread north. The Mexican influence makes for a hot spicy concoction.

Ketteman says, "I love Mexican food. I loved it before I lived in Texas, and living in Texas for ten years made me love it even more! I can't get enough of it. However, I love things extra spicy, so when I cook Mexican, I don't mess around."

Ketteman wrote a book *Armadilly Chili* in which Billie Armadilly sets out to make her "hot armadilly chili." When her friends—Tex the tarantula, Mackie the bluebird, and Taffy the horned toad—are too busy to help, Billie proceeds to make her own version of her chili with beetles, peppers, and prickly pear cactus. Just as Little Red Hen did in many stories that preceded this one, Billie denies her friends a chance to share the chili, but she soon realizes that without friends her chili wasn't nearly as enjoyable.

White Lightening Chili

- 1 pound boneless, skinless chicken breasts, boiled and shredded
- 4 teaspoons ground cumin
- 2 teaspoons dried oregano
- 1 large onion, chopped
- 2 cans (16 ounce) great white northern beans, rinsed and drained
- 1 1/2 cups fat free chicken broth
- Medium jalapeno pepper, seeded and finally chopped
- 1 small can chopped green chilies
- Salt and pepper to taste

Suggested toppings:

- Pickled jalapeno peppers
- Sharp grated cheddar cheese
- Sliced scallions
- Hot sauce

Mix all ingredients together, bring to a boil, then turn on low to medium for about an hour. May serve on rice, if desired.

The Little Red Hen

When Helen Ketteman wrote *Armadilly Chili,* she was actually writing a literary version of the classic "Little Red Hen" tale. After readers become familiar with the classic version of the Little Red Hen's tale, they might what to reread *Armadilly Chili* and other literary versions of the tale before trying to tell or write their own unique version.

Classic Versions of "Little Red Hen"

Downard, Barry. *The Little Red Hen.* (Simon & Schuster, 2004)

Galdone, Paul. *Nursery Classics: A Galdone Treasury.* (Clarion Books, 2001)

McQueen, Lucina. *The Little Red Hen.* (Scholastic, 1985)

Miller, J. P. *The Little Red Hen.* (Golden Books, 2004)

Literary Versions of the Classic Tale

Ada, Alma Flor. *With Love, Little Red Hen.* Illustrated by Leslie Tryon. (Atheneum, 2001)

Crummel, Susan Stevens, and Janet Stevens. *Cook-A-Doodle-Doo!* Illustrated by Janet Stevens. (Harcourt, 1999)

Fleming, Candace. *Gator Gumbo: A Spicy-Hot Tale.* Illustrated by Sally Anne Lambert. (Farrar, Straus & Giroux, 2004)

McGrath, Barbara Barbieri. *The Little Green Witch.* Illustrated by Martha G. Alexander. (Charlesbridge, 2005)

Walrod, Amy. *The Little Red Hen (Makes a Pizza).* Illustrated by Philemon Sturges. (Puffin, 2001)

Helen Ketteman

Helen Ketteman grew up in the American South during the 1950s. She says, "Living in a small Southern town in that era was fabulous. I had freedom kids just don't have today. I had three sisters, and my sisters and I played together constantly, using our imagination and making up games, plays, and just pretending. We didn't sit and watch television, and we didn't have lots of organized activities. When I visit schools, I love to do storytelling. That's part of my heritage, too. I grew up with storytellers. Well, what Southerner worth his [or her] salt doesn't have a few stories to tell? I also grew up listening to people talk—and I noticed the music of language early on. I remember an aunt giving me a copy of Kipling's *Just-So Stories* for my seventh birthday. I was a good reader and could read the stories. I didn't know what many of the words meant, but I distinctly remember one thing—I loved the way the words sounded when I read them aloud. And I read them over and over. There was something magical about Kipling's language, and it caught my imagination right away."

Selected Books Written by Helen Ketteman

Armadillo Tattletale. Illustrated by Keith Graves. (Scholastic, 2000)

Armadilly Chili. Illustrated by Will Terry. (Albert Whitman, 2004)

Bubba, the Cowboy Prince: A Fractured Texas Tale. Illustrated by Warhola. (Scholastic, 1997)

The Great Cake Bake. Illustrated by Matt Collins. (Walker, 2005)

I Remember Papa. Illustrated by Greg Shed. (Dial, 1998)

Mama's Way. Illustrated by Mary Whyte. (Dial Books for Young Readers, 2001)

Shoeshine Whittaker. Illustrated by Scott Goto. (Walker, 1999)

Waynetta and the Cornstalk: A Texas Fairy Tale. Illustrated by Diane Greenseid. (Albert Whitman, 2007)

I love bagels! Hot from the oven. Solid as a brick. I can eat them right out of the bag. Add lox and cream cheese and I'm in heaven. Smoked sturgeon and whitefish —the gods on Mount Olympus never had it so good!

—Eric A. Kimmel

Eric A. Kimmel

Birthday: October 30

Favorite place: Venice, Italy

Favorite foods: Bagels

Family:

    Spouse—Doris Ann Kimmel

Home state:

    Childhood—Brooklyn, New York

    Now—Portland, Oregon

Here Eric Kimmel tells us about Bagels: "You like bagels, too, you say? Hah! We'll see about that. What kind of bagels are we talking about? Those puffy things from the supermarket, with blueberries and cinnamon? Feh! They have as much to do with a real bagel as a stick of cotton candy has to do with a cheesecake.

"Let me teach you about bagels. A real bagel, like a real person, has to have character. It has to have substance. You have to know something is there in your mouth. Bagels aren't like potato chips or Doritos. You can eat a whole bag and never know where they went. Not with bagels! If you eat a real bagel, you'll know you had a meal. You'll know you've been chewing something. And you probably won't be hungry again for a couple of hours, unless it's a craving for more bagels.

"A real bagel has to be boiled, not just baked. It has to be made from special ingredients, high gluten flour and malt sugar. A lot of complicated steps go into making a bagel, which is why some highly skilled home bakers—such as myself—don't bother with them. It would take me all day to make a couple dozen bagels, and they still wouldn't be as good as the ones I could get at the bagel bakery. Assuming there's a REAL bagel bakery near you.

"According to one legend, the first bagel was created to honor a famous war victory. In 1683, a Turkish army marched into Europe from the Balkans. The Turks were unstoppable until they arrived at the gates of Vienna. For a time it appeared that the city would fall, and with that, the rest of Europe. At the last moment, when all seemed lost, an army of Polish cavalry led by King Jan Sobieski came riding to the rescue. It was out of the movies. George Lucas could have made this film. The Poles caught the Turks completely by surprise. They sent them running back to Istanbul and saved the day.

"To commemorate Jan Sobieski's victory, the bakers of Vienna created a special round bread in his honor. They called it a *buegel,* meaning "stirrup," to immortalize the king and his gallant horsemen who saved Western civilization from disaster.

"It's hard to imagine anything more wonderful than a bagel. But guess what! There is. It's called a *bialy.*

"Remind me to tell you about *bialys* sometime."

Eric A. Kimmel

Eric A. Kimmel grew up in Brooklyn, New York, and undoubtedly was there during the time when dozens of bialy bakeries were in New York City. Now the number of bialy bakeries has dwindled considerably. Bialys (or *Bialystok kuchen*) came to the United States from Bialystok, Poland, in the early 1900s, when thousands of Eastern European Jews immigrated to America.

Bialystok, the city of origin, was part of Russia until 1918, so some will say that bialys originated in Russia depending on the exact date they feel bialys were first made. The city was founded in 1310. Bialystok was taken by Prussia in 1795 and by Russia in 1807, captured by Germany in 1915, but restored to Poland in 1921. During World War II, the city was overrun by Germans (1941) and then retaken by Soviet troops in 1944. At the end of the war, the city was returned to Poland once again (1945). However, many if not all of the city's Jewish citizens had been taken and murdered in the gas chambers. Today there are only a handful of Jewish citizens in Bialystok, and the only bread to be found resembling bialy seem to be New York bagels. The identity of many families and of the bialy have been lost in the city of their origin.

Bialys became a staple in New York delicatessens and in the Jewish communities. The best bialys were baked in Manhattan's Lower East Side, once known as "Bialy Central."

The bialy and the better-know bagel are similar. Instead of a hole as the bagel has, the bialy has an indentation that holds a filling, often onion, garlic, or poppy seeds. Bagels are boiled, and bialys are baked. Bialys are best eaten fresh, and they do not ship well, as they begin to stale after about six hours. For years in the United States, bialys were only popular in New York; but in places where "real" bagels are enjoyed you will often find the bialy. The bagel probably holds a slight edge in popularity, but the bialy, a dimpled bun with an onion filling, is closing in fast.

Selected Books Written by Eric A. Kimmel

The Adventures of Hershel of Ostropol. Illustrated by Trina Schart Hyman. (Holiday House, 1995)

Anansi Goes Fishing. Illustrated by Janet Stevens. (Holiday, 1992)

The Birds' Gift: A Ukrainian Easter Story. Illustrated by Katya Krenina. (Holiday House, 1999)

Blackbeard's Last Fight. Illustrated by Leonard Everett Fisher. (Farrar, Straus & Giroux, 2006)

Cactus Soup. Illustrated by Phil Huling. (Marshall Cavendish, 2004)

A Cloak for the Moon. Illustrated by Katya Krenina. (Holiday House, 2001)

The Frog Princess: A Tlingit Legend from Alaska. Illustrated by Rosanne Litzinger. (Holiday House, 2006)

Gershon's Monster: A Story for the Jewish New Year. Illustrated by Jon J. Muth. (Scholastic, 2000)

Hershel and the Hanukkah Goblins. Illustrated by Trina Schart Hyman. (Holiday House,1989)

A Horn for Louis. Illustrated by James Bemardin. (Random House, 2005)

The Lady in the Blue Cloak: Legends from the Texas Missions. Illustrated by Susan Guevara. (Holiday House, 2006)

Nanny Goat and the Seven Little Kids. Illustrated by Janet Stevens. (Holiday House, 1990)

The Runaway Tortilla. Illustrated by Randy Cecil. (Winslow, 2000)

The Spotted Pony: A Collection of Hanukkah Stories. Illustrated by Leonard Everett Fisher. (Holiday House, 1992)

Bialys with Onion–Poppy Seed Topping

Eric A. Kimmel's favorite food is the bagel, but he also likes bialys; and they are some-what (according to some bakers) easier to make. Bialys are less likely to be available commercially as they are only "fresh" for a short length of time, although they can be frozen and warmed up later. Here's a favorite New York recipe.

Ingredients

- Cornmeal (a tablespoon, more or less)
- 1 3/4 cups warm water (110 to 115 degrees F), divided in half
- 1 package active dry yeast
- 3 teaspoons sugar
- 2 teaspoons salt
- 4 1/2 cups all-purpose flour or bread flour

Before beginning to mix the bialy ingredients, prepare two baking sheets with parchment paper and sprinkle lightly with the tablespoon or so of cornmeal.

In a large bowl, mix 1/2 cup of the warm water, the yeast, and sugar. Let stand for 10 minutes or until foamy.

While the yeast is working, mix the topping.

Onion–Poppy Seed Topping

- 1 tablespoon vegetable or olive oil
- 1 1/2 teaspoons poppy seeds
- 1/3 cup very finely minced onion
- 1/2 teaspoon coarse kosher salt

In a small bowl, combine vegetable or olive oil, poppy seeds, onions, and salt; set aside.

Now turn your attention back to the bialys themselves.

After the yeast has become foamy, add the remaining 1 1/2 cups water, the salt, and the bread or all-purpose flour. Knead by hand or with dough hook of mixer for 8 minutes until smooth (the dough will be soft). If the dough is too moist, add a ta-blespoon or more of flour, one tablespoon at a time. If the dough is too dry, and looks gnarly, add warm water, a tablespoon at a time.

Shape the dough into a ball and place in a lightly oiled bowl, turning the dough to oil on all sides. Cover with plastic wrap and let rise 1 1/2 hours or until tripled in

(Continued)

bulk. Punch dough down in bowl, turn it over, cover again with plastic wrap, and let rise another 45 minutes or until again doubled in bulk.

Once the dough has doubled the second time, punch it down and roll into a fat, 8-inch-long cylinder. Slice the cylinder into eight 1-inch long slices and lay the dough rounds flat onto a lightly floured board. Cover with a towel, and let the rounds rest for ten minutes. Gently pat the edges of the rounds into 3- to 4-inch diameters. The middles might be higher than the edges. Place dough rounds—bialys—on the cornmeal dusted baking sheets and cover once again, with plastic wrap. Let rise an additional 30 minutes or until increased by about half in bulk (don't let them over-rise).

Use two fingers to make a depression in the middle of each dough round; press from the center outward, leaving a 1-inch rim. Place 1 teaspoon of the onion–poppy seed topping in the hole of each bialy. Cover lightly with plastic wrap or a damp towel and let rise for 30 minutes.

Preheat oven to 425 degrees F. Use both upper and lower shelves of the oven to bake the bialys, but rotate after 6 minutes, front to back, up to down. Bake another 6 minutes until lightly brown. Do not bake too long or the bialys will be very dry. Remove from oven and let cool on wire racks. Makes 12 bialys.

Eat bialys fresh or store in a tight container. A bialy is delicious sliced in half horizontally, toasted, and buttered, or spread with cream cheese. Bialys may also be filled as for a sandwich.

Eric A. Kimmel grew up in Brooklyn, New York, surrounded by his family. His grandmother told him stories from western Ukraine, where she had grown up. Eric also loved the stories of Dr. Seuss and read over and over the tales collected by the Grimm Brothers. Eric's father, Morris Kimmel, told his son stories about growing up in a family seven children in a tenement on Kosciusko Street in the 1920s.

Kimmel eventually became a storyteller himself, telling the stories he loved. During his childhood, Eric and his friends spent Saturdays going "all over town." After college, Kimmel spent a year teaching in Harlem and later lived on St. Thomas Island in the Virgin Islands. By 1973, he had earned a Ph.D. from the University of Illinois. After some time as an assistant professor at Indiana University at South Bend, Eric and his wife, Doris Ann, moved with her daughter, Bridgett, to Portland, Oregon, where Eric and Doris still live.

Eric was a professor at Portland State University for many years but left in 1994 to devote himself full time to creating and telling his stories. He is a skilled knitter and an accomplished bread baker. He loves coarse peasant rye bread. As for knitting, he loves the classic folk patterns—Irish Arans and Guernseys. He has had his own spinning wheel since 1992.

Eric A. Kimmel explains the origin of bagels, and we know the area of Russia (now Poland) where bialys originated. There are a couple of books that explain how other types of bread have come to be.

Panettone is a sweet fruit bread that comes from Milan, Italy. It is sometimes called "big bread" or "Tony's bread." Read:

dePaola, Tomie. *Tony's Bread: An Italian Folktale*. (Putnam, 1996)

Legend has it that the pretzel was developed when a baker is challenged to make a dough with water and to make a good-tasting roll that the rising sun can shine through three times. Read:

Carle, Eric. *Walter the Baker*. (Simon & Schuster, 1995)

Sandy Lanton—Latkes

Sandy Lanton

Sandy Lanton

Birthday: June 19

Favorite place: San Diego, California

Favorite foods: Lobster, shrimp, spaghetti, corn on the cob, pea soup, Greek salad, cheesecake, pistachio ice cream

Family:

   Spouse—Sy

   Son—Dave

   Daughter—Ruth

Home:

   Childhood—Queens, New York City

   Now—Woodbury, Long Island, New York

I chose latkes for a very practical reason. I wanted to write a Hanukkah story.

—About writing *Lots of Latkes* by Sandy Lanton

Sandy Lanton decided to be a writer when she was in the fifth grade. After winning an essay contest that she wrote about Theodore Roosevelt, she was invited with other winners from every school to a party at the Theodore Roosevelt home in New York City. She was hooked. She says, "I loved seeing my words and my name in print."

Sandy grew up in New York City. When she was very young, her mother bought her the little golden books. Her favorite was *The Pokey Little Puppy.* When Lanton was seven, the family moved from a six-story apartment building on Manhattan's Lower East Side to a first-floor garden apartment in Queens. Not only did she have grass and trees right outside her window—windows she often climbed through—but the local library was right around the corner. She considered the library to be "her library," and she had a goal of reading every book in the children's department. She didn't quite make that goal, but the librarians certainly became familiar with who she was. As she got older, she came to love *Heidi, Black Beauty,* and *Little Women.* She also enjoyed the Nancy Drew series, but she says, "The library didn't have them; they weren't considered 'literature,' but my friend, Bonnie, had the entire set and let me borrow them one at a time if I was careful with them."

Selected Books Written by Sandy Lanton

Daddy's Chair. Illustrated by Shelly Haas. (Lanton Haas Press, 2001)

Lots of Latkes: A Hanukkah Story. Illustrated by Vicki Jo Redenbaugh. (Lerner/KarBen Publishing, 2003)

Jelly Doughnuts

In Lots of Latkes, *various guests were to bring specific items for a potluck meal. Manya was known for her homemade jelly, so she had been asked to bring jelly doughnuts. But when she found she had no sugar, she made latkes instead (as did the many other guests). Here is a child-friendly recipe that might be used to involve children in the food preparation, although since these doughnuts are also fried in oil, an adult should be present to supervise.*

Use a tube of baking powder biscuits. With a turkey baster filled with jelly (apricot, raspberry, or cherry), inject a 1/2 teaspoonful of jelly into the center of each biscuit. You might wish to pinch shut the hole made by the baster so that the jelly does not ooze out. Heat 1 1/2 inches of oil in a cooking pan. When oil is hot (and spits if a drop of water is put into the pan), use tongs to place biscuits into the oil. Lower heat just enough to maintain temperature. Cook biscuits until lightly brown and roll over to cook the other side. Remove from the oil and drain on a cooling rack or paper towels. When cool enough to handle, roll in confectioner's (powdered) sugar or granulated sugar. Makes as many doughnuts as you have biscuits. Best served warm.

Latkes, Latkes, Latkes!

Edwards, Michelle. *Papa's Latkes*. Illustrated by Stacey Schuett. (Candlewick Press, 2004)

Glaser, Linda. *The Borrowed Hanukkah Latkes*. Illustrated by Nancy Cote. (Albert Whitman, 1997)

Howland, Naomi. *Latkes, Latkes, Good to Eat*. (Clarion, 1999)

Kimmelman, Leslie. *The Runaway Latkes*. Illustrated by Paul Yalowitz. (Albert Whitman, 2002)

Manushkin, Fran. *Latkes and Applesauce: A Hanukkah Story*. Illustrated by Robin Spowart. (Scholastic, 1990)

Penn, Malka. *The Miracle of the Potato Latkes: A Hanukkah Story*. Illustrated by Giora Carmi. (Holiday House, 1994)

Yorinks, Arthur. *The Flying Latke*. Illustrated by William Steig. (Simon & Schuster, 1999)

Zalben, Jane Breskin. *Papa's Latkes*. (Henry Holt, 1994)

My family always got together for Hanukkah at Aunt Irene's and Uncle George's house. Aunt Irene always made latkes with Uncle George's help—he did the [potato] peeling. We all brought dishes to complete the feast. I always brought the salad. We also brought menorahs, and we lined them up on the table to light. Uncle George led the singing in his booming voice. My cousin Lynne made song sheets with all the traditional songs. Even though my aunt and uncle are gone, the tradition continues. We take turns hosting the Hanukkah party and several people make the latkes, but we all bring something good to eat. We all bring our menorahs, some handmade by the children out of clay or wood. We line them up on the table to light. We sing the traditional songs using Lynne's song sheets. Now I also read *Lots of Latkes* to the youngest children.

Every July, the Long Island Children's Writers and Illustrators has a picnic in a member's backyard with our families, and everyone brings something. We sign up at the June meeting for various dishes. Sometimes people sign up for one dish and bring something completely different. I thought about what would happen if every one brought the same thing. These two images came together in *Lots of Latkes*. I set the story long ago so people couldn't go to the supermarket to buy the item they were planning to bring and for one reason or another couldn't.

—Sandy Lanton

Latkes

Rivka Leah's Latkes recipe is available in Lots of Latkes. *The following recipe is another variation that is easy to make.*

- 2 pounds or about 4 large potatoes, peeled
- 2 large eggs
- 1 teaspoon salt (or more to taste)
- Oil for frying

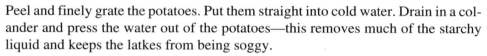

Peel and finely grate the potatoes. Put them straight into cold water. Drain in a colander and press the water out of the potatoes—this removes much of the starchy liquid and keeps the latkes from being soggy.

Add the salt to the eggs and beat. Add well-beaten egg mixture to potatoes and stir. Coat the bottom of a frying pan or griddle with oil and heat. Place 1/4 cup of potatoes onto the griddle, flatten a little and lower heat so the latkes will cook thoroughly before browning around the edges. Fry on both sides. Serve hot with sour cream or applesauce.

Variations for serving: Vary the presentation by serving with dill sauce and a bit of cooked salmon garnishing the top or instead of applesauce make an apple-pear sauce (with lemon and a hint of cinnamon), or even a cranberry sauce. Add your favorite spices to create a new flavor; add chunked apples (and cinnamon) to the potato mixture, or add some grated cheese (for cheese latkes), grated zucchini, and grated carrots (and even a red pepper) to make vegetable latkes.

Laurie Lawlor—Thai Stir Fry

Laurie Lawlor

Birthday: April 4

Favorite place: Wisconsin Wetland near Kettle Morraine State Park

Favorite foods: Yogurt, Thai stir fry from my favorite restaurant in Evanston (Illinois), and donuts!

Family:

    Spouse—John "Jack" (married 30+ years)

    Son—John

    Daughter—Megan

Home:

    Childhood—LaGrange, Illinois

    Now—Evanston, Illinois

I found that as I was working on this book, I became hungrier and hungrier! This is what happens when you become very involved in writing about your characters. You empathize with them completely— including their hunger pains.

— Laurie Lawlor, on writing *Dead Reckoning: A Pirate Journey with Captain Frances Drake*

Because I am from a big, hungry family (the eldest in a family of six) and because my mother did not know how to drive, our trips to the grocery store were times of great anticipation and sly eating tactics. By the time we unloaded the bags of groceries, there was often little food left. That was because my brothers and sisters and I had "snacked" heavily on everything in the parking lot and the car before the groceries could be unloaded.

I learned to cook at a fairly early age— mainly because I had to. One of my earliest memories of cooking food for my brothers and sisters was burning scrambled eggs badly. A terrible smell I despise to this day.

When I write about the past in many of my historical novels it is important to me to understand what people wore, how they lived, and what they did for fun. What they ate is very important to know—whether I'm writing about the sixteenth century or the early twentieth century. I often use newspaper accounts, diaries, and early cookbooks to discover details about food my characters have eaten.

—Laurie Lawlor

Selected Books Written by Laurie Lawlor

In addition to writing books for three series, "American Sisters" (Pocket Books), "Addie Across the Prairie" (Albert Whitman), and "Heartland" (Pocket Books), Laurie Lawlor has written picture books, fiction, and information books.

Dead Reckoning: A Pirate Voyage with Captain Drake. (Simon & Schuster, 2005)

He Will Go Fearless. (Simon & Schuster, 2006)

Helen Keller: Rebellious Spirit. (Holiday House, 2001)

Magnificent Voyage: An American Adventurer on Captain James Cook's Final Expedition. (Holiday House, 2002)

Old Crump: The True Story of a Trip West. Illustrated by John Winch. (Holiday House, 2002)

The School at Crooked Creek. (Holiday House, 2004)

This Tender Place: The Story of a Wetland Year. Illustrated by photographs. (Terrace Books/University of Wisconsin—Madison, 2005)

Wind on the River (Jamestown Publishers, 2001)

Corn Soup

The School at Crooked Creek *is set in the Indiana frontier in 1820. When the early settlers came to Indiana, they learned from the Native Americans how to use many wild or cultivated plants and game. One of the first crops that the early settlers cultivated was corn. Almost every meal they ate had corn as one of the dishes. They ate things like dried corn, cream corn, hull corn, dried corn mush, and sometimes they ate corn bread.*

In the nineteenth century, corn was usually boiled on the cob with hardwood ash; they were left in the husk for this process to soften the kernels. The kernels were then scraped from the cob and dried for later use, especially during the cold winters when they made corn soup and corn bread. The corn was husked, boiled, and dried and used in some of the same dishes we enjoy today.

Ingredients

- Water as needed
- Four cups dried corn (or frozen if you don't have access to dried)
- Four to five pork hocks, beef cubes, spareribs, or venison (or combination)
- Salt and pepper

Cook your choice of meat, in sufficient water to cover, until tender. Let cool and take meat from bone. Discard bone, but save stock and skim off all fat. In a large stockpot, combine stock, corn, and meat and bring to a boil. Cook for about three hours. Salt and pepper to taste. During the days of the early settlers, spices and herbs were rarely used. Today, we might add chopped celery, onion, and some dried parsley to make this soup savory.

Johnny Cake

Also called Journey Cake, so called because this cake/bread was easy to make and take on a journey

- 2 cups flour
- 1 1/2 tablespoons baking powder
- 3/4 teaspoon salt
- 1 cup cornmeal
- 3 eggs
- 1 cup milk
- 1/2 cup maple syrup
- 3/4 cup melted shortening

Combine flour, baking powder, and salt. Add cornmeal and mix thoroughly. Combine remaining ingredients and add to dry ingredients, stirring only to dampen all the flour. Pour into greased pan or iron skillet and bake for 30 minutes until all sides are brown.

Booklist

Laurie Lawlor's education in the field of journalism stimulated her curiosity and made her want to know all the details of a favorite great aunt, who, at the age of nine, accompanied her family across the Iowa prairie to homestead in Dakota Territory. She was able to read some of her aunt's journals and later spent several years researching. Once she had enough details, she wrote the first novel in her Addie series, *Addie across the Prairie* was published in 1986 (Albert A. Whitman). Since the book was based on her Great Aunt Laura's life, Laurie at first named the girl "Laura," but her editor, in a reference to Laura Ingalls Wilder's Little House series, felt there were "too many Lauras on the prairie." Laurie agreed to call her character "Addie."

The Addie books are set in the middle 1800s, and they provide a lot of details about moving west, and life on the prairie. Other books that contribute to readers' knowledge about the westward movement include:

Ackerman, Karen. *Araminta's Paint Box.* Illustrated by Betsy Lewin. (Aladdin, 1998)

Armstrong, Jennifer. *Black-Eyed Susan: A Novel.* (Knopf, 1995; Yearling, 1997)

Cannon, A. E. *Charlotte's Rose.* (Wendy Lamb Books, 2002; Yearling, 2004)

Conrad, Pam. *Prairie Songs* (HarperCollins, 1985)

Conrad, Pam. *Prairie Visions* (HarperCollins, 1991)

Erdrich, Louise. *The Birchbark House* (Hyperion, 1999)

Hopkinson, Deborah. *Apples to Oregon: Being the (Slightly) True Narrative of How a Brave Pioneer Father Brought Apples, Peaches, Pears, Plums, Grapes, and Cherries (and Children) ... the Plains.* Illustrated by Nancy Carpenter. (Simon & Schuster, 2004)

Kurtz, Jane. *I'm Sorry, Almira Ann.* Illustrated by Susan Havice. (Henry Holt, 1999)

MacLachlan, Patricia. *Sarah, Plain and Tall.* (HarperTrophy, 1987)

McCaughrean, Geraldine. *Stop the Train!* (HarperCollins, 2003)

Rylant, Cynthia. *Old Town in the Green Groves.* Illustrated by Jim LaMarche. (HarperCollins, 2002; HarperTrophy, 2004)

Stotts, Stuart. *Books in a Box: Lutie Stearns and the Traveling Libraries of Wisconsin.* (Big Valley Press, 2005)

Turner, Ann. *Grasshopper Summer.* Illustrated by Erika Meltzer. (Macmillan 1989)

Wilder, Laura Ingalls. Little House series. Illustrated by Garth Williams. (HarperCollins, various dates and editions)

Thai Stir-Fried Rice Noodles

One of Laurie Lawlor's favorite foods is Thai stir fry from her favorite restaurant. There are many Asian stir-fry recipes, but Thai food is sometimes described as a hybrid between Chinese and Indian cuisine. The peppers and curries (seasoned with a mixture of spices) usually associated with Indian entrées are ever-present in the Chinese-style noodles and rice dishes of Thai food.

Ingredients

- 8 ounces (1/8 inch wide) rice noodles
- 1 whole chicken breast, boned, skinned
- 8 medium-size shrimp, shelled, deveined
- 1/2 cup water
- 1/4 cup fish sauce (available at specialty and Asian markets)
- 3 tablespoons sugar
- 1 tablespoon lime juice
- 1 teaspoon paprika
- 1/8 teaspoon red (cayenne) pepper
- 1/2 pound fresh bean sprouts
- 3 green onions, white part only, cut into 1-inch shreds
- 3 tablespoons vegetable oil
- 4 large garlic cloves, finely chopped
- 1 egg
- 4 tablespoons finely crushed roasted peanuts

Cover the rice noodles with water in a large bowl and soak for 45 minutes. While the noodles are soaking, cut chicken into 1 1/2-inch by 1/3-inch strips. Cut shrimp in half lengthwise; set chicken and shrimp aside. Combine the 1/2 cup water, fish sauce, sugar, lime juice, paprika, and red pepper in a small bowl; set aside. Set aside one-quarter of bean sprouts for topping. Combine the shredded green onions and the rest of the bean sprouts. Drain noodles.

Heat the vegetable oil in a wok, over medium-high heat. Once the oil is heated, add the garlic. Fry until garlic starts to brown. Increase heat. Add chicken and stir fry until almost cooked, about 2 minutes. Push chicken to one side. Break egg into wok. Stir quickly to break up yolk and scramble egg. When egg is set, mix with chicken.

Add drained noodles, shrimp, fish-sauce mixture, and 3 tablespoons peanuts. Cook and stir over high heat 2 to 3 minutes or until noodles are soft and most of liquid is absorbed. Add green-onion mixture; cook, stirring, for 1 more minute. Spoon onto a heated platter. Sprinkle with reserved bean sprouts, then with remaining peanuts.

Loreen Leedy—Spritz Cookies

Every family has special foods they like to eat. When we were growing up, my mom made a special kind of cookie every year during the holidays.

—Loreen Leedy

My mother's mother came from Sweden, and it is traditional in Scandinavian countries to make Spritz Cookies at Christmas. The cookie dough is put into a cylinder that has odd-looking holes at the other end and is pushed out in various shapes such as hearts, stars, and wreaths. Nowadays there are easy-to-use cookie presses available, even electric ones, but my mother always used a simple metal one that required a very steady hand and arm to operate. We would help decorate the cookies with colored sprinkles, nuts, and Red Hots. With five children, Mom had to make a double batch (at least!). [A couple of years ago,] my two nieces helped me make some Spritz cookies, and though the kitchen ended up with sprinkles and colored sugar everywhere, everyone enjoyed eating the yummy results.

—Loreen Leedy

Loreen Leedy

Birthday: June 15

Favorite place: Outdoors in a
natural area such as a forest

Favorite foods: cookies, crunchy
raw veggies

Family:

Spouse—Andrew Schuerger

Home:

Childhood—Wilmington,
Delaware

Now—central Florida

Writing a Recipe Book

Many people have a collection of cookbooks. But Leedy suggests that readers may wish to create their own special cookbook with family recipes. Her book, *Look at My Book: How Kids Can Write and Illustrate Terrific Books,* has a lot of ideas for creating a personal cookbook.

Suggestions by Loreen Leedy

First: Do some research (see page 7 of Loreen's book) by asking relatives for their favorite recipes. It would also be fun to add a special story that goes with the dish, such as the time the dog ate Aunt Julie's Cherry Explosion Cake.

Do a rough draft (page 14) then practice some fancy lettering (page 28) to write out the recipe.

Add an illustration (pages 15 and 24–27).

Leedy's book illustrates ways to bind your book (page 29), but you can also use clear plastic page protectors in a three-ring binder to store the cookbook pages. (This also keeps the pages safe from splattered ingredients.) Keep adding to the cookbook, and it will become a treasured keepsake—you might even have to make copies for all your relatives.

Spritz Cookies

Illustrations by Loreen Leedy

Sift together:

- 2 1/4 cups flour
- 1/2 teaspoon salt

In a different bowl, mix to a creamy consistency:

- 3/4 cup sugar
- 1 cup butter

Add:

- 2 egg yolks
- 1 teaspoon vanilla or almond extract

Stir in the flour, mixing well. Chill in refrigerator for at least an hour. Preheat the over to 350 degrees F. Put dough into cookie press and press carefully onto an ungreased cookie sheet. Decorate as desired. Bake for about 10 minutes until set and very lightly browned.

Signature Recipe—Loreen Leedy

Loreen Leedy is well known for her fiction and information books. She has written about writing letters and solving mathematical problems. Her books are characterized by her use of speech bubbles, which allows characters to ask questions and to provide interesting information and comments.

Selected Books Written and Illustrated by Loreen Leedy

E-mail from Mars, with Andrew Schuerger. (Holiday House, 2006)

The Great Graph Contest. (Holiday House. 2004)

Look at My Book: How Kids Can Write and Illustrate Terrific Books. (Holiday House, 2004)

Mapping Penny's World. (Henry Holt, 2000)

Subtraction Action. (Holiday House, 2000)

There's a Frog in My Throat: 440 Animal Sayings a Little Bird Told Me, coauthored with Pat Street. (Winslow Press, 2001)

Creating a Book—Writing a Story

Loreen Leedy's book *Look at My Book: How Kids Can Write and Illustrate Terrific Books* gives a lot of information about how to create and make a personal book. Here are some other books that will give additional information that may be used in creating one's own family recipe book.

Aliki. *How a Book Is Made.* (HarperTrophy, 1988)

Bang, Molly. *Picture This: How Pictures Work.* (SeaStar Books, 2000)

Christelow, Eileen. *What Do Authors Do?* (Clarion, 1997)

Christelow, Eileen. *What Do Illustrators Do?* (Clarion, 1999)

Duke, Kate. *Aunt Isabel Tells a Good One.* (Puffin, 1994)

Lester, Helen. *Author: A True Story.* (Houghton Mifflin/Walter Lorraine Books; Reprint edition, 2002)

Stevens, Janet. *From Pictures to Words: A Book about Making a Book.* (Holiday House, 1995)

Loreen Leedy

Loreen Leedy grew up in Wilmington, Delaware. Even as a very young child, she loved to draw and create artistic works. She knew she wanted to be an artist, but by the time she was at college, she did not know what kind of art she wanted to pursue. After graduating from the University of Delaware, she turned to creating whimsical animal jewelry and chess pieces from polymer clay. She traveled to craft shows selling her creations. In the early 1980s, she turned her attention to children's books and began to create book characters of her whimsical animals. At first she used traditional artist's tools (pencils, paints, and brushes) to make her art, but her most recent books have been illustrated using computer technology, which she says gives her a degree of flexibility that she did not have before. With a computer, she is able to incorporate scans of real objects into her illustrations and to manipulate drawings she has made to create a new composition.

Loreen has published more than thirty books. Her husband, Andrew "Andy" Schuerger, is a scientist who works on space biology research at Kennedy Space Center. Together they wrote the book *E-mail from Mars*.

Swedish Pepparkakor (Ginger Snaps)

Pepparkakor *is a special holiday treat, in Sweden, especially on St. Lucia's day (December 13).* Pepparkakor *is also the cookie that Pippi Longstocking rolls out in enormous quantities on her kitchen floor. (*Pippi Longstocking *by Astrid Lindgren [Viking, 1950]).*

- 1 cup butter (or margarine)
- 1 cup firmly packed light brown sugar
- 3 tablespoons dark molasses
- Grated rind of one lemon
- 3 cups all-purpose flour
- 1 1/4 teaspoons ground cardamom

1 1/4 teaspoons baking soda
4 teaspoons ground cinnamon
2 teaspoons ground cloves
1/4 teaspoon ground ginger
1/4 cup water

Cream together the butter and brown sugar, in a large bowl. Add in the molasses and lemon rind. Set aside. In a smaller bowl, combine the flour, baking soda, and spices. Mix the first half of the dry ingredients into the molasses mixture. Add the 1/4 cup water. Once the water has been incorporated into the mixture add in the remaining dry ingredients and mix well. Shape the dough into a ball and wrap in waxed paper. Refrigerate for several hours or overnight.

Preheat oven to 350 degrees F. Divide the ball of dough in half and roll it 1/8 inch thick on a floured board. Use cookie cutters to cut cookies in desired shapes. Place cookies on a lightly greased cookie sheet. Repeat until all the dough is used. Bake each sheet of cookies, 8 to 10 minutes or until cookies are lightly brown on the edges. They should be soft when removed from the cookie sheet but will crisp as they cool.

Cynthia Leitich Smith and Greg Leitich Smith—Chocolate-Covered Strawberries

Most of all I remember the Rocky Mountain trout. I guess because it was something I could get only there. My dad would talk about how he'd eaten it as a boy, and it made me feel more connected to him somehow, ordering the same thing.

—Cynthia Leitich Smith

Photo Credit: Greg Leitich Smith

Cynthia Leitich Smith

Birthday: December 31

Favorite place: my sunroom

Favorite foods: sake sashimi, garlic hummus, cucumbers, caviar, dark-chocolate covered strawberries, scrambled eggs, and ostrich

Family:

Spouse—Greg Leitich Smith

Cats— Leo Galilei, Blizzard Bentley, Sebastian Doe, Mercury Boo

Home:

Childhood—Kansas City—Missouri and Kansas suburbs

Now—Austin, Texas

Greg Leitich Smith

Greg Leitich Smith

Birthday: August 18

Family:

Spouse—Cynthia Leitich Smith

Home:

Childhood—Chicago, Illinois

Now—Austin, Texas

Photo Credit: Cynthia Leitich Smith

Greg Leitich

Greg Leitich was born in Evanston, Illinois, and grew up in the Chicago area where he attended Lane Tech High School, a science magnet school very similar to the fictional school that is the setting for his first two novels, *Ninjas, Piranhas, and Galileo* and *Tofu and T. Rex*. Greg earned an undergraduate degree from the University of Chicago and a graduate degree from the University of Texas—both in electrical engineering. Later he attended University of Michigan Law School, and he now spends his days as a patent attorney.

Cynthia Smith was born in Kansas City, Missouri. She grew up in that area, but often spent summer months in Oklahoma. She is a tribal member of the Muscogee (Creek) Nation. She graduated from the University of Kansas in 1990 and entered the University of Michigan Law School, where she and Greg met. Cynthia earned her law degree in 1994—the same year Greg earned his degree from that same school.

They married in September of 1994 and lived in Texas and Chicago before settling in Austin, Texas, where they are renovating a historic home. When they married, Cynthia Smith took Greg's surname as a "middle name"—distinguishing her more common surname by adding Leitich. Her name became Cynthia Leitich Smith. Greg Leitich continued to use his birth name in his role as a patent attorney, but when he began to write children's books he added Cynthia's surname to his, becoming Greg Leitich Smith.

Greg is an author of middle grade–teen novels, and Cynthia is a renowned author of contemporary Native American stories. She has written picture books (her most recent with husband Greg), middle grade stories, and young adult novels.

Selected Books Written by Greg Leitich Smith

Ninjas, Piranhas, and Galileo. (Little, Brown, 2003)

Tofu and T. Rex. (Little, Brown, 2005)

Selected Books by Cynthia Leitich Smith

Indian Shoes. (HarperCollins, 2002)

Jingle Dancer. Illustrated by Cornelius Van Wright and Ying-Hwa Hu. (Morrow/HarperCollins, 2000)

Rain Is Not My Indian Name. (HarperCollins, 2001)

Selected Book Written by Cynthia Leitich Smith and Greg Leitich Smith

Santa Knows. Illustrated by Steve Bjorkman. (Dutton, 2006)

Photo Credit: Frances Hill

I'm in the rare and fortunate position to be living with a fellow children's/teen author—my very cute husband, Greg Leitich Smith. It lends itself to our working together on projects, as readers and researchers, even though we may be writing independently. Together, we built a pasta bridge while I was writing *Rain Is Not My Indian Name*. Together we mixed up stuffing for a vegan sushi *Kielbasa* for his *Tofu and T. Rex*.

Tofu and T. Rex is about a young vegan who goes to live with her cousin's family who own an East European deli and butcher shop. Her name is Freddie Murchison-Kowalski, and she is enthusiastically principled in her veganism. Having lived mostly along the cattle trail—from Austin to Chicago, I've always been a die-hard carnivore, but sometime during my twentieth or fortieth reading of *Tofu and T. Rex*, Freddie's arguments really got to me.

I'm not a vegan, but I have stopped eating mammals entirely.

My husband, the author of the book and He-Who-Cooks-at-Our-House, is a big steak-and-prime-rib guy. He's appalled, "It's fiction!" he keeps telling me.

But what can I say? His story sucked me in.

I grew and changed.

That's what heroes are supposed to do, though, isn't it?

—Cynthia Leitich Smith

TOFU

Basically tofu is a "cheese-like food made of curdled soybean milk." Tofu is to the Orient what the potato is to the West. Both can be baked, boiled, grilled, or fried; eaten whole, smashed, in cubes, or mixed with any number of other ingredients. And just like the potato, tofu is rather bland tasting without seasonings. However, some taste tests have resulted in the opinion that tofu, unseasoned, is tastier than potatoes unseasoned. Tofu is a source of protein, whereas potatoes are mostly a source of carbohydrates.

Tofu is an important part of most vegetarians' diet and as such figured prominently in Greg Leitich Smith's *Tofu and T. Rex* book.

Baked Tofu Bites

This hors d'oeuvre can be served hot or cold or used as a salad topping.

Ingredients

- 2 (16-ounce) packages extra firm tofu
- 1/2 cup soy sauce
- 4 tablespoons maple syrup
- 4 tablespoons ketchup
- 2 tablespoons vinegar
- 2 dashes hot sauce
- 2 tablespoon sesame seeds
- 1/2 teaspoon garlic powder
- 1/2 teaspoon ground black pepper
- 2 teaspoons liquid smoke flavoring

Directions

Preheat the oven to 375 degrees F. Prepare a baking sheet by lightly spraying or greasing with oil.

Slice the tofu into 1/2-inch slices and gently press the excess water out of the tofu. Cut the sliced tofu crossways into 1/2-inch slices; making 1/2-inch cubes.

Mix together, the soy sauce, maple syrup, ketchup, vinegar, and hot sauce. Stir in sesame seeds, garlic powder, black pepper, and liquid smoke. Add the tofu and gently stir. Cover and marinate at least 5 minutes.

Place the cubes of tofu on the prepared baking sheet (single layer). Bake in oven for 15 minutes. Turn the tofu and bake another 10 to 15 minutes or until the tofu turns golden brown. Serves 8.

Tofu and Rice Stuffed Red Peppers

Ingredients

- 1 cup uncooked brown rice
- 2 cups water
- 2 tablespoons olive oil
- 1 clove garlic, minced
- 1 (12 ounce) package extra-firm tofu, drained and diced in approximately 1/2 inch cubes
- 1 3/4 cups marinara sauce, divided
- salt to taste
- Ground black pepper to taste
- 2 red bell peppers, halved and seeded
- 2 orange bell peppers, halved and seeded
- 2 cups shredded mozzarella cheese
- 8 slices tomato

Directions

Preheat oven to 350 degrees F and then cook the rice as directed on the package, boiling until rice is tender. Set aside.

In a skillet, heat olive oil over a medium heat. Stir in the garlic and tofu. Cook about 5 minutes.

Mix in 1/4 cup of the marinara sauce, season with salt and pepper and continue to cook and stir until tofu is evenly brown.

Now it's time to stuff the peppers. Spoon an equal amount of rice into each pepper half, press rice to compact it in the cavity of the pepper. Layer rice with remaining marinara sauce, and half of the cheese. Press equal amounts of tofu into the pepper halves. Place 1 tomato slice on each pepper, and top peppers with remaining mozzarella.

Arrange stuffed peppers in a baking dish. Bake 25 minutes in the preheated oven, until cheese is melted. Serve half of a colored pepper to each person.

Dark-Chocolate-Covered Strawberries

One of Cynthia Leitich Smith's favorite foods is dark-chocolate-covered strawberries. This is an easy and quick recipe for making your own.

Ingredients

- 12 ounces dark chocolate
- 6 tablespoons half and half cream
- 1 tablespoon unsalted butter
- 40 large strawberries with stems (carefully wiped clean with damp towel)

Combine the chocolate and cream in a two-quart glass bowl. Heat in microwave oven on high 3 to 4 minutes. Stir occasionally to smooth the mixture. When chocolate is melted and smooth, add butter and stir until butter is melted.

Dip each strawberry into the chocolate mixture. Allow the excess chocolate to drip back into the bowl. If the chocolate is not the right consistency for coating the strawberries, add additional cream.

Place each coated strawberry on a baking sheet lined with foil or waxed paper. Let the chocolate-covered strawberry cool at room temperature, and then chill the strawberries in the refrigerator until chocolate is set, about 20 to 30 minutes.

Strawberry Shortcake

If you enjoy chocolate-covered strawberries, strawberry shortcake should be on your list of favorites as well. A simple, not too sweet shortcake is made with biscuits.

Prepare 2 quarts strawberries by stemming and hulling the berries, wash them, and place in a large bowl with 2/3 cup sugar. Mash lightly to create some juice, but leave many berries whole. Cover and refrigerate while making biscuits.

Biscuits

In a medium bowl, combine the following ingredients. Mix with a spoon until dry ingredients are incorporated into the wet mixture.

- 2 cups all-purpose flour
- 1 tablespoon baking powder
- 1/2 teaspoon salt
- 3 tablespoons sugar
- 1 stick butter, chilled (cut into chunks)
- 2/3 to 3/4 cup half and half, milk, or cream

Spoon biscuit mixture (making 8 biscuits) onto a lightly buttered baking pan. Preheat the oven to 425 degree and bake the biscuits for 10 to 15 minutes, until biscuits are golden brown. While the biscuits are baking, whip 1 1/2 cup heavy cream until it forms soft peaks.

Once the biscuits are finished baking, move them to a platter, and split each biscuit horizontally with a serrated knife. Place each split biscuit onto a dessert plate and remove the top of the biscuit. Cover the bottom biscuit with 2/3 cup berries/juice. Replace the top of the biscuit and spoon on a tablespoon or so of berries. Top with whipped cream for topping and serve while the biscuit is still warm.

E. B. Lewis—Waffles

My favorite foods—waffles and pancakes —I love maple syrup. And fish—especially salmon—baked, grilled, or broiled.

— E. B. Lewis

Earl Bradley (E. B.) Lewis

Birthday: December 16

Favorite foods: waffles, pancakes—with maple syrup, salmon (grilled, broiled, baked)

Family:

Sons—Aaron and Joshua

Home:

Childhood—Philadelphia, Pennsylvania

Now—New Jersey

Earl Bradley (E. B.) Lewis was born in Philadelphia, Pennsylvania, where he grew up as the oldest child in his family. He has been interested in drawing since his childhood. E. B. remembers drawing on walls. He was five years older than his sister—and jealous. He sought attention at school and became the class clown. One day in sixth grade, his teacher asked the students, "What do you want to be?" Charlie, another student, answered, "Doctor." E. B. raised his hand and said, "Lawyer." Everyone laughed—including his teacher. That was a turning point. E. B. decided that he would be someone and would make a contribution. He would not be the one others laughed at or about.

Two of E. B.'s uncles were artists. His Uncle Bradley began to come every Saturday from New Jersey to take E. B. to the Temple University School of Art League, an art school that Uncle Bradley ran. E. B. knew he wanted to go to the same art school that his uncle had attended. Uncle Bradley also bombarded him with books, and E. B. began reading about something he liked—art.

In 1975, after graduating from high school, E. B. formally entered the Temple University Tyler School of Art. During art school, he found the medium he preferred—watercolor. He graduated in 1979 with a major in graphic design and illustration, and art education. E. B. taught art for eight years. During that time, he did not pick up a paintbrush. Then he began to stay at school after hours to paint. One of his first paintings was of a lighthouse scene in Bermuda—a scene from his honeymoon. He loved painting children and also has "an affinity for water." He lived on the Delaware River and found many locations for painting. Eventually he accumulated enough paintings for an art gallery show—and the show sold out. As he began to build his success with more sold-out art exhibits, he was given an invitation to illustrate a children's book.

"There is," says Lewis, "a thin line between illustration and fine art. The difference is—one makes money and one doesn't." Once he agreed to illustrate his first children's book he was offered nine more contracts in two weeks. He quit his teaching job. His first illustrated book was Jane Kurtz's *Fire on the Mountain* (Simon & Schuster, 1984). He completed the illustrations for five books in the first year. Now he generally completes four books a year. He lives in Folsom, New Jersey, where his studio is a large warehouse—the "other side" has a pool table for when he wants to relax. He most often uses watercolor and stages photograph shots to help him get the right angles and stances for people and objects. Sometimes his two sons pose for him; other times he goes searching for the right model for his photography sessions.

Selected Books Illustrated by E. B. Lewis

Across the Alley. Text by Richard Michelson. (Putnam, 2006)

Bippity Bop Barbershop. Text by Natasha Anastasia Tarpley. (Megan Tingley, 2002)

Circle Unbroken. Text by Margot Theis Raven. (Farrar, Straus & Giroux, 2004)

Coming on Home Soon. Text by Jacqueline Woodson. (Putnam, 2004)

Danitra Brown, Class Clown. Text by Nikki Grimes. (Amistad, 2005)

Dirt on Their Skirts: The Story of the Young Women Who Won the World Championship. Text by Doreen Rappaport and Lyndall Callan. (Dial, 2000)

Happy Feet: The Savoy Ballroom Lindy Hoppers and Me. Text by Richard Michelson. (Gullivar, 2005)

Joe-Joe's First Flight. Text by Natasha Tarpley. (Knopf, 2003)

My Best Friend. Text by Mary Ann Rodman. (Viking, 2005)

Sometimes My Mommy Gets Angry. Text by Bebe Moore Campbell. (Grosset & Dunlap, 2003)

Talkin' about Bessie. Text by Nikki Grimes. (Orchard, 2002)

This Little Light of Mine. Text from a classic song by the same title. (Simon & Schuster, 2005)

When You Were Born. Text by Dianna Hutts Aston. (Candlewick, 2004)

Waffles

Waffles and pancakes are among E. B. Lewis's favorite foods, and he loves maple syrup. Here's a special basic waffle recipe that has been a favorite since the early 1970s.

Preheat your waffle iron.

Separate the whites and yolks of three eggs.

In a small mixing bowl, beat the egg whites until they are stiff. Set aside.

Then in a medium to large mixing bowl, sift together:

- 1 3/4 cups flour
- 2 teaspoons baking powder
- 1/2 teaspoon salt
- 1 tablespoon sugar

Add and mix into the dry ingredients:

- Yolks of the three eggs
- 7 tablespoons vegetable oil
- 1 1/2 cups milk

Beat until there are no lumps in the batter. Put aside the beaters and fold the egg whites into the batter using a spatula or other flat utensil. Put a full 1/2 cup of batter in your waffle iron to make a 9-inch round waffle. This recipe makes about eight 9-inch waffles.

Left-over waffles can be cooled and frozen in a plastic bag. Heat in a microwave when you are ready to eat. Serve waffles with warm cinnamon applesauce or maple syrup.

MAPLE SYRUP

Maple syrup comes from maple trees. Maple trees are tapped and from the tap drips sap from the tree. When the pilgrims arrived, Native Americans were already tapping maple trees. They used a hatchet to tap the trees for sap. Sugar maple trees (also known as rock or hard maple) are the best sap producers. Red maples also produce sweet sap. One to three taps can be placed in each tree, depending on the tree's size. Each tap hole will yield from five to fifteen gallons of sap. Sometimes tap holes will yield as much as forty to eighty gallons of sap in a single year. Ten gallons of sap produces about one quart of syrup. Cooking the sap reduces it to make syrup.

Haas, Jessie. *Sugaring*. Illustrated by Joseph A. Smith. (Greenwillow, 1996)

Keller, Kristin Thoennes. *From Maple Trees to Maple Syrup*. (First Facts from Farm to Table) (First Facts Books, 2004)

Lasky, Kathryn. *Sugaring Time*. Illustrated by Christopher G. Knight. (Aladdin, 1986)

Maxson, Tammy Skiver. *Grandpa's Maple Syrup*. (PublishAmerica, 2005)

Mitchell, Melanie. *From Maple Tree to Syrup*. (Start to Finish). (Lerner, 2004)

Play Ball!

When E. B. Lewis signed on to illustrate *Dirt on Their Skirts: The Story of the Young Women Who Won the World Championship,* he knew he would have to do some research. The story is based on an event that took place in Racine, Wisconsin. Lewis traveled there and found that the field was still there. He needed models for photographs, so he talked some women, mostly teachers from a local school, into dressing in "uniforms" that he located. The uniforms were waitress dresses from the era. Some of the women had never played ball in their life. The pitcher was a second-grade teacher.

Jack's Caramel Corn and Peanuts

Although the food at many ballparks across the country has become more sophisti-cated, the standard and most popular fare may still be peanuts, Cracker Jacks, and hot dogs.

Popping corn was part of the Native American diet in colonial days. The idea of covering popcorn and peanuts with molasses was an idea that emerged in 1893 and showed up at the 1896 Columbian Exposition in Chicago. Two brothers, Fred and Louis Ruekheim, developed the process and then refined it when customers commented about the stickiness of the early concoction. Louis developed a for-mula that made a great molasses coating that was crispy and dry. The Cracker Jack formula is still a secret of the company. In 1908, the Cracker Jack name was incorporated into the famous song, "Take Me Out to the Ball Game." "Buy me some peanuts and Cracker Jacks" is still heard at ballparks throughout the United States. Cracker Jacks became a standard snack food at baseball games. Read:

> Norworth, Jack. *Take Me Out to the Ballgame.* Illustrated by Jim Burke. (Lit-tle, Brown, 2006).

Although the Cracker Jack recipe is secret, you can make your own caramel corn with this easy recipe.

Pop enough popcorn to yield 4 cups freshly popped corn. Salt lightly. Put corn in a shallow roasting pan (large cake pan) and add 1 cup peanuts.

In a heavy sauce pan mix:

- 1 cup packed brown sugar
- 1/2 cup butter or margarine
- 1/2 cup corn syrup (light)

Stir over medium heat until boiling. Boil for 5 minutes without stirring. Remove from heat and stir in:

- 1/2 teaspoon vanilla
- 1/2 teaspoon baking soda

Pour syrup mixture over the popcorn and stir to coat well.

Bake in a preheated 250 degree F oven for 1 hour. Stir several times as it is baking. Cool, break apart, and store in a tightly covered container.

Peter Mandel—Steamed Chinese Dumplings

Photo Credit: Kathy Mandel

One of the best things about growing up in Manhattan was the food—especially the street vendor, on-the-run sort.

—Peter Mandel

Peter Mandel

Birthday: June 7

Favorite place: A particular pedestrian bridge that crosses Paris's River Seine

Favorite foods: Steamed Chinese dumplings, Sabrett hot dog with mustard, onions, sauerkraut (from a New York City street vendor)

Family:

Spouse—Kathy Byrd Mandel

Home:

Childhood—Manhattan, in Chelsea, on 16th Street and 7th Avenue

Now—Providence, Rhode Island

Peter Mandel grew up in Manhattan, where both of his parents were associated with *Life* magazine and where Peter's own creativity was nurtured at the progressive New York City elementary school—the City and Country School. The school's curriculum included a lot of writing, research, and art. Peter was fascinated with facts about his home city and read about the skyscrapers in Manhattan—learning about the transportation in the city, the buildings, and the neighborhood.

Years later, as a writer known to adults, he contributed to many major publications. But his memories of Manhattan and its sights and sounds have emerged as part of his books for young readers—the boats, the planes, the sounds (and tastes) of Shea Stadium.

Peter says, "Around the corner from the apartment building my family lived in, there was a Sabrett hot dog man who always set up shop with his cart, mixing his own onion recipe, selling the world's best hot dogs under the trademark blue-and-yellow Sabrett brand umbrella.

"One of my favorite spreads in my picture book, *Say Hey! A Song of Willie Mays,* shows not only Mays at bat, but the crowd at the polo grounds with a hot dog vendor hawking franks. This is another New York Style dog that I have trouble duplicating anywhere else: the lightly-steamed, soft-textured kind that I used to get at Shea Stadium, as a kid at Mets games.

"Other top-drawer NYC street snacks include, of course, hot pretzels and—if you can still find them—roasted chestnuts in the shell. Boy do I miss those."

Selected Books Written by Peter Mandel

Boats on the River. Illustrated by Ed Miller. (Cartwheel/Scholastic, 2004)

My Ocean Liner: Across the North Atlantic on the Great Ship Normandie. Illustrated by Betsey MacDonald. (Stemmer House, 2000)

Planes at The Airport. Illustrated by Ed Miller. (Cartwheel/Scholastic, 2004)

Say Hey: A Song of Willie Mays. Illustrated by Don Tate. (Jump at the Sun/Hyperion Books for Children, 2000)

New York Style Hot Dog #1

Peter Mandel's favorite foods include a "Sabrett Hot dog with mustard, onions, and sauerkraut—from a NYC street vendor." We can't give you this hot dog from a street vendor, but the Sabrett hot dog, an all-beef skinless frankfurter in a natural casing, can be purchased at specialty food stores. The hot dogs are made with beef and spices and are then smoked in hickory smoke houses. Street vendors add toppings that include mustard, sauerkraut, relish, and onions—finely chopped and in a tomato sauce. Now the signature condiments that are used on Sabrett hot dogs are also available commercially packaged. So for an authentic Sabrett hot dog, the "recipe" is rather simple:

- Purchase Sabrett brand hot dogs
- Steam the dogs to the recommended internal temperature of 160 degrees F
- Place the hot dog in a quality bun
- Dress the hot dog with your choice of Sabrett condiments.

True hot dog lovers would caution that one never dresses the bun but rather places the hot dog in the bun and then dresses the dog.

New York Style Hot Dog #2

Peter Mandel's second mention of a hot dog includes those sold at Shea Stadium. Again the recipe includes obtaining the right hot dog and the condiments to dress the dog. The hot dog used at Shea Stadium is a Nathan's Famous hot dog. The Nathan dog is also an all-beef frankfurter, skinless, and with a natural casing. Most often the ballpark dog is served with mustard—specifically Gulden's Spicy Brown Mustard. Gulden's seems to be the mustard of choice at dozens of ballparks, including Shea Stadium.

As a child, Mandel enjoyed food from vendors on the streets of New York—hot dogs, steamed Chinese dumplings, and other savory foods. The variety featured here are those sometimes dubbed "cook and sell." There are many varieties of dumplings made by the Chinese. The Chinese have made dumplings since the Sung dynasty. The dumplings come in a variety of shapes, most often round or crescent-shaped, but sometimes in small round "pouches" or trianglar shapes. There are gow gees, har gow, jiaozi, potstickers, Shanghai steamed buns, and siu mai. The dumplings can be steamed, pan-fried, or boiled. Fillings vary as well—meat and vegetables or vegetarian, sweet or savory. The following recipe is shaped like the siu mai (or shu mai)—"cook and sell dumplings." The siu mai has a unique shape in which the wrapper is gathered up into several folds before steaming. The filling sticks out at the top, and the entire dumpling is soft and puffy.

Steamed Chinese (Pork) Dumplings (Siu Mai)

To make these dumplings, you will need 1 package (approximately 30) round wonton wrappers. These wrappers will be used to hold the filling, and then the entire "dumpling" will be steamed.

Mix together in a medium sized mixing bowl:

- 1/2 pound fresh ground pork (do not use lean)
- 3 ounces fresh and minced uncooked (green) shrimp
- 3 ounces water chestnuts, finely chopped
- 1/2 cup finely chopped bamboo shoots
- 1 cup finely chopped scallions
- 1/2 cup minced celery

Season mixture with:

• 2 teaspoons salt	2 teaspoons light soy sauce
• 1/4 teaspoon white pepper	1/2 teaspoon sesame oil
• 2 teaspoons sugar	2 tablespoons cornstarch

Put the filling mixture into the refrigerator to chill for at least 30 minutes.

Take each wrapper, one at a time, in the palm of one hand. Put a tablespoonful of the filling in the center of the wrapper. Wrap the sides of the wrapper up and around—squeezing the wrapper as close to the filling as possible. The top will be pleated and resemble, somewhat an opening flower blossom. Take care to gently push the filling down from the top to pack the ball of filling firmly, adding extra filling if needed. The filling should be seen above the wrapper. Flatten the base slightly. Place the dumplings in a lightly oiled steamer basket and steam over simmering water for 15 to 20 minutes. Serve with the soy and sesame dip.

Soy and Sesame Dip

- 1/2 cup light soy sauce
- 1/4 cup sesame oil

Transportation

Mandel's more recent books have focused on transportation, and because they are in board-book format, they are excellent to use as stand-up anchor books in a book display for children who are investigating modes of transportation.

Augarde, Steve. *We're Going on an Airplane: Steve Augarde's Interactive Pop-Up Book.* (Handprint, 2003)

Barton, Bryon. *Airport.* (HarperTrophy, 1987)

Barton, Bryon. *Boats.* (HarperCollins, 1986)

Barton, Bryon. *Planes.* (HarperCollins, 1986)

Barton, Bryon. *Trains.* (HarperCollins, 1986)

Barton, Bryon. *Trucks.* (HarperCollins, 1986)

Corey, Shana. *Boats* (Step-Into-Reading, Step 1). Illustrated by Mike Reed. (Random House, 2001)

Evans, Frank. *All Aboard Airplanes.* (Grosset & Dunlap, 1998)

Gibbons, Gail. *Boat Book.* (Holiday House, 1983)

Millard, Anne. *DK Big Book of Airplanes.* (DK Children, 2001)

Pallotta, Jerry. *The Boat Alphabet Book.* Illustrated by David Biedrzycki. (Charlesbridge, 1998)

Pallotta, Jerry. *Dory Story.* Illustrated by David Biedrzycki. (Charlesbridge, 2004)

Pallotta, Jerry, and Fred Stillwell. *The Airplane Alphabet Book.* Illustrated by Rob Bolster. (Charlesbridge, 1997)

Scarry, Richard. *Richard Scarry's A Day at the Airport.* (Random House, 2001)

Submarine (Eyewitness Books). (DK Publishing, 2003)

Rafe Martin—*Rava Masala Dosai*

Photo Credit: Mark Mason

> *I really don't spend much time in the kitchen; I enjoy my wife's cooking too much…. [However,] we get [rava masala dosai] in an Indian vegetarian restaurant in Rochester.*
>
> **—Rafe Martin**

Rafe Martin

Birthday: January 22

Favorite place: home

Favorite foods: rava masala dosai

Family:

   Spouse—Rose

   Son—Jacob (b. 1970)

   Daughter—Ariya (b. 1974)

Home:

   Childhood—New York City

   Now—Rochester, New York

Rafe Martin was a writer first, but he put that occupation aside for a time when he began to tell stories. He became very well known as a storyteller. Martin continues to tell stories throughout the United States and in other countries, but he has also returned to writing.

During Martin's graduate school years, when the Vietnam War was going on, he began sitting with Philip Kapleau Roshi, the founder of the Rochester Zen Center, in Upstate New York. At first he studied as a student, and then he became a disciple—and a storyteller. As a disciple, he told the Jataka tales from the Buddhist tradition. Jataka tales are known as the stories of the Buddha's former incarnations. Rafe began to learn of the power of told stories and developed techniques as a storyteller. Later, when he and his wife Rose became parents in 1970, Martin became reacquainted with children's literature as he read stories aloud to his children. He realized that children's literature and traditional tales are really records of stories.

"A storyteller," Martin says, "is always in the process of rewriting the story." One never gets to a final text. A writer, however, does come to a place when a final version must be put on paper."

Rafe Martin heard many stories while he was growing up. His mother read fairy tales and Aesop's Fables to him. One of his favorites was "The Tortoise and the Hare." After holiday celebrations, he would hear family stories from his father's family, especially stories about growing up in the old days in New York City's Lower East Side. Members of his father's family were first-generation Russian Jews, and they had both hilariously funny stories and stories of hardship as well. His father told stories from rescue missions in the Himalayas during World War II. Each of his grandmothers had been teenage immigrants and had their own stories of fleeing the Russian Revolution. His childhood was filled with story, and that has contributed to his development as a storyteller and as a writer.

Martin tells of two incidents during his children's childhood. He says, "Once [when the Martin children] were fighting at breakfast, as siblings sometimes do, I threatened to pour the maple syrup over my head if they didn't stop. They continued fighting so, true to my word, I doused my head with maple syrup! We all became so hysterical laughing that all discord was forgotten. My children, now grown, often reminisce about that breakfast. It always brings laughter."

Another story involves Martin's efforts to keep his children away from real chocolate. "When our children were young, in an effort to make sure that they ate healthy food, I concocted a dessert made from tofu, carob, and honey, pureed in our blender. I called it "chocolate pudding." Our children ate it dutifully until they got a taste of *real* chocolate pudding, courtesy of some friends. After that they never ate mine again!"

"Chocolate" Mousse Pie

Use the carob chips alternative in this recipe, and the mousse will approximate the "chocolate" pudding Martin made for his children.

Chocolate or "Chocolate" Pudding or Pie Filling

- 10 ounces chocolate chips (or carob chips)
- 2 packages firm tofu
- 3 tablespoons honey or maple syrup

Heat chips in double boiler or microwave until melted. Add honey and stir until smooth. In a blender or processor, blend tofu until smooth. Add the chocolate (or carob) and honey (or syrup) mixture to tofu and whip until creamy. Pour filling into a prepared or purchased graham cracker crust or eat as a pudding.

Booklist

In Martin's version of *The Twelve Months,* Marushka is sent into the wintry cold by her aunt and cousin to gather violets, then strawberries, and then apples. Beatrice Schenk deRegniers's version, as well as Vojtech's, also have the girl seeking violets and strawberries. Marshak's version includes other details.

deRegniers, Beatrice Schenk. *Little Sister and the Month Brothers.* Illustrated by Margot Tomes. (Clarion, 1976)

Marshak, Samuel. *The Month-Brothers: A Slavic Tale.* (Morrow, 1983)

Vojtech, Anna, and Philemon Sturges. *Marushka and the Month Brothers: A Folktale.* (North-South, 1996)

Rava Masala Dosai

This dish is basically a wheat or rice flour crepe that is used as a wrap for an onion and potato filling. This recipe has a rather mild masala filling; a curried filling will be much spicier. Some of the more unusual ingredients (such as the besan, rice flour, rasa) will have to be purchased at a specialty food store.

Prepare the masala filling

- 3 potatoes boiled, peeled, and cubed
- 1 onion, sliced or chopped
- 2 chilies, chopped

Season with powdered mustard or 1/2 teaspoon mustard seed and

- 1 teaspoon besan
- 1 teaspoon turmeric
- Salt to taste

In an oiled pan, place the mustard powder or the mustard seeds. Add the chilis and onions.

Fry for a couple of minutes, then add potato, salt, and turmeric.

Cook for some time until potatoes soften. Mix the besan with water and add to the potato mixture. Cook for a couple of minutes more, then garnish with cilantro.

Dosai

- 1 cup rice flour
- 1 cup wheat flour
- 1 cup all-purpose flour
- 1 tablespoon rasa
- 3 finely chopped green chilies (mild or hot, to your taste)
- 1 teaspoon mustard seeds
- 1 teaspoon cumin seeds
- curry leaves—a few dried
- Salt to taste

Mix all the flours with salt and green chilies. Add enough water to make a semi-liquid batter. Add the mustard, cumin, and curry leaves to the batter.

In a griddle or a nonstick flat pan, pour a ladle of batter. Make the batter into a round shape. Pour some oil around it and turn the dosa after bubbling spots appear. Take a spoonful of masala filling, fill in the center, and close the dosa.

Serve hot with chutney or sambhar.

Sambhar is an accompaniment often served in southern Indian cuisine. It is a stew of highly spiced lentils and vegetables eaten mixed with rice. Chutney, another relish that originated in India, is a pungent relish made of fruits, spices, and herbs.

Selected Books Written by Rafe Martin

Birdwing. (Arthur A. Levine, 2005), Young Adult

A Girl and the Sea. Illustrated by Dave Lafleur. (Houghton Mifflin, 2005)

The Language of Birds. Illustrated by Susan Gaber. (Putnam, 2000)

The Shark God. Illustrated by David Shannon. (Arthur A. Levine, 2001)

The Storytelling Princess. Illustrated by Kimberly Bulcken Root. (Putnam, 2001)

The Twelve Months. Illustrated by Vladyana Krykorka. (Fitzhenry & Whiteside, 2001)

Ann Morris—*Vdolky*

Ann Morris

Birthday: October 1

Favorite place: Haly and Greece

Favorite foods: Cheesecake, ice cream, lobster, shrimp, coffee, stuffed cabbage, *tzimmes*, bagels.

Home:

    Childhood—New York

    Now—New York

The grandmothers [featured in the What Was It Like, Grandma? series] are all good cooks, ready to share recipes and of course, offer anything from samples to banquets.

—Ann Morris

Anne Morris shared these thoughts on how food can be a special part of peoples lives: "If I didn't eat three helpings of everything my mother cooked when I went to visit her, she would invariably say, 'You always come to my house when you're not hungry.'

"When my Aunt Helen used to come visit our home for afternoon cake and coffee, she would say, 'I'll just have a sliver.' Her slivers extended through the afternoon until she'd finished most of the cake.

"I now live in a neighborhood filled with superb markets. One day a big sign appeared in the window of one of them, Fairway, saying 'we sell the best gefilte fish.' Just a few days later, the Citerella market next to Fairway sported the following sign: 'We sell the worst gefilte fish.'

"Then there's Zabar's, the market of markets with a coffee shop at one end where I make daily trips to refresh my brain with their excellent coffee. But this is no ordinary coffee bar—it's a shmoozer's paradise, everyone listens to everyone else's conversation, friendships are forged over bagels and lox, and you never know who you'll meet there. Buses of Japanese tourists arrive to get a whiff of the place. Once, when I was riding the subway, a family of German tourists holding a map approached me and asked: 'Ver ich Zabar's?'

"So, food brings people together. My book *Bread Bread Bread* helped me discover some of the similarities and differences of bread making, the enjoyment of eating and marketing. The symbolism of bread, whether religious, psychological, or sociological, was invariably there to be observed and thought about. Hunks of life's most sustaining food."

Selected Books Written by Ann Morris

Bread, Bread, Bread. Illustrated by Ken Heyman. (HarperCollins, 1989)

Light the Candle! Bang the Drum! A Book of Holidays around the World. Illustrated by Peter Linenthal. (Dutton, 1997)

Families. (HarperCollins, 2000)

That's Our School Series. Includes *That's Our Principal, That's Our Teacher, That's Our Custodian, That's Our Librarian, That's Our Nurse, and That's Our Gym Teacher.* (Millbrook, 2003)

Tsunami: Helping Each Other. Illustrated by Heidi Larson. (Lerner, 2005)

What Was It Like Grandma Series. Illustrated with photographs by Peter Linenthal. Includes *Grandma Esther Remembers* (2002), *Grandma Lai Goon Remembers* (2002), *Grandma Susan Remembers* (2002); *Grandma Francisca Remembers* (2002), *Grandma Lois Remembers* (2002), *Grandma Maxine Remembers* (2002), and *Grandma Hekmat Remembers* (2003). (Millbrook)

Ann Morris

Her bag is always packed. She has traveled to destinations throughout the world gathering information and pictures for her many books—more than one hundred—that she has written in the past decades. She has toured the world seeking a diverse look at hats, houses, bread, shoes, and even weddings! She has visited schools to profile those who work there: a teacher, a principal, a custodian, a librarian, a nurse, and a gym teacher. She has visited with grandmothers from seven ethnicities and told their stories of growing up. She has written about what people around the world eat, what they wear, how they work, and how they play. Her books are reflective of her own curiosity about people and places.

Ann Morris attended Hunter Elementary School and had the good fortune of having professors from Hunter College visit the school with their extraordinary tales (and visuals) of their travels around the world. She spent many rainy Saturdays at the nearby Museum of Natural History and at a favorite bookstore where she planned what book she would request for her birthday. Her love of books carried her through her college years and into her teaching career. Soon she was teaching teachers and working on a Ph.D. Three years into the program, she left to become part of educational publishing with Scholastic. The creative possibilities seemed to be unlimited. She utilized many resources to develop books, recordings, educational materials, and slide programs. Inspired to write her own books, she persisted until an editor accepted her first book. Soon thereafter she left Scholastic to became a full-time writer. That was just the beginning. Her writing and traveling have taken her to circuses, a goat farm, a teddy bear factory; around the world to Russia, Italy, Israel, Greece; and across the United States from New York to San Francisco.

VDOLKY—LITTLE CAKE FOR WEDDING CEREMONY

When immigrants from Bohemia, Moravia, and Silesia arrived in the United States, they were identified by their origins as Bohemians or Moravians. Once Czechoslovakia was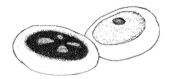
established at the end of World War I, they were identified as Czecho-slovakian or simply "Czech." Now following the establishment of the Czech Republic and Slovakia at the end of the Cold War, they are often identified as either Czech or Slovak. There are many regional recipes for the *vdolky,* which are traditional wedding pastry. Moravians and people in other regions made a turnover type of pastry with the filling inside a three-cornered folded pastry. The Bohemians made a circle of dough with an indentation in the center to hold the filling. Originally a wedding treat, the pastry is now enjoyed throughout the year on any occasion. The more generic name for the wedding pastry is *kolace.*

Two books that feature *kolace* or *vdolky* as a part of the story are:

Nelson, Nan Ferring. *My Day with Anka.* Illustrated by Bill Farnsworth. (HarperCollins, 1996)—This is the story of Karrie's relationship with her family's housekeeper, Anka, who comes each week to clean. While she is there, she makes noodles and *kolaches.* On the book flap is a picture of the traditional *kolaches* made in Cedar Rapids, Iowa, where this story takes place.

Machalek, Jan. *Eva's Summer Vacation: A Story of the Czech Republic.* (SoundPrints, 1999)—Eva travels from her home city of Prague to attend her aunt's wedding in the Moravian countryside village of Hluk. On pages 18–19, readers see Eva's aunt with a plate full of plum scones—*vdolky.*

South Moravian Vdolky

Ann Morris travels far and wide, always visiting with people and observing how they work and play and what they eat, including what they eat at wedding feasts. Here's a recipe for kolace *that she might have found in South Moravia.* Kolace *is a general name for the poppy-seed or fruit-filled pastry found in the Czech and Slavic countries,* Vdolky *is a type of* kolace.

Ingredients

- 1 cup milk, scalded
- 1/2 cup sugar
- 1/2 cup butter
- 1 package dry yeast
- 3 eggs, beaten
- 1 teaspoon salt
- 5 cups all-purpose flour

Mix together, in a large bowl, the scalded milk, sugar, and butter. Stir to dissolve. Allow it to cool to warm, then add the yeast and let it begin to work. Add eggs. Mix all ingredients.

Measure out the flour and add the salt. Set the flour aside.

Using an electric mixer begin to add in small portions of the flour until the mixer is no longer able to handle the mixing.

At that stage begin to work the dough by hand. When the dough begins to come together and leave the sides of the bowl, it is ready to remove from the bowl. Roll into a ball and cover.

Let the dough rest and rise in a warm place until it doubles in bulk.

Once the dough has doubled, turn it out on a floured surface and knead gently until it becomes soft and elastic. Pinch off egg-sized pieces of dough and form them into rounds. Place each round on a cooking sheet, about 2 inches apart. Use a floured thumb to make a depression in the center. Fill the depression with filling and then let the rounds rise for about 20 minutes. Just before baking brush tops of the dough with beaten egg mixed with a little milk and sugar.

Bake at 350 degrees F for 15 to 20 minutes or until lightly browned.

Fillings may be any variation you would like. The following are some of the most common.

(Continued)

Kolache Filling

Apricot: Soak 1 pound of dried apricots, in a cooking pan filled with enough cool water to cover the apricots, for several hours. Put the pan over low heat and bring to slow simmer. Add sugar to taste. Cook until the apricots are very soft. Stir vigorously to get a smooth consistency, or run them through the food processor. Cook the apricots until the water has cooked off and you have the desired consistency. A few drops of lemon juice will give the apricot filling a little tang.

Prune: Use the same procedure as described for the apricot filling.

Pineapple: Use a can of crushed pineapple, cook down and continuously stir until the pineapple is smooth and the desired consistency is achieved.

Cottage Cheese: Melt 1 tablespoon butter and cool slightly.

Add:

- 1 pound dry cottage cheese (farmer's cheese)
- 1/4 cup sugar
- 1 egg, beaten
- 1/4 teaspoon lemon zest
- Taste and adjust for sweetness.

Poppy Seed: This filling should be made the night before you plan to use it.

Combine:

- 1/2 pound ground poppy seeds
- 1/2 teaspoon salt
- 1 cup sugar
- 1 teaspoon vanilla extract

Add enough milk to make a thick mix. Let stand overnight to absorb the liquid.

Almost any fruit filling can be used as the filling in *kolaches*. However, jam and jelly do not work well because they liquefy in the heat of the oven and make a mess. Commercial pie filling can be used successfully.

Kolaches—Kids Kitchen

These are not as good as the real thing, but it is a child-friendly recipe, and they serve as a quick and simple substitute when you want to have a quick treat for guests.

Use a package of commercial biscuits. Separate and place each one on a lightly greased cookie sheet. Use a floured thumb to make a depression in the center of each biscuit. Add a teaspoon of pie filling into the depression. Brush the biscuit with beaten egg, a little water, and sugar.

Bake until the biscuit is lightly brown.

Sprinkle the *kolaches* with powdered sugar before serving. Eat while still warm.

Robin Pulver—Szegediner Goulas

I grew up in Phelps, a small town in up-state New York, known as "the sauer-kraut capital of the World." In spring and summer, the town was bordered with fields of the cabbage that would be made into sauerkraut.

—Robin Pulver

Robin Pulver

Birthday: October 1

Favorite place: Keuka Lake

Favorite foods: My parents encouraged me to try everything, and I love just about everything! It's hard to choose—dark chocolate, kale and carrots, Thai food, sauerkraut! … and blackberries.

Family:

    Spouse—Don

    Son—David

    Daughter—Nina

    (and pets)—dog, Sadie (a Labrador); goldfish, Hakeem

Home:

    Childhood—Phelps, New York

    Now—Pittsford, New York

The hazy blue-green [cabbage] fields reminded me of rippling lakes. In the roads, we would find cabbages that had fallen from trucks on their way to the factory. Sauerkraut is one of my favorite foods. Not only do I love the taste of it, I also love the memories it brings back to me. My husband grew up in Phelps, too. In fact, he lived practically across from the original sauerkraut factory.

One childhood summer vacation, my older brother David and I decided to take our own "field trips" to explore our area. We visited the telephone office. We visited an apple farm. We even took a tour of the then brand-new Silver Floss Sauerkraut Factory.

Finally, that summer, David and I challenged ourselves to ride our bikes down Tiger Hill, the biggest hill in town, just around the corner from the school. Tiger Hill was so steep, it was closed to traffic in the winter. The townspeople used it to for sledding and tobogganing, especially on snow days, when school was closed. Biking or sledding down Tiger Hill was terrifying, but exciting. Tiger Hill was an inspiration for my book about the intrepid school bus driver, Axle Annie.

Axle Annie's reply was always the same: "Do snowplows plow? Do tow truck tow? Are school buses yellow? Of course, I can make it up Tiger Hill!" and she always did.

Tedd Arnold, the illustrator, made Tiger Hill look even more gloriously monstrous than the hill of my memories. ("Hale Snow's machine had turned Tiger Hill into a monstrous mounting of swirling snow.")

The sauerkraut factory in Phelps has been closed down now for many years. Tiger Hill isn't as steep as it used to be. The town made a decision to have it graded, to make it traffic friendly. Still, every summer, Phelps has a Sauerkraut Festival, which includes a big parade, a carnival, and even a sauerkraut recipe contest. For me, the smell of sauerkraut cooking always brings back memories of Phelps and Tiger Hill.

—Robin Pulver

Selected Books Written by Robin Pulver

Author Day for Room 3T. Illustrated by Chuck Richards. (Clarion, 2005)

Axle Annie. Illustrated by Tedd Arnold. (Dial Books for Young Readers, 1999)

Axle Annie and the Speed Grump. Illustrated by Tedd Arnold. (Dial Books for Young Readers, 2005)

Christmas for a Kitten. Illustrated by Layne Johnson. (Albert A. Whitman, 2003)

Mrs. Toggle's Zipper. Illustrated by R. W. Alley. (Four Winds Press, 1990). Other books about Mrs. Toggle: *Mrs. Toggle and the Dinosaur* (1991), *Mrs. Toggle's Beautiful Blue Shoe* (1994), *Mrs. Toggle's Class Picture Day* (Scholastic, 2000)

Nouns and Verbs Have a Field Day. Illustrated by Lynne Rowe Reed. (Holiday House, 2006)

Punctuation Takes a Vacation. Illustrated by Lynne Rowe Reed. (Holiday House, 2004)

Way to Go, Alex! Illustrated by Elizabeth Wolf. (Albert Whitman, 1999)

SZEGEDINER GOULAS (GYPSY GOULASH)

"I don't know where this recipe first came from, but it was a favorite of mine as a child, and it still is, although I have modified it somewhat over time. I have taken this dish to the annual holiday party of the Rochester-area group of children's authors and illustrators, and it's always a hit! My mouth starts watering, just thinking about it."

—Robin Pulver

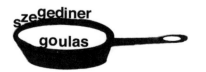

Szegediner Goulas

In a large skillet sauté 1/3 cup onion in olive oil. Add 2 pounds mixed lean meat (pork and beef), cut in 1-inch pieces. Stir in 2 one-pound cans sauerkraut, Add 1 bay leaf,

Simmer for 1 1/2 hours, covered, until the meat is tender.

Before serving, stir in 1 cup low-fat sour cream.

This recipe may be made using only pork or beef. It's still tasty.

Sauerkraut Chocolate Cake Supreme

Here's a more unusual use of sauerkraut—in a delicious chocolate cake.

In a large mixing bowl, cream together:

- 2/3 cup butter
- 1 1/2 cups sugar
- 3 large or 4 medium eggs, beaten
- 1 teaspoon vanilla

In a second bowl combine dry ingredients:

- 1/2 cup cocoa
- 2 1/4 cup flour
- 1 teaspoon baking powder
- 1/4 teaspoon salt

Slowly combine the dry ingredients with the butter-sugar mixture, alternately adding a portion of the dry ingredients with 1 cup water.

When butter mixture and dry ingredients are thoroughly combined, gently fold in

- 2/3 cup chopped sauerkraut, drained

Preheat oven to 350 degrees F. Grease and flour two 8- or 9-inch cake pans. Bake for 25 to 30 minutes. Frost the cake with a cream cheese or buttercream frosting.

Books with a "Helping" of Sauerkraut

Sauerkraut is finely sliced and chopped white cabbage that has been allowed to ferment (sour) in a salt brine (a strong solution of salt and water used for pickling). Sauerkraut is not usually at the top of list of favorite foods for most children, and they might not even know what sauerkraut is, but it is mentioned in several books. Share a taste of sauerkraut and read one of these books.

In the Midwest, a favorite pizza is made with Canadian Bacon (chopped ham) and sauerkraut spread over the pizza in a weblike fashion. Bake the pizza in the usual fashion. Although sauerkraut is not usually used on pizzas in New England where Robin Pulver lives, this use of pizza is very popular in the Midwest, and those who eat a Canadian Bacon and sauerkraut pizza will surely discover why one of Robin Pulver's favorite foods is sauerkraut.

DeVos, Philip. *Carnival of the Animals*. Illustrated by Piet Grobler. (Front Street, 2000)—There are tortoises that waltz, honky-tonk pianists, and lions who do not like sauerkraut or brussels sprouts

Greenberg, David T. *Slugs*. Illustrated by Victoria Chess. (Megan Tingley, 1983)—Fun and zany: slurping slugs with straws, and slugs in your pasta … and slugs with your sauerkraut.

Numeroff, Laura. *Sometimes I Wonder If Poodles Like Noodles*. Illustrated by Tim Bowers. (Simon & Schuster, 1999)—One of Numeroff's verses has lunch being made in the microwave—with yams and sauerkraut.

Pinkwater, Daniel. *Looking for Bobowicz: A Hoboken Chicken Story*. Illustrated by Jill Pinkwater. (HarperCollins, 2004)—Nick moves with his somewhat disinterested family to Hoboken. When his bike is stolen, he sets out to find it and in the process uncovers the secret of Arthur Bobowicz and his 266-pound chicken. Figuring into the story is fermented sauerkraut.

Steig, William. *Tiffky Doofky*. (Farrar, Straus & Giroux/Michael di Capua, 1987; Sunburst pb)—Tiffky is a (dog) garbage collector who is told by a fortuneteller that he will find his true love before the sun sets. However, during his usual searching through the dump for treasures, Tiffky Doofky finds an emerald necklace lying on a bed of sauerkraut. The necklace puts him under the spell of a malevolent witch—a spell that leads to more complications.

Candice Ransom—Apple Butter and Biscuits

Photo Credit: Frank W. Ransom

My family's roots grow deep in the Virginia Mountains. These hardy people brought their superstitions, crafts, and heritage from England and Germany. My mother described apple-butter "boilings" she attended as a child, which I wrote about in a picture book.

—Candice Ransom

Candice Ransom

Birthday: July 10

Favorite place: Blue Ridge Mountains

Favorite foods: Donuts, cake, cookies ... and yes homemade biscuits with homemade apple butter

Family:

  Spouse—Frank Ransom

Home:

  Childhood—Centreville, Virginia

  Now—Fredericksburg, Virginia

When Candice Ransom wrote of the apple-butter "boilings" in her book *Apple-Butter Time,* she was writing about an experience that her mother had told her about, many times over. Ransom said, "Though I never participated in an old-time 'boiling,' I could eat my mother's apple butter all day long. This is her recipe for stove-top apple butter from the Shenandoah Valley, near where she grew up."

Candice Ransom

Candice Ransom grew up in Virginia with an older sister who seems to have became the model for the older sister in several of Candice's earlier books. Candice began her writing as a second grader and wrote about contemporary events—many from her own life. Once she was in high school, she found she still enjoyed writing, and continued her interest once she entered the world of work as a secretary. After her first novel was published, she felt confident that the publisher would be asking her to write more. She was fortunate in that the publisher did call. Ransom soon settled into writing contemporary realistic fiction and in recent years has moved to writing nonfiction and historical novels. Her work has been lauded as accurate and lively.

Sixty percent of the Civil War was fought on Virginia soil, and many of the nation's presidents came from there as well, so Ransom is surrounded by history. She often walks the same streets once walked by George Washington, Robert E. Lee, and Thomas Jefferson. Much of her inspiration comes from those surroundings and from the places she and her husband visit. Candice currently lives in Fredericksburg with her husband, Frank, and their four cats.

Apple Butter

Cook cored apples with the skin on and then press through a colander. To one quart of apples, add 1/4 cup vinegar, 1 cup sugar, and 1 tablespoon cinnamon. Heat over burner flame long enough to dissolve sugar, stirring with wooden spoon, then place in a stone crock (or Dutch oven) and place in 275 degree F oven. Cook for 1 to 2 hours. The apple butter mixture gets thicker as the moisture cooks down, cook the apple mixture as long as you wish depending on desired thickness.

Signature Recipe—Candice Ransom

Apple butter without biscuits is like a hug without a squeeze! I loved my mother's lard biscuits (yes, lard!) so much they nearly became a character in my novel set in the Blue Ridge Mountain in the 1950s. My mother baked biscuits nearly every day, sometimes as the base for milk gravy, sometimes slathered with grape jam made from the arbor that grew in our back yard. But her biscuits tasted best with apple butter. Yum!

—Candice Ransom

Old Time Biscuits

In Finding Day's Bottom, *the family makes biscuits on Christmas morning—the big meal of the day. They took turns beating the biscuits—"Three hundred times?" "Five hundred times," Mama said. "In honor of the day."*

- 4 cups flour
- 1 teaspoon soda
- 1 teaspoon salt
- 2 teaspoons baking powder
- Lard (about size of large egg)
- Sour milk (Add one to two teaspoons of vinegar or lemon juice to 1 cup sweet milk and let stand for 10 minutes or so until the milk begins to curdle, or sour.)

Sift dry ingredients. Add lard and work in with a fork. Add enough milk to make dough easy to handle. Knead gently. Roll 1/2-inch thick, cut into squares, and bake in 400 degree F oven.

Signature Recipe—Candice Ransom

Anyone who has read Candice Ransom's *Willie McLean and the Civil War Surrender* and would like to read other stories set during the Civil War period will be interested in some of the stories from the following list.

Allen, Thomas B. *Harriet Tubman, Secret Agent: How Daring Slaves and Free Blacks Spied for the Union during the Civil War.* (National Geographic, 2006)

Bolotin, Norman, and Angel Bolotin. *Home and Country: A Civil War Scrapbook.* (Lodestar, 1994)

Erickson, Paul. *Daily Life on a Southern Plantation, 1853.* (Lodestar, 1998)

Freedman, Russell. *Lincoln: A Photobiography.* (Clarion, 1987)

Fritz, Jean. *Just a Few Words, Mr. Lincoln.* (Grosset & Dunlap, 1993)

George Ella Lyon. *Cecil's Story.* Illustrated by Peter Catalanotto. (Orchard, 1991)

Herbert, Janis. *The Civil War for Kids: A History with 21 Activities.* (Chicago Press Review, 1999)

Hopkinson, Deborah. *Billy and the Rebel: Based on a True Civil War Story.* (Simon & Schuster, 2005)

Murphy, Jim. *The Boys' War: Confederate and Union Soldiers Talk about the Civil War.* (Clarion, 1990)

Polacco, Patricia. *Pink and Say.* (Philomel, 1994)

Ransom, Candice. *Children of the Civil War.* (CarolRhoda, 1998)

Selected Books Written by Candice Ransom

Apple-Butter Time. (Macmillian/McGraw-Hill, 1997)

Danger at Sand Cove. Illustrated by Den Schofield. (Carolrhoda, 2000)

Finding Day's Bottom. (CarolRhoda, 2006)

George Washington. (Lerner, 2002)

John Hancock. (Carolrhoda, 2005)

Lewis and Clark. (Lerner, 2002)

Liberty Street. Illustrated by Eric Velasquez. (Walker, 2003)

Maria von Trapp: Beyond the Sound of Music. (Carolrhoda, 2001)

Martha Washington. (Carolrhoda, 2003)

Mother Teresa. Illustrated by Elaine Verstraete. (Carolrhoda, 2001)

The Promise Quilt. Illustrated by Ellen Beier. (Walker, 1999)

Rescue on the Outer Banks. Illustrated by Karen Ritz. (Carolrhoda, 2002)

Robert E. Lee. (Lerner, 2005)

Sam Collier and the Founding of Jamestown. Illustrated by Matthew Archambault. (CarolRhoda, 2005)

Willie McLean and the Civil War Surrender. Illustrated by Jeni Reeves. Lerner/Carolrhoda, 2004

Shenandoah Apple Cinnamon Cake

From the same valley as Candice's mother's apple butter recipe comes this variation of an age-old favorite cake from Shenandoah Valley where apples are plentiful.

Peel and thinly slice 5 apples (any variety of baking apple will produce good results).

Toss the apple slices with:

- 2 tablespoons cinnamon
- 5 tablespoons sugar

Set apple mixture aside.

Cream together:

- 4 eggs
- 2 cups granulated sugar

Then add:

- 3 cups flour
- 1 cup vegetable oil
- 3 tablespoons baking powder
- 1/2 teaspoon cinnamon
- 1/4 teaspoon nutmeg
- 2 1/2 teaspoons vanilla
- 1/4 cup fresh orange juice

Put 1/3 batter in a greased and floured Bundt or other baking pan.

Layer 1/2 the apples on the batter.

Layer another 1/3 of the batter over the apples.

Layer the last 1/2 of the apples on the batter.

Layer the last 1/3 of the batter over the second layer of apples.

Bake at 350 degrees F for 70 minutes. Cool on a wire rack and remove from pan. Serve with sweetened whipped cream.

James Ransome and Lesa Cline-Ransome—Crab Cakes

> *[My] job as an illustrator is to put the sprinkles on the ice cream.*
>
> **—James Ransome**

Lesa Cline-Ransome

Birthday: July 12

Favorite place: After a trip to London in 2005, it became her favorite place.

Favorite foods: fish, sweet potatoes, spinach, summer squash

Family:
    Spouse—James Ransome

Home:
    Childhood—Massachusetts and later New Jersey
    Now—Upstate New York

James Ransome

Birthday: September 25

Favorite place: New Orleans—even in the summertime

Favorite foods: fish, sweet potatoes, spinach, summer squash

Family:
    Spouse—Lesa Cline-Ransome
    Son—Malcolm (b. 1997)
    Daughters—Jamie (1994), Maya (1996), and Leila (2000)

Home:
    Childhood—North Carolina and later New Jersey
    Now—Upstate New York

James Ransome and Lesa Cline-Ransome

James Ransome grew up in North Carolina with his grandmother. Rich Square was a small town, and behind his grandmother's house was a swamp. His grandmother seldom spanked him, but one day he came home all muddy from being in the swamp and she did spank him—not because he got muddy but because there were alligators in the swamp, and he wasn't supposed to be there. Years later when Ransome created the illustrations for *Under the Quilt of Night,* he drew on his experiences and memories of the swamp to create a sense of danger in the swamps that were part of the story.

As a boy, Ransome and his cousin often went to the comic book store, and that helped develop a taste for art. During his teen years, he left his grandmother's home and moved to New Jersey to live with his mother who had married and settled there. While living in New Jersey, he became interested in filmmaking, and he ended up enrolling at the Pratt Institute.

Lesa grew up in Massachusetts. She and her sisters regularly visited the public library with their mother. Some days her mother would spend the whole day reading. Lesa learned to love books and at first wanted to become a journalist. She had an idea that she wanted to be a fashion writer. The idea of being a journalist persisted during her high school years, but her interest in journalism waned when she decided she did not like to interview people.

During her sophomore year at Pratt Institute, she met James Ransome, a fellow classmate. They met at a *Purple Rain* (all Prince music) dance and soon were exploring New York together. She helped James with his writing projects, and he helped her with her art projects. They married in 1989. After meeting illustrator Jerry Pinkney James became fascinated with children's book illustration. Pinkney became James's mentor.

Lesa ended up in fashion advertising, but she eventually tired of debates about turquoise versus teal and decided she did not want to continue in that line of work. So she went back to school to study early childhood education. Before Lesa graduated with her education degree, the couple was expecting their first child, Jamie.

One of their first homes was in Poughkeepsie, New York, where the family lived in a large frame home once owned by a doctor. The former waiting room was James Ransome's studio, and the hallway to the dining room was an art gallery of sorts. James also had a room for an office, where he dealt with the business side of his work. There in his office, he kept extensive research files, books, magazines, and photos and pictures filed by category. In the late 1990s, Lesa began to write. With three young children underfoot, she squeezed writing time between caring for the children and the household responsibilities. She carved out writing time on Tuesdays and Thursdays. On those days, James got the children ready for school—the two older girls were in school, and Malcolm was in nursery school on those two days. James was back in the office by 9:00 A.M., and in the afternoon, Lesa would pick up the children from school. After spending family time together from 5 to 8 P.M., James would return to his studio. When their fourth child, Leila, arrived, writing time became more difficult for Lesa until the baby became old enough for nursery school. Later, the family moved a short distance from Poughkeepsie, into a new home near Rhinebeck, where James and Lesa continue to illustrate and write.

Lesa and James work independently from one another, although James sometimes becomes involved in what Lesa does. In fact, Lesa says she "stands in line" to have James illustrate her books.

Bits and pieces of the family sometimes end up in James's illustrations. The family Dalmatian, Clinton, often appears in his books. James's friend and mentor, Jerry Pinkney, posed as Uncle Jed's brother; Lesa's father posed as Uncle Jed; and the house Uncle Jed lives in is actually an old Ransome family home, where the family gathers for a reunion each year. Ransome returned to his boyhood home in North Carolina to research the setting and even used his grandfather's chickens as models for those that appear in the book. Lesa can be seen in *Aunt Flossie's Hats.* Their daughter Maya's drawings are incorporated into *Visiting Day* as drawings made by the young girl who is visiting her dad.

James Ransome's ancestors were slaves on a plantation, and that ancestral home, the Ransom Plantation (the family added an "e" after slavery ended), served as a model for the plantation in *Sweet Clara and the Freedom Quilt.*

Selected Titles Illustrated by James Ransome

James Ransome has illustrated many books, and since 2000 he has illustrated several written by his wife Lesa Cline-Ransome. The following list includes selected titles illustrated by James.

Bunting, Eve. *Peepers*. (Harcourt Brace, 2000)

Cline-Ransome, Lesa. *Major Taylor, Champion Cyclist*. Illustrated by James E. Ransome. (Atheneum, 2004)

Cline-Ransome, Lesa. *Pelé*. (Atheneum, 2007)

Cline-Ransome, Lesa. *Quilt Alphabet*. (Holiday House, 2001)

Cline-Ransome, Lesa. *Quilt Counting*. (SeaStar Books, 2002)

Cline-Ransome, Lesa. *Satchel Paige*. (Simon & Schuster, 2000)

Haskins, James, and Kathleen Benson. *Building a New Land: African Americans in Colonial America*. (HarperCollins, 2001)

Hooks, William H. *Freedom's Fruit*. (Knopf, 1996)

Hopkinson, Deborah. *Sky Boys: How They Built the Empire State Building*. (Schwartz & Wade Books, 2006)

Hopkinson, Deborah. *Sweet Clara and the Freedom Quilt*. (Knopf, 1993; 2003 10th anniversary edition.)

Hopkinson, Deborah. *Under the Quilt of Night*. (Atheneum/Anne Schwartz Books, 2002)

Howard, Elizabeth Fitzgerald. *Aunt Flossie's Hats (and Crab Cakes Later)*. (Clarion, 2001; 10th Anniversary edition)

Mitchell, Margaree King. *Uncle Jed's Barbershop*.

Woodson, Jacqueline. *Visiting Day*. (Scholastic, 2002)

AUNT FLOSSIE'S HATS (AND CRAB CAKES LATER)

James Ransome's illustrations captured the lively story of Sarah and Susan's afternoon with Great-Great Aunt Flossie. In the tenth-anniversary edition, author Elizabeth Fitzgerald Howard added an eight-page section telling about her own family history and the real Aunt Flossie. In the story Sarah and Susan are served tea and Maryland crab cakes by their Great-Great Aunt Flossie.

Crab Cakes Supreme

In a small skillet, sauté 1/2 small onion, chopped, in 1 tablespoon butter and a 1/2 teaspoon coarse kosher salt. Set aside.

Whisk together:

- 2 large eggs
- 1 1/2 teaspoons Worcestershire sauce
- 1/2 teaspoon coarse kosher salt
- 1 teaspoon sweet paprika
- Pinch of cayenne pepper
- 1/2 teaspoon freshly ground black pepper
- 2 tablespoon prepared tartar sauce

Carefully fold in 1 pound fresh lump crabmeat (make sure the crabmeat has had all bits of shell and cartilage removed; be careful not to break up the lumps of crab) and 2 slices of firm white sandwich bread torn into small pieces. The mixture will be relatively wet.

Gently form the mixture into six cakes approximately 3 inches in diameter and 3/4 inches thick. Place the cakes on a pan lined with waxed paper and sprinkle 3 tablespoons dried bread crumbs over the top. Turn the cakes over, and sprinkle with another 3 tablespoons dried bread crumbs. Cover the cakes with another sheet of waxed paper and chill for 1 hour or overnight.

Melt 3 tablespoons of unsalted butter in a large nonstick skillet over medium high heat until the foam subsides. Cook the crab cakes until golden brown, about 3 minutes on each side. Serve warm and with one of these sauces.

Horseradish Red Sauce

- 1/4 cup catsup
- 1/4 cup minced parsley
- 1 tablespoon horseradish
- 2 teaspoons white vinegar
- 1 teaspoon grated lemon peel
- 1 teaspoon hot pepper sauce

Mix together in a small bowl, cover and refrigerate until ready to use.

Sour Cream-Dijon Sauce

- 3/4 cup Dijon mustard
- 3/4 cup sour cream
- 3/4 cup mayonnaise
- 1 tablespoon white vinegar
- 1/4 teaspoon mustard powder
- Pinch of white pepper

Ham and Sweet Potato Skillet Scramble

Both James and Lesa list sweet potatoes as a favorite food. Here's a southern recipe that might be in their favorite recipe box.

- 1/2 cup chopped onion
- 8 tablespoons butter or margarine
- 4 tablespoons flour
- 2 cans (total 30 ounces) pineapple chunks, drained, reserve syrup
- 2/3 cup water
- 2/3 cup brown sugar, firmly packed
- 2 cans (total 48 ounces) sweet potatoes, drained and sliced
- 2 fully cooked ham steaks, cut in serving-sized pieces

Sauté the onion in butter or margarine (2–3 minutes). Once the onions are translucent, stir in the flour and add the pineapple syrup and water. Stir constantly and allow liquid to thicken as for a gravy. Stir in pineapple and brown sugar. Top with potatoes and ham pieces. Cover the skillet and simmer for 20 to 25 minutes. Serves 4 to 6 people.

Quilts

Quilts are a major feature in several of James's and two of Lesa's books. Here is a list of additional titles to extend a quilt theme. In addition, selected collaborative themes might be incorporated into the use of individual titles presented: Civil War, mathematics, generosity, family heritage, westward movement, family relationships (especially among the generations), cooperation, resourcefulness, and so forth.

Bial, Raymond. *Needle and Thread: A Book about Quilts*. (Houghton Mifflin, 1996)

Bourgeois, Paulette. *Oma's Quilt*. Illustrated by Stephane Jorisch. (Kids Can Press, 2001)

Brumbeau, Jeff. *The Quiltmaker's Gift*. Illustrated by Gail De Marcken. (Scholastic, 2001)

Coerr, Eleanor. *The Josefina Story Quilt*. Illustrations by Bruce Degan. (HarperCollins, 1986)

Ernst, Lisa Campbell. *Sam Johnson and the Blue Ribbon Quilt*. (Lothrop, Lee, and Shepard, 1983)

Flournoy, Valerie. *The Patchwork Quilt*. Illustrated by Jerry Pinkney. (Dial, 1985)

Gibbons, Gail. *The Quilting Bee*. (HarperCollins, 2004)

Hines, Anna Grossnickle. *Pieces, A Year in Poems and Quilts*. (Greenwillow, 2001)

Hines, Anna Grossnickle. *Winter Lights: A Season in Poems and Quilts*. (Greenwillow, 2005)

Howard, Ellen. *The Log Cabin Quilt*. Illustrated by Ronald Himler. (Holiday House, 1996)

Johnston, Tony, and Tomie dePaola. *The Quilt Story*. (Putnam, 1985)

Kinsey-Warnock, Natalie. *The Canada Geese Quilt*. Illustrated by Leslie Bowman. (Dutton, 1989

Paul, Ann. *Eight Hands Round*. (HarperCollins, 1991)

Polacco, Patricia. *The Keeping Quilt*. (Simon & Schuster, 1988)

Ransom, Candice F. *The Promise Quilt*. Illustrated by Ellen Beier. (Walker, 2002)

Root, Phyllis. *The Name Quilt*. Illustrated by Margot Apple. (Farrar, Straus & Giroux, 2003)

Stroud, Bettye. *The Patchwork Path: A Quilt Map to Freedom*. Illustrated by Erin Susanne Bennett. (Candlewick, 2005)

Turner, Ann, and Thomas B. Allen. *Sewing Quilts*. (Simon & Schuster, 1994)

Vaughan, Marcia. *The Secret to Freedom*. Illustrated by Larry Johnson. (Lee & Low, 2001)

Patchwork Muffins

Women (and sometimes men) who created quilts sometimes gathered to quilt at one of the participant's homes and worked together to create a quilt for one of them or for a special occasion. These social (and work) gatherings not only yielded a finished quilt but also an opportunity for neighbors to socialize and get to know one another better. The participants might bring a covered dish for a pot-luck meal, spouses might come in the early evening to share an evening of socializing and dancing, or the fare might have been much simpler with the hostess supplying a simple bread or muffins to be served with tea or lemonade.

Mix together:

- 1 tablespoon sugar
- 1 egg
- 4 tablespoons shortening
- 1 cup sour milk (Either use milk soured naturally or add 1–2 teaspoons of vinegar or lemon juice to 1 cup sweet milk. Let stand for 10 minutes or so until the milk begins to curdle—sour.)

Set aside, and sift together:

- 1/2 teaspoon baking soda
- 2 teaspoons baking powder
- 1/4 teaspoon salt
- 1 cup graham or whole wheat flour
- 3/4 cup white flour

Mix the sugar and shortening mixture with the sifted dry ingredients. Do not overmix—the batter will be slightly lumpy. Add your choice of blueberries, raspberries, raisins, nuts, or a patchwork of various berries and nuts.

Spoon into paper lined or greased muffin tins. Bake at 400 degrees F for 12 to 20 minutes. Serve warm.

.

Peter Roop and Connie Roop—Clam Chowder

Photo Credit: Martha Roop Turner

That afternoon, Abbie helped Mahala write her letters. Esther helped Lydia cook supper. Everyone helped take care of Mama.

—From *Keep the Lights Burning, Abbie* by Peter Roop and Connie Roop

Peter Roop

Birthday: March 8

Favorite place: Spruce Island, Maine

Favorite foods: lobster, clams, buffalo burgers, and pizza

Family:

    Spouse—Connie

    Son—Sterling

    Daughter—Heidi

Home:

    Childhood—Born in Massachusetts, lived in Memphis, Tennessee

    Now—Appleton, Wisconsin

Connie Roop

Birthday: June 18

Favorite place: Star Lake Fire Pit

Favorite foods: coffee ice cream, raspberries, dark chocolate, crab—"I love food."

Family:

    Spouse—Peter

    Son—Sterling

    Daughter—Heidi

Home:

    Childhood—Born in Elkhorn, Wisconsin, lived in Delevan, Wisconsin

    Now—Appleton, Wisconsin

Peter Roop shared his experiences clamming with his family in New England: "We have long had a connection to Maine where we have sailed, boated, kayaked, camped, gone swimming, and eaten seafood.

"One of our favorite family activities is to put on our boots, grab our clamming forks, pick up our clamming hod, hop into our boat *Island Hopper,* and head for our secret clamming flat on a secret island.

"We first wait for the tide to go far enough to uncover the clam flat. Then we plop through the muddy clam flats watching for the telltale jets of water which tells us where the clams are hiding.

"We dig into the mud with out clamming forks, turning over big, smelly chunks until we spot a clam or two. We pick the clams out of the mud and measure them to make sure they are "keepers," big enough to eat. The "keepers" go into the hod. The ones that are too small to keep, we gently return to their muddy homes so they can grow big enough to maybe become "keepers" one day. Every once in awhile a clam gets its revenge by squirting a jet of water into our faces!

"When we have two dozen "keepers," we rinse them in the ocean and head home, enjoying the salty spray all the way. There we make our delicious, steamy clam chowder, much in the same way the Burgess family probably did out on Matincus Rock when Abbie bravely kept the lights burning in 1856."

How to Steam Clams

Soak any quantity of clams in a salt brine of 1/3 cup salt to 1 gallon cold water. This brine will help rid the clams of any sand or grit before the clams are cooked. Soak for 15 minutes, drain, and soak in fresh brine for an additional 15 minutes.

Then:

Use a stiff brush to scrub the clams under cold running water.

In a kettle or pot place 1/2 inch water. Place clams on a rack over the water (but not in the water), cover and bring the water to a boil.

Steam the clams in the covered pot for 5 to 10 minutes until the clam shells open. As each clam opens, remove the clam meat for use in the chowder.

Clam Chowder

Fry 4 to 6 strips of bacon, crumble) and reserve bacon fat.

Cook 1 chopped onion and 1 large chopped potato in some of the bacon fat until the potato is soft.

Add 1 quart of 2 percent milk and 1 pint of half and half to potato, onion, and crumbled bacon (in the sauce pan).

Add steamed clams (or mussels or fish). The quantity is variable depending on how "clam filled" you wish your chowder to be.

Simmer gently, but do not boil. Serve hot. Chowder will be more flavorful after the first day.

Signature Recipe—Peter Roop

Peter and Connie Roop

Peter Roop was born in Winchester, Massachusetts, but counts his childhood home as Memphis, Tennessee, where he grew up. After earning a degree in education from Lawrence University (Appleton, Wisconsin), he went on to earn a graduate degree in children's literature at the Center for the Study of Children's Literature at Simmons College in Boston. He was able to study with authors Scott O'Dell and Nancy Bond. The influence of these writers, and that of the coursework itself, helped Roop understand the critical elements in writing for children.

Connie Roop was born and raised in Wisconsin. Despite being recognized for her writing during her middle school and high school years, she did not consider being a writer until later in life. She entered Lawrence College with the intent of becoming a physician, but during her coursework she changed her mind and earned credentials to become a science teacher.

During the late 1970s the couple enrolled for graduate work in Boston universities— Peter studied children's literature at Simmons College, and Connie undertook a degree in science teaching at Boston College. During that time, as a diversion Connie began to read some of the children's books Peter was reading for his studies. She developed a list of science books to correlate with her science curriculum, and she became interested in the world of children's books.

The couple returned to live in Appleton, Wisconsin, and both worked as educators. Peter involved himself more heavily into writing. After writing for about six years, he and Connie began to collaborate. Their first book together was a joke book, and it's success resulted in several similar titles. Eventually the two writers turned to their joint interest in Maine. They wrote about a historical figure they had discovered while researching an article about Maine. In 1856, Abbie Burgess's father was the lighthouse keeper at a Maine lighthouse. When Abbie's mother fell ill and her father was trapped away from the lighthouse during a month of violent storms, Abbie managed to keep two lighthouses going. The Roop's common interest in the story of brave children who made a footprint in history resulted other books, *Buttons for General Washington* and *Ahyoka and the Talking Leaves*.

To get details right, the couple has traveled to locations and have experienced events that influence their writing. They have watched fifty whooping cranes at dawn and incorporated the excitement into *Seasons of the Cranes*. They traveled to the outreaches of the Maine coast to feel the chilling blasts of a nor'easter, as Abbie Burgess did. During their writing of *Buttons for George Washington,* they walked the cobbled streets of Philadelphia; and as they wrote *Off the Map: The Journals of Lewis and Clark*, they camped at the actual campsites of Lewis and Clark.

Connie's interest in science has also come through several of their titles. Together they wrote four titles in a Great Mysteries series that presented situations that have yet to be solved by science.

Peter taught elementary school, in Appleton for almost three decades before devoting himself full time to writing and meeting readers in schools throughout the United States. His passion for history and other cultures continues to influence his research and writing. As of 2006, Connie continued in her career as an environmental science teacher in Appleton, as well as a collaborator with her husband in the research and writing of children's books.

Selected Books Written by Peter Roop and Connie Roop

Ahyoka and the Talking Leaves. Illustrated by Yoshi Miyake. (Lothrop, Lee and Shepherd, 1992)

Backyard Beasties: Jokes to Snake You Smile. Written with Diane L. Burns. Illustrated by Brian Gable. (Carolrhoda, 2004)

Buttons for General Washington. Illustrated by Peter E. Hanson. (Carolrhoda, 1986)

California Gold Rush. (Scholastic, 2002)

The Diary of Mary Jemison, Captured by the Indians. (Marshall Cavendish, 2000)

Down the Colorado: John Wesley Powell. (Marshall Cavendish, 2001)

Escape from the Ice: Shackleton and the Endurance. Illustrated by Bob Doucet. (Scholastic, 2001)

An Eye for an Eye: A Revolutionary War Novel. (Jamestown Publications, 2000)

Go Fly a Kite, Ben Franklin! (Scholastic, 2003)

Goodbye for Today: A Girl's Whaling Journal (Atheneum, 2000)

Keep the Lights Burning, Abbie. Illustrated by Peter E. Hanson. (Carolrhoda, 1985)

Let's Drive, Henry Ford! (Scholastic, 2004)

Let's Play Soldier, George Washington! (Scholastic, 2002)

Let's Split Logs, Abe Lincoln! (Scholastic, 2002)

The Louisiana Purchase. Illustrated by Sally Wern Comport. (Aladdin, 2004)

Off the Map: The Journals of Lewis and Clark. Illustrated by Tim Tanner. (Walker, 1993)

Over in the Rain Forest. Illustrated by Carol Schwartz. (Scholastic, 2003)

Sacagawea: Girl of the Shinning Mountains. (Hyperion, 2003)

Sew What, Betsy Ross? (Scholastic, 2002)

Sitting Bull. (Scholastic, 2002)

Sojourner Truth. Scholastic, 2002.

Starfish. (Scholastic, 2001)

Take Command, Captain Farragut! (Atheneum (New York, 2001)

Take a Giant Leap, Neil Armstrong! (Scholastic, 2005)

Take a Stand, Rosa Parks. (Scholastic, 2005)

Turn on the Light, Thomas Edison! (Scholastic, 2003)

Whales and Dolphins. (Scholastic, 2000)

Abbie Burgess Grant—One of Maine's Lighthouse Keepers

(A Narrative Timeline)

Matinicus Rock is on a thirty-two-acre island, covered with granite rocks, eighteen miles offshore and twenty-five miles from the nearest port, Rockland, Maine. The lighthouse at Matinicus Rock was a dual-light tower. The original lighthouse was authorized by President John Quincy Adams in 1827. The first lighthouse keeper was John A. Shaw who lived on the island with his wife until 1831. After Shaw died, there were four more lighthouse keepers until Abbie Burgess's father Samuel Burgess took over in 1853. Abbie helped her father, and for many purposes was the lighthouse keeper while her father attempted to add to the family income by lobster fishing.

Political events caused Samuel Burgess to be relieved of his station in 1861. A Burgess family friend came to take over the lighthouse keeper's duties. His two sons, William G. and Isaac Grant, became their father's assistant. Abbie stayed on to teach them the duties. Within a year, a romance with Isaac led the two young people to marry. Isaac and Abbie lived at the rock and became parents to four children there. Abbie was officially appointed as assistant keeper. They stayed at Matinicus Rock until 1869, and in 1873 Isaac Grant was appointed keeper at Whitehead Light. When Isaac died in 1875, Abbie Burgess was named head lighthouse keeper, a post she kept for fifteen years. She raised their four children on Matinicus Rock. Abbie left the Whitehead Lighthouse in 1890 due to ill health. In 1892, at age fifty-three, she died in a house on Maple Street, in Portland, Maine. Abbie's grave (with that of Isaac Grant) is marked by a small lighthouse in nearby Spruce Head.

Lighthouses

Connie Roop and Peter Roop wrote *Keep the Lights Burning, Abbie* after discovering Abigail Burgess Grant, who lived in the lighthouse at Matinicus Rock, Maine. Several lighthouse heroines, including Abigail Burgess Grant, were the inspiration for another author's story, Deborah Hopkinson's *Birdie's Lighthouse.* Hopkinson tells her story in the form of a journal—*Birdie's Lighthouse* spans one year in Birdie Holland's life.

Other stories on this list incorporate heroes and heroines and tales of life in a lighthouse.

Briggs, Kelly Paul. *Lighthouse Lullaby.* (Down East Books, 2001)

Buzzeo, Toni. *The Sea Chest.* Illustrated by Mary GrandPré. (Dial, 2002)

Gibbons, Gail. *Beacons of Light: Lighthouses.* (HarperCollins, 1990)

Hopkinson, Deborah. *Birdie's Lighthouse.* Illustrated by Kimberly Bucklen Root. (Atheneum/Anne Schwartz, 1997)

Lewis, Anne Margaret. *Lighthouse Fireflies*. Illustrated by Mary Frey. (Mackinac Island Press, 2005)

O'Hara, Megan. *Lighthouse: Living in a Great Lakes Lighthouse 1910–1914*. (Capstone Press, 1998)

Olson, Arielle North. *The Lighthouse Keeper's Daughter*. Illustrated by Elaine Wentworth. (Little, Brown, 1987)

Perrow, Angeli. *Lighthouse Dog to the Rescue*. Illustrated by Emily Harris. (Down East Books, 2003)

Pfitsch, Patricia Curtis. *Keeper of the Light*. (Simon & Schuster, 1997; novel length)

Thaxter, Celia. *Celia's Island Journal*. Illustrated by Loretta Krupinski. (Little Brown, 1992)

Raspberry Cream Chocolate Drizzle

Preheat oven to 325 degrees F. While it is preheating, melt 4 tablespoons of butter in an 8-inch square baking dish.

While the butter is melting, in a medium-sized mixing bowl combine:

- 3/4 cup flour
- 3/4 cup granulated sugar
- 1 1/2 teaspoons baking powder
- Dash of salt
- 1/2 cup evaporated milk

Beat until the batter is smooth.

Pour the batter over the melted butter, and top the batter with 2 cups fresh raspberries.

Sprinkle 2 tablespoons brown sugar evenly over the raspberries.

Bake for 45 to 55 minutes, or until browned.

Topping

- 1–2 ounces semisweet dark chocolate (melted)
- 1 cup heavy whipping cream (whipped)

While the cake is baking, melt an ounce or two of dark chocolate and whip a cup of heavy whipping cream for the topping. (A convenient alternative is to use Dream Whip with warmed Hershey's hot fudge sauce.)

Serve raspberry cake warm with a generous dollop of whipped cream drizzled with melted dark chocolate.

RASPBERRIES

Among Connie Roop's favorite foods are raspberries and dark chocolate. The recipe on the previous page combines a taste of each. Red and yellow raspberries can be grown throughout the Roops's home state of Wisconsin, while the purple and black raspberries grow best in the southern regions of the state. Raspberries come in red, black, purple, and yellow varieties. There are summer varieties and fall bearing raspberry bushes. The fall-bearing raspberries yield a large crop in the fall and a smaller crop the following summer.

Nicole Rubel—Matzo Ball Soup

Photo Credit: Geoff Shapiro

I cook it [matzo ball soup] every other month because I love it, my husband loves it, and I think it keeps one well.

—Nicole Rubel

Matzo ball soup plays a major role in one of the chapters in my novel, *Its Hot and Cold in Miami,* which I wrote and illustrated. It's about twins Rachel and Rebecca growing up in Miami. Rachel feels Rebecca stole half her brain when they were still in their Mom's stomach, and that's why she [Rebecca] is so smart.

In the chapter "Granny Fanny," Rachel asks her grandmother for a bowl of soup stuffed with a million matzo balls. She mentions earlier in the story that Granny Fanny brings matzo ball soup when anyone in the family is sick.

Many years ago, my grandmother brought matzo ball soup to our house when anyone was sick. I'm sure it made us well because all four of us kids were very healthy.

—Nicole Rubel

Nicole Rubel grew up in Miami (just like Rachel and Rebecca), and, just like Rachel and Rebecca, she was a twin. Her relationship with her identical twin sister, Bonnie, became the inspiration for several of her books. Her parents named Nicole "Leslie," and that is how she was known as a child and into her adulthood. When it was time to head off to college, Leslie's (Nicole's) sister Bonnie qualified for admittance into the University of Wisconsin at Madison; she was smart and had good grades. Nicole (Leslie) did not qualify for admittance. To be close to her sister, Nicole enrolled in a college in Beloit. That year was one that allowed Nicole to realize that she was her own person. After deciding to go to art school, she enrolled in the Boston Museum School of Art, a move that eventually propelled her into the world of children's books. While in college, Rubel met authors James Marshall and Walter Lorraine, and both helped her. At the time, author Jack Gantos was her friend, and he collaborated with her to write the Rotten Ralph series of books. The first title was published in 1976. Gantos was credited for the writing; and Nicole was credited as the illustrator.

During her college years in Boston, Nicole decided to change her name from Leslie to Nicole, and she sent out announcements to all of her family and friends. This was the beginning of her life with a new sense of purpose. For a number of years, Nicole lived in Boston and New York, continuing to illustrate the Rotten Ralph books and as well as others. Her books are often described as humorous, and the illustrations as fun and somewhat whacky.

In 1987, she married Richard C. Langsen, a family therapist, and eventually the couple left their New York apartment to move across the country to an eight-and-a-half acre refuge in Aurora, Oregon. There they enjoy their cats, horses, and even a sheep or two. Anyone who visits their "Red Cat Farm" is greeted by a large red cat carved from a tree trunk. Inside their home are whimsical touches, not unlike the whimsical touches that characterize her watercolor illustrations for her many books. Images from her growing up years in Miami populate her illustrations, and twin images often show up in her books even if the book is not about twins. Her sister Bonnie is involved in the family import business in Miami, and Nicole often travels overseas with Bonnie on buying trips. Identical twins with red hair walking along the streets of Hong Kong—an interesting image that just might show up in one of her books one day.

Selected Books Written and Illustrated by Nicole Rubel

A *Cowboy Named Ernestine.* (Dial, 2001)

Cyrano the Bear. (Dial, 1995)

Double Trouble: A Field Guide fro Twins. (Farrar, Straus & Giroux, 2004)

Grody's Not So Golden Rules. (Harcourt, 2003)

Ham and Pickles First Day of School. (Harcourt, 2006)

It's Hot and Cold in Miami. (Farrar, Straus and Giroux, 2006)

Rotten Ralph series, authored by Jack Gantos, including *Best in Show for Rotten Ralph: A Rotten Ralph Rotten Reader* (Farrar, Straus & Giroux, 2005), *Rotten Ralph Feels Rotten: A Rotten Ralph Rotten Reader* (Farrar, Straus & Giroux, 2004), *Rotten Ralph Helps Out: A Rotten Ralph Rotten Reader* (Farrar, Straus & Giroux, 2004), *Rotten Ralph's Rotten Romance* (HarperCollins, 1997), and *Wedding Bells for Rotten Ralph* (HarperCollins, 1999)

Twice as Nice: What's It Like to Be a Twin. (Farrar, Straus & Giroux, 2004)

Matzo Ball Soup

"The trick is to start with a good chicken, and that means finding a fresh kosher one. They just taste better. I figured this out after years of failure with regular chickens," says Nicole Rubel.

Fill a pot with water to almost cover the chicken. Add three chopped carrots, one large chopped onion, chop six celery stalks, and a large handful of fresh dill, salt and pepper. Cook until chicken falls from the bone.

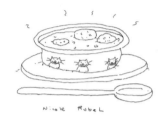

While the soup simmers, make your matzo balls.

- 2 tablespoons vegetable oil
- 2 large eggs, slightly beaten
- 1/2 cup matzo meal
- 1 teaspoon salt
- 2 tablespoons seltzer (or some kind of fizzy water)

Mix all ingredients and refrigerate for one hour, covered.

Remove chicken from boiling broth to be served later as a side dish. Lightly shape mixture into balls and drop gently in for about 25 minutes. Serve soup with the chicken on the side.

Signature Recipe—Nicole Rubel

Booklist

Matzo ball soup is legendary for curing the sick. Soup of all kinds shows up in books, and January is National Soup Month. So share the passages from *Hot and Cold in Miami,* read a title or two from this booklist, and enjoy your favorite soup.

Brown, Marcia. *Stone Soup.* (Atheneum, 1947; Aladdin, 2005 reissue)

Cocca-Leffler, Maryann. *Bravery Soup.* (Albert A. Whitman, 2005)

Cooper, Helen. *Pumpkin Soup.* (Farrar, Straus & Giroux, 1999)

Creech, Sharon. *Granny Torrelli Makes Soup.* (Joanna Cotler, 2003)

Duncan, Alice Faye. *Christmas Soup.* Illustrated by Phyllis Dooley. (ZonderKidz, 2005)

Gershator, David, and Phillis Gershator. *Kallaloo!: A Caribbean Tale.* Illustrated by Diane Greenseid. (Marshall Cavendish, 2005)

Jones, Christianne. *Stone Soup.* Illustrated by Micah Chambers-Goldbert. (Picture Window Books, 2005)

Kimmel, Eric A. *Cactus Soup.* Illustrated by Phil Huling. (Marshall Cavendish, 2004)

McGovern, Ann. *Stone Soup.* Illustrated by Winslow Pinney Pels. (Scholastic, 1986)

Rylant, Cynthia. *Mr. Putter & Tabby Stir the Soup.* Illustrated by Arthur Howard (Harcourt, 2004)

Seeger, Pete, and Paul Dubois Jacobs. *Some Friends to Feed: The Story of Stone Soup.* Illustrated by Michael Hays. (Putnam, 2005)

Segal, John. *Carrot Soup.* (Margaret K. McElderry, 2006)

Smith, Connie Macdonald. *Pea Soup Fog.* Illustrated by Jen Cart. (Down East Books, 2004)

Blackberry Cobbler

Nicole particularly enjoys a raspberry, blackberry, or blueberry cobbler. Here is a simple cobbler recipe that is baked in an iron skillet. The cobbler calls for blackberries but any type of berry—raspberries, blackberries, or blueberries could be used. Make a sauce on the stove top. Drop the cobbler dough into the berry sauce by the spoonfuls. Transfer to the oven and bake.

Making the Berry "Sauce"

Dissolve 2 tablespoons cornstarch in 1/4 cup cold water

Add:

- 1 cup sugar
- 1 tablespoon lemon juice
- 4 cups blackberries, picked over, rinsed, and drained (or substitute raspberries or blueberries)

Put into an 8- or 9-inch cast iron skillet and place on a stovetop burner. Bring to boil.

Making the dough for the cobbler

In a large bowl combine:

- 1 cup flour
- 1/2 cup sugar
- 1 teaspoon baking powder
- 1/2 teaspoon salt

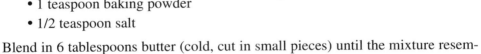

Blend in 6 tablespoons butter (cold, cut in small pieces) until the mixture resembles a course meal.

Add in 1/4 cup boiling water to make a soft dough.

Bring the blackberry mixture to a boil, stirring. Drop spoonfuls of the dough carefully onto the boiling mixture. Reduce heat and cook for 3 to 5 minutes. Place the iron skillet on a foil-lined baking sheet (to catch the overflow and to avoid a mess) and bake on the center shelf in a preheated 400 degree F oven for 20 to 25 minutes or until the topping is golden. Spoon a dumpling out onto a serving plate. Spoon some of the berry sauce over the dumpling. Top with vanilla ice cream or whipped cream. Sprinkle a bit of nutmeg on the ice cream or whipped cream for an extra tang.

Claudia Rueda—Toasted Big-Bottomed Ants

Photo Credit: Jorge Giraldo

There is a pantry story I would like to tell, related to my country and to the books I've been doing lately. It's not about my grandma's muffins or the potato soup we used to have every Sunday at family re-unions. It is more exotic than that, and you are going to like it if you like peculiar stories.

—Claudia Rueda

Claudia Rueda was raised in Colombia and moved to the United States in the late 1990s. While she was preparing the illustrations for *Nacho and Lolita*, a story set in the California mission of San Juan Capistrano, she visited Stanford (California) and carefully researched missions, swallows, and Juaneo Indians. The result was extraordinary and detailed colored pencil drawings. In 2004, Claudia Rueda found herself working on two picture books about insects. The spider who ate the fly swallowed by "The Old Lady" led her to the real story of the *Eency Weency Spider*. "At the end," said Rueda, "it is all about eating. And in this case, about bug-eating! So this is where the story begins."

Claudia Rueda

Birthday: July 28

Favorite place: A plane or a train with a new destination.

Favorite foods: bread, cheese, mussels, olives, herbs and spices, ginger, mushrooms, dark chocolate … Asian, French, Mexican… I am getting hungry!

Family:

Spouse—Jorge Giraldo

Daughters—Catalina (1997) and Camila (1999)

Home:

Childhood—Bogota, Colombia

Now—lives between Bogota, New York City, and California!

Ants in the Pantry

Here is what Claudia has to say about a very unusual delicacy: "I was about eighteen. I had just come back home from watching *The Silence of the Lambs*. I went to the kitchen to grab something to eat, and I saw a can of chocolate candy on top of the fridge. The perfect snack to get rid of the bitter flavor of a scary movie, I thought. But I almost dropped the can, when instead of chocolate, I found a bunch of giant toasted ants! I was not hungry anymore.

"*Hormigas culonas,* which translates to big-bottomed ants, were that night's surprise. They were a rare and exotic delicacy brought as a very special gift to my mother from Santander, a region in the North East of Colombia, where she had been raised as a child. Those ants might have been the result of one of my grandma's recipes!

"The *hormigas culonas* are named after the extremely big size of their rear abdomen. Thousands of *culona* queens come out of their giant mud nests only once a year, after April's rains, to begin their nuptial flight. The drone ants patiently wait for that precious moment hoping to fertilize one of them. After a first and only happy act of love, they fall to the ground and die. But the strength of this fertilization is such that it's enough for a queen to lay eggs for twenty years!

"This love story explains why the Guanes Indians, who lived in the region for over five hundred years, and now many people in Colombia and around the world, consider the toasted *culonas* an aphrodisiac. It was actually considered the ideal wedding present among the *Guanes.*

"But people also like to eat them because they are aromatic, crunchy, and exquisite. After removing their wings, head, and legs, the ants are toasted in a mud pot over an open fire, salted, and packed. And you can now find them in London, Los Angeles, and Barcelona.

"Even if it sounds yucky, we are not the only ones around to appreciate bug snacks. There are about 1,600 edible insects around the world. And most of them are actually a very good source of protein!"

Selected Books Illustrated by Claudia Rueda

Eency Weency Spider, The Real Story. Text by Margaret Wang. (Piggy Toes Press/Intervisual Books, 2005)

Going to Grandma's Farm. Text by Betsy Franco. A Rookie Reader. (Children's Press, 2004; Scholastic paperback)

I Know an Old Lady Who Swallowed a Fly. (Piggy Toes Press/Intervisual Books, 2004)

Nacho And Lolita. Text by Pam Muñoz Ryan. (Scholastic, 2005)

Toasted Big-Bottomed Ants

Chances are, you won't try this recipe—partly because it's nearly impossible to find big bottomed ants in the United States, and partly because if you could find them, you probably wouldn't want to eat them.

- 1 pound of live big-bottomed ants (NOT the ones in your backyard!)
- 12 ounces water
- 2 tablespoons salt
- A wok or frying pan

Remove wings, legs, and head from the live ants (be careful: they bite really hard!). Rinse them in salty water. Dry them. Add the ants to the wok/pan and toast them without adding oil or butter, until they look brown and crunchy, for about 45 minutes. While cooking, stir constantly with a wooden spoon. Let them cool on a basket or a rack for ventilation.

Signature Recipe—Claudia Rueda

EDIBLE INSECTS

Some think that ants taste similar to crispy fried bacon and they use the toasted ants as a party snack in place of the more traditional nuts or candies. Eating ants is not as strange as it may seem. Many cultures eat foods that other cultures would find strange—or at least interesting. The Japanese have canned bees (fried bee pupae with soy sauce), and according to the *Food Insects Newsletter* ("Some Insect Foods of the American Indians: And How the Early Whites Reacted to Them," 1994 [November 7]: 3), the Paiute (a Native American Tribe) ate the pupae of a fly (*kutsavi*) dried in the sun and mixed with acorns, berries, grass seed, ground, and then made into bread. The pupae of worms were also fried in their own grease, and became a crunchy treat. Mormon crickets (more like a katydid) were also dried and ground with pinenuts and grass seed to make a dark bread. Other insects were also included in the early Native American diet: grasshoppers, cicadas, ants and ant pupae, wasp pupae and prepupae, certain beetle larvae, and several kinds of caterpillars. Insects found their way into other cultures as well with canned ants and silkworm pupae from Japan, maguey worms

from Mexico, fried grasshoppers showing up in gourmet shopping marts. And a tiny insect, the cochineal scale, has been crushed and used as red pigment for use in food, cosmetics, and for clothing dyes since the eighteenth century. Currently the dyes produced by crushing the cochineal is the only natural red dye approved by the United States Food and Drug Administration.

For those serious about investigating the bug-eating world, the following books might yield some interesting information to share or read. These are books written for the older reader, but selected portions can be read aloud, and some of the information will be accessible directly by younger readers.

Gordon, David G. *Eat-a-Bug Cookbook*. (Ten Speed Press, 1998)

Menzel, Peter and Faith D'Aluisio. *Man Eating Bugs: The Art and Science of Eating Insects*. (Ten Speed Press, 1998)

Bugs, Bugs, Bugs!

Barner, Bob. *Bugs! Bugs! Bugs!* (Chronicle, 1999)

Greenaway, Theresa. *Big Book of Bugs*. (DK Children, 2000)

Hughes, Monica. *Bugs*. (Bearport Publishing, 2006)

Llewellyn, Claire. The Best Book of Bugs. (Kingfisher, 1998)

Phillips, Dee. *Bugs and Spiders*. (Two Can Publishers, 2006)

Polacco, Patricia. *When Lightning Comes in a Jar*. (Philomel, 2002)

Sayre, April Pulley. *The Bumblebee Queen*. Illustrated by Patricia J. Wynne. (Charlesbridge, 2005)

Pseudo-Insect Snacks

Even if eating insects isn't something you are interested in doing, you might still be interested in preparing some of these pseudo-insect snacks.

Ants-on-a-Log

Clean stalks of celery and cut into 2-3 inch pieces. Fill the groove with peanut butter and sprinkle raisins on the peanut butter.

Aphids-on-a-Log

Clean stalks of celery and cut into 2-3 inch pieces. Fill the groove with peanut butter and sprinkle sunflower seeds on the peanut butter.

Gnats-on-a-Log

Clean stalks of celery and cut into 2-3 inch pieces. Fill the groove with peanut butter and sprinkle currants on the peanut butter.

Flies in the Pudding

Make vanilla pudding and stir in raisins.

Bug Juice

Mix lemonade with blue Kool-aid and you will get a neon green juice.

Spider Cake

Use a chocolate cake mix, make and bake as directed, except bake in two metal bowls—one larger than the other. Once the cake has been removed from the oven, cool and remove from the bowls. Slice the bigger cake in half horizontally. Carefully scoop out a cavity in each portion of the sliced cake. Fill the cavity with pistachio pudding (or vanilla pudding colored green with food coloring). Place the portions of the cake back together and then arrange both cakes on a serving platter and frost with black frosting (either purchase black food coloring to color your favorite frosting recipe, or add blue food coloring to chocolate frosting). Use green candies (such as gumdrops, M&M's or other round candy) to create eyes on the "head" of the spider. Use eight licorice sticks for spider legs. When the cake is cut, it will spurt green goop—like a squashed spider.

Pam Muñoz Ryan—Rice and Beans

Photo Credit: Sharron L. McElmeel

My favorite foods: I really love pizza and I also love noodles ... and chocolate! And barbecued chicken.

—Pam Muñoz Ryan

Pam Muñoz Ryan

Birthday: December 25

Favorite foods: barbequed chicken, and pizza—and noodles and chocolate.

Family:

> **Spouse—Jim Ryan**
>
> **Daughters—Marcie and Annie**
>
> **Sons—Matt and Tyler**

Home:

> **Childhood—San Joaquin Valley (Bakersfield, California)**
>
> **Now—northern area of San Diego County near the Pacific Ocean**

When she was growing up in Bakersfield, California, it never occurred to Pam Muñoz that she could be a writer. She never kept a journal, but many days she told stories—created in her head and put on plays in her backyard. When she grew up, she became a bilingual teacher. But after marrying and becoming a mother of two daughters and twin sons, she went back to college to earn her graduate degree in education. One of her professors suggested she try writing. She thought that was a good idea, so she accepted an offer to help a friend write an adult book, but soon she realized what she wanted to do with her career—she wanted to write children's books. She now is a full-time writer and has written many books, several that reflect her own cultural background—a background that includes Spanish, Mexican, Basque, Italian, and Oklahoman.

Pam Muñoz Ryan's grandparents were from Mexico and Italy. At her Italian grandmother's house, she ate fried okra, black-eyed peas, and peach cobbler. She ate enchiladas and rice and beans at her Mexican grandmother's house. For Pam, these foods are associated with fond memories of being with her grandparents. She also loves a variety of other foods, including noodles, pizza, and chocolate. Rice and beans became part of one of her picture books—*Mice and Beans*. That story brings together her fond memories of large noisy family get-togethers and food that was shared with her twenty-three cousins: enchiladas, red mole, and rice and beans.

Selected Books Written by Pam Muñoz Ryan

Amelia and Eleanor Go for a Ride: Based on a True Story. Illustrated by Brian Selznick. (Scholastic, 1999)

Becoming Naomi León. (Scholastic, 2004)

Esperanza Rising. (Scholastic, 2000)

How Do You Raise a Raisin? Illustrated by Craig Brown. (Charlesbridge, 2003)

Mice and Beans. Illustrated by Joe Cepeda. (Scholastic, 2001)

Nacho and Lolita. Illustrated by Claudia Rueda. (Scholastic, 2005)

Riding Freedom. Illustrated by Brian Selznick. (Scholastic, 1999)

There Was No Snow on Christmas Eve. Illustrated by Dennis Nolan. (Hyperion, 2003)

When Marian Sang: The True Recital of Marian Anderson. Illustrated by Brian Selznick. (Scholastic, 2002)

Mouse Tales

When reading *Mice and Beans,* you can "read" a second story line taking place among the resident mice. They manage to steal away birthday party items. Each day something new is missing, and Grandma Rosa Maria thinks she is just forgetful ("Que boba soy! Silly me"). But the mice help by filling the piñata when Rosa Maria forgets, and if you look carefully, you will notice that the enterprising mice manage to have their own birthday celebration as well. Tomie dePaola uses a similar technique with a lone mouse in his story "*Charlie Needs a Cloak.*" In dePaola's story the lone mouse watches as Charlie gathers the wool, cards it, spins it, and weaves the wool yarn into fabric, and eventually observes the cutting and making of a new cloak. The mouse gathers thread, a candle, an old shoe, and other materials. When Charlie finishes making a cozy new cloak, the little mouse snuggles into his cozy new shoe home. This story runs parallel to Charlie's story just as the mice's story in *Mice and Beans* takes place in concert with Rosa Maria's story.

Skillet Beef and Noodles

One of Pam Muñoz Ryan's favorite foods is noodles. This noodle dish is very popular and can be prepared quickly in a skillet.

In a large skillet over medium heat, cook and stir:

- 1 pound ground beef (ground round or chuck)
- 1/2 cup chopped onion
- 1 cup thinly sliced celery (about 3 stalks)

Cook until the meat is no longer pink

Drain off the excess fat.

Stir in:

- 1 can (4 ounces) sliced mushrooms, undrained
- 1 can (about 10.5 ounces) cream of mushroom soup
- 1 medium green bell pepper, chopped
- 1 small jar (2 ounces) diced pimientos, drained
- 1 cup milk
- 1 tablespoon Worcestershire sauce
- 1 teaspoon salt
- 2 cups uncooked noodles, about 4 ounces

Bring mixture to a boil and quickly reduce heat, cover, and simmer. Stir occasionally, for about 25 minutes or until noodles are tender. May need to add a little more water to skillet mixture during cooking. Serves 4.

Making Egg Noodles

For this beef and noodle dish, you can either use purchased noodles or make your own. Here's a simple recipe for fresh homemade noodles.

In a large bowl, combine:

- 2 cups all-purpose flour
- 1 teaspoon salt

Make a well in the center of the flour mixture.

In a small dish slightly beat

- 2 eggs

Add eggs into the flour. Mix eggs and flour together to make a stiff dough. If it is too stiff, add 2 to 3 tablespoons water.

On a lightly floured surface, knead dough for about 3 to 4 minutes. Using a floured rolling pin, roll the dough out to desired thinness. Roll as thin as a dime, but no thicker than a nickel. Allow the sheet of noodle dough to air dry for 20 to 30 minutes and then use a sharp knife or noodle cutter to cut the noodles into thin slivers. These noodles can be used fresh or dried for use in the next few days. Refrigerate or freeze if not used immediately. They will keep frozen for a week or more.

RICE AND BEANS

Pam Muñoz Ryan remembers many dinners of enchiladas and red mole—and of course, rice and beans. Her grandmother's tiny kitchen bustled with activity, and many of her twenty-three cousins squeezed into her grandmother's home. Memories of those family gatherings formed the basis for Ryan's book, *Mice and Beans*. The illustrator, Joe Cepeda, brought his own memory of family birthday parties to the book, which is a joyous celebration of family and children, and a joyous birthday party for a seven-year-old.

Rice and Beans

Beans

Soak 2 cups of pinto beans overnight in water.

The following day, when you are ready to cook them, drain and rinse. Then put the beans in a large cooking pot with:

- 1 teaspoon garlic powder or 2 garlic cloves
- 3 quarts of water or 3 quarts of chicken broth

Bring to a boil, turn the heat to medium, and cook for 2 1/2 to 3 hours. Add water if necessary. If you use chicken broth, you will probably not need to add salt, but if using water you may wish to add 1 teaspoon salt per cup of beans, just before turning off the heat.

Mexican Rice

- 1 clove garlic, minced
- 1 cup uncooked rice
- 1 teaspoon of salt
- 1/2 cup chopped bell pepper
- 1/2 cup chopped onion
- 1/2 cup tomato puree or canned tomato sauce
- 2 cups chicken broth
- 3 tablespoons cooking oil

Heat the oil and add rice to cook until golden. Add chopped onion and sauté. Add chopped bell pepper and garlic. In a blender blend tomato, broth, and salt. Add the tomato and broth mixture to the rice. Cook until tender and the liquid is absorbed. The cooking time will be approximately 20 minutes over low heat.

Books with "Other Stories"

Several books have minor stories that take place as parallel stories to the main story. Jan Brett is an illustrator who often puts these side "stories" in the borders of her tales, so check her titles listed below as well as any other book authored/illustrated by Jan Brett.

Anno, Mitsumasa. *Anno's Aesop: A Book of Fables*. (Orchard Books, 1989)

Brett, Jan. *Annie and the Wild Animals*. (Houghton Mifflin, 1985)

Brett, Jan. *Honey … Honey … Lion!* (Putnam, 2005)

Brett, Jan. *The Mitten*. (Putnam, 1989)

Brett, Jan. *Trouble with Trolls*. (Putnam, 1992)

Brett, Jan. *The Umbrella*. (Putnam, 2004)

Brown, Margaret Wise. *Goodnight Moon*. (HarperCollins, various dates/editions)

dePaola, Tomie. *"Charlie Needs a Cloak."* (Prentice-Hall, 1973; Simon & Schuster, 1988)

Gilman, Phoebe. *Something from Nothing*. (Scholastic, 1993)

Martin, Jacqueline Briggs. *Snowflake Bentley*. Illustrated by Mary Azarian. (Houghton Mifflin, 1998)

McPhail, David. *Mole Music*. (Henry Holt, 1999)

Moore, Clement C. *The Night before Christmas*. Illustrated by Jan Brett. (Putnam, 1998)

Noble, Trinka Hakes. *Meanwhile Back at the Ranch*. Illustrated by Tony Ross. (Dial, 1987; Puffin, 1992)

Ryan, Pam Muñoz. *Mice and Beans*. Illustrated by Joe Cepeda. (Scholastic, 2001)

Diane Stanley—Blackberry Pie

Photo Credit: Karen Sachar

Diane Stanley

Birthday: December 27

**Favorite place: Anyplace
   beautiful—how can I possibly
   choose between Italy and France
   and China and Hawaii and my
   own home town, Santa Fe? I
   love them all!**

**Favorite foods: Pasta, cheese,
   duck, fruity desserts, summer
   tomatoes, peaches, berries,
   ethnic foods of every kind.**

Family:

   Spouse—Peter Vennema

   Son—John Venneman

   **Daughters—Catherine
      Zuromski, Tamara Zuromski**

Home:

   Childhood—Abilene, Texas

   Now—Santa Fe, New Mexico

I love to cook.... Cooking keeps me in touch with the seasons. Now that I live in Santa Fe, I go every Saturday to the farmer's market down at the Rail Yard. First, in late spring, there are arugula and winter lettuces, plus lots of jams and jellies from last year's harvest. But soon the full flowering of summer produce is upon us with eggplant and asparagus and tomatoes and onions and twelve different kinds of garlic and zucchini and raspberries and peaches. Later the melons come and the honey and the apples and the wonderful smoky aroma of roasting chilis.

—Diane Stanley

Diane Stanley grew up in a house filled with stories. Her mother was a writer and loved language. She often read to Diane, who savored the words she heard. Although the margins of her school notebooks were crammed with pencil sketches, Diane did not think about art as a career until her senior year of college. Her interest in creating children's books came later. Today, as a full-time author and illustrator, she is perhaps best known for her picture-book biographies, but she has written several fictional books as well.

Diane spends most of her days in her studio, writing and illustrating. But she also has always enjoyed making other things—and cooking. She says, "Everyone in my family is this way, going back several generations. Give us a project and we are happy campers. Whether it is weaving, knitting, throwing pots, or making fudge, learning new skills and then taking flight with our own creations is what we were born to do. Perhaps that is why I so seldom use recipes—and even when I do use them, they are just the starting point. I know what tastes good together and I know what is in my refrigerator and I know more or less what I can do to make them taste good and look pretty."

229

And she says, "Since cooking is something I know and love, it naturally makes its way into my books. Each of my three novels has at least one cooking scene. In *The Mysterious Matter of I. M. Fine,* Fanny and Beamer make pancakes while waiting for the climatic event to occur. They don't have everything the recipe calls for, so they improvise, just as I do."

Stanley's other two novels have historical elements, so the cooking scenes are limited to the methods and ingredients that would have been available.

"In *A Time Apart,* my heroine Ginny is participating in an Iron Age experiment and so is required to limit herself to methods and ingredients that would have been available to a British villager two thousand years ago. She makes her own authentic tarts from wild blackberries and strawberries she picks, honey from the hives, butter from the goats, and flour from the grain they grew. She bakes them in a clay oven.

"I was so intrigued by the Iron Age way of cooking that I tried making a few of her recipes myself. I made tarts much like Ginny's (although the berries came from the market) and cooked them on tin foil over the gas grill. The crust was a little hard, but they were pretty and they tasted good. My bread resembled hardtack of yore. And my attempt to make farmer's cheese utterly failed—it just got smelly. The goat's milk I bought at Whole Foods Market was apparently pasteurized.

"My novel, *Bella at Midnight,* is set in the Middle Ages. And so I bought two delightful books about medieval cooking. I thought children would be fascinated by the combination of sweet and savory that was so common in cooking of that time, bizarre dishes like salmon and fruit tart or bone-marrow pie."

In that book, there is mention of eel pie and other such common fare as well as dainties like "bone-marrow pie, with its many layers of marrow mixed with currants, and artichoke souls, and great raisins, and damson prunes, and cinnamon, and dates, and rosewater."

Stanley says, "Of course, food tastes much better if you grow it or pick it yourself. Though I travel too much to take proper care of a vegetable garden, I pick wild berries every chance I get. We spend part of every summer on the lovely island of Nantucket, Massachusetts. If we are there in August, when the blackberries are ripe, I always make a pie, not all that different from Ginny's tarts. My daughter got a terrible case of poison ivy helping me pick them one year—but it was one of the best pies I ever ate."

Nantucket Island

Nantucket is a fifty-square-mile island about thirty miles off the coast of southeastern Massachusetts. For more than 150 years, Nantucket served as the center of the world's whaling industry. The community once famed for its fleets of whaling ships now promotes the study of marine mammals and hosts whale-watching cruises. Many visit the islands for vacations or long-term seasonal visits. The height of the berry-picking season is late summer to early fall (August), when tourists enjoy the availability of blackberry brambles for picking the juicy ripe berries. Tourists also regularly visit in Nantucket for Daffodil Weekend and the Cranberry Festival.

Edward Lear mentioned the location in one of his well-known limericks:

> *There once was a man from Nantucket*
> *Who kept all his dough in a bucket*
> *His daughter, named Nan,*
> *Ran away with a man.*
> *And as for the bucket, Nantucket.*

Books Written by Diane Stanley

Being Thankful at Plymouth Plantation. Illustrated by Holly Berry. (Joanna Cotler Books, 2003)

Bella at Midnight: The Thimble, the Ring, and the Slippers of Glass. Illustrated by Bagram Ibatoulline. (HarperCollins, 2006)

The Giant and the Beanstalk. (HarperCollins, 2004)

Goldie and the Three Bears. (HarperCollins, 2003)

Good Queen Bess. Coauthored with Peter Vennema. (HarperCollins, 2001)

Joining the Boston Tea Party. Illustrated by Holly Berry. (HarperCollins, 2001)

The Last Princess: The Story of Princess Ka'iulani of Hawai'i. Text by Fay Stanley. (Four Winds, 1991)

Michelangelo. (HarperCollins, 2000)

Saladin: Nobel Prince of Islam. (HarperCollins, 2002)

Thanksgiving on Plymouth Plantation. Illustrated by Holly Berry. (Joanna Cotler Books, 2004)

The Mysterious Matter of I. M. Fine. (HarperCollins, 2001)

The Time-Traveling Twins. (HarperCollins, 2001)

Blackberry Pie

The Pastry

- 1 cup cold unsalted butter
- 1/2 teaspoon salt
- 2 cups all-purpose flour, plus more for rolling
- 2–3 tablespoons cold water
- 1 teaspoon grated lemon or orange zest (optional)

The Filling

- 4–5 cups of blackberries (However, you may use any kind of berries or fruit you like—strawberries, blueberries, raspberries, peaches, cherries, apples, pears—whatever is handy and to your taste. Use one kind or mix together. If using large fruit such as apples, cut into small pieces.)
- 1 cup sugar

Combine the flour, salt, and sugar in a bowl. Cut the butter into little bits and add them to the flour. It helps to put the butter in the freezer for a while before you do this, because you want the butter to stay cold. With the tips of your fingers, work the butter into the flour, continuously mixing, until it starts to look like cornmeal. Add the cold water and mix together quickly, forming the dough into a ball. Put it on your kitchen counter or a pastry board. With the heel of one hand, push a small portion of the dough away from you, smearing it across the board. This is the final mixing (kneading) of the butter and the flour. Continue until you have mixed all the dough. Scrape it back together, form it into a ball, wrap it well in waxed paper, and put it in the refrigerator for a couple of hours or overnight.

When you are ready to make your pie, take the pastry out of the refrigerator and divide it in half. Sprinkle some flour on the counter or board, put half the pastry on the counter and roll it out in a 13-inch circle using a rolling pin. With each stroke of the pin, start in the middle and roll out, going in different directions each time. This will help keep the thickness of the pastry even. Place the pastry in a pie pan.

Preheat your oven to 350 degrees F.

Put the fruit into a bowl, add the sugar and mix well. You can add nuts, grated lemon zest, or anything else that strikes your fancy. Pour the fruit into the pastry shell and begin making the top.

(Continued)

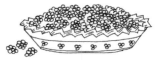

Roll out the other half of the pastry, just as you did with the first half. Lay your second circle of pastry over the fruit and pinch the dough together all around the edge to seal it. Cut several little slits in the top crust, radiating out like the spokes of a wheel. (This is for the steam to escape when you are cooking it.) Sprinkle a little sugar over the top of the tart (pie). Add a few little slivers of butter on the top, too. Pop it in the oven and cook for about 45 to 50 minutes. You will know it is ready when the crust is brown and the filling is juicy and bubbling. If your pie is really full of fruit, it might bubble out and make a mess in the oven. If it looks like it is doing that, slip a bit of tin foil under it to catch the spill.

You can eat your pie hot or at room temperature, with ice cream or sour cream mixed with sugar.

Signature Recipe—Diane Stanley

Hope Vestergaard—Yellow Cake

I've outgrown the cherries, but yellow cake with chocolate frosting still makes me feel like I'm six years old and queen of the world. And in my imagination, I am.

—Hope Vestergaard

Hope Vestergaard

Birthday: June 7

Favorite place: Where my kids are—often outside, especially by the water.

Favorite foods: Seven grain bread, most kinds of cake, fresh seafood.

Family:

Spouse—Michael (he's Danish)

Sons—Max (1994) and Carsten (1998)

Dog—Buck

Home:

Childhood—Ann Arbor, Michigan, and New Orleans, Louisiana

Now—Ann Arbor, Michigan (on a small farm)

Hope shares the following memories from her childhood: "During family vacations to my hometown of New Orleans, spending the night with my great-grandparents was a special treat. Dinner at Mimi and Papa's was usually seafood: a bowl of jambalaya or boiled crawfish, piled on a table covered with newspaper. It felt wonderfully uncivilized to peel the crawfish and gobble them up one after the other, though I never could bring myself to suck the heads as the grownups did. After dinner, we'd almost always bake a cake: an ordinary three-layer yellow cake made extraordinary by conversations with the cook and two perfectly placed maraschino cherries on top.

"After a drawn-out, chatty dinner, Mimi would give me a shower with egg shampoo and brush my long hair until it shined. I always conveniently forgot my nightgown so I could borrow a top from her silky polyester pajamas. We spent the evening cheering for game shows and playing poker and canasta. In the morning, Mimi would serve up eggs, bacon, grits, biscuits, and orange juice in the tiniest glasses I had ever seen. All my memories of Mimi's house are peppered with delicious smells and sounds: eggs sizzling in a fry pan; steam rising from a pot of seafood; sweet smoke from Papa's cigars; Mimi's gorgeous metallic slippers shuffling on the linoleum.

"After I married and had my first son, I took him to visit Mimi and my grandmother, Granny. Mimi's house was very much the same, sadly minus the smell of Papa's cigars, but

Mimi was no longer mobile enough to cook. As I lifted her from her wheelchair to her bed, I noticed her famously soft, crepy skin had grown smooth and firm and her comfortable curves had vanished. It was as though she were shrinking, growing younger. I wanted to wash her hair and bake a cake like she had done for me, but she worried about falling in the tub and didn't have a big appetite.

"Playing with the baby elicited lots of childhood reminiscing. When I was younger, my relatives' voices had been mostly background noise: a soundtrack for all the games and meals. This time, I paid more attention to the stories Mimi and Granny told. As Granny spoke, she traced the tablecloth with her index finger as though she were writing in cursive, something my mother, a published author, had done for as long as I could remember. I had always assumed the storytelling gene started and ended with my mom, but listening to Mimi and Granny hold court and watching Granny's fingers write invisible words, I realized that a fine sense of story and the compulsion to share was a family tradition.

"Many generations of sharing stories over supper had set the stage for me to eventually find my own voice. A few years after this trip to New Orleans, I began writing my own books. My childhood immersion in stories and rich sensory experiences shaped my career path as surely as Mimi's hands placed two cherries, perfectly centered, on top of her tasty cakes. I've outgrown the cherries, but yellow cake with chocolate frosting still makes me feel like I'm six years old and queen of the world. And in my imagination, I am.

Selected Books Written by Hope Vestergaard

Baby Love. Illustrated by John Wallace. (Dutton Children's Books, 2002)

Driving Daddy. Illustrated by Thierry Courtin. (Dutton Children's Books, 2003)

Hello, Snow! Illustrated by Nadine Bernard Westcott. (Farrar, Straus & Giroux/Melanie Kroupa Books, 2004)

Hillside Lullaby. Illustrated by Margie Moore. (Dutton Children's Books, 2006)

Wake Up, Mama! Illustrated by Thierry Courtin. (Dutton Children's Books, 2003)

What Do You Do When a Monster Says Boo? Illustrated by Maggie Smith. (Dutton Children's Books, 2006)

Yellow Layer Cake à la Mimi

Grease and lightly flour 3 (8 x 1 1/2 inch) round cake pans. Set aside.

In a large bowl, sift together the following ingredients and mix well:

- 2 2/3 cups cake flour
- 2 cups sugar
- 1 tablespoon baking powder
- 1/2 teaspoon salt

With a pastry blender, cut in until evenly distributed:

- 3/4 cup plus 1 tablespoon vegetable shortening

To the dry mixture, add:

- 1 1/8 cups milk and beat until moistened
- 3 eggs
- 1 1/2 teaspoons vanilla

Beat 2 minutes at medium speed. Spread batter evenly in prepared pans. Bake in a 350 degree F oven for about 20 minutes or until a wooden pick inserted near center comes out clean. Cool cakes in pan on wire rack for 10 minutes. Remove from pans and allow to completely cool on the wire rack.

Frost each layer as they are stacked one on top if the other and then frost all over.

Hope Vestergaard

When Hope was growing up, she was surrounded by eleven sisters and brothers. Family trips often included a visit to the children's Great-Grand-mother Mimi's and Papa's home. There was storytelling and the three-layered yellow cake with two cherries on top. While Hope was attending Smith College in North hampton, Massachusetts, Jane Yolen, Patricia Maclachan, and Jane Dyer came to talk about children's books and writing. Hope returned to Ann Arbor

Great-Grandmother Mimi and two grandchildren.

Photo from Hope Vestergaard's family album

and became associated with Gretchen's House (an early child care/education center). As a teacher, she read hundreds of books to the young children with whom she was working. She participated in a picture-book class facilitated by author Nancy Shaw and Tracy Gallup. That class put Hope into the world of writing children's books. In 1999, she became a full-time consultant, turning her work to teacher education and writing. In 2002, her first book, *Baby Love,* was published by Dutton Children's Books. Now she and her family live on a small farm outside or Ann Arbor, Michigan, where she is surrounded by animals—including a dog, several cows, hundreds of birds, and millions of spiders.

Chocolate Fudge Frosting

- 3 1/2 cups granulated sugar
- 1 1/2 cups milk or evaporated milk
- 6 squares unsweetened chocolate (4 ounces)
- 4 1/2 tablespoons corn syrup
- 1/2 cup butter
- 1 1/2 teaspoon vanilla

In a 3- or 4-quart saucepan, combine sugar, milk, chocolate, and corn syrup. Bring mixture to a boil over medium-high heat, stirring frequently. Reduce heat to medium and put a candy thermometer in the pan. Continue to cook, stirring occasionally, until mixture reaches 234 degrees F (soft ball stage).

Remove from heat—do not stir. Add butter and vanilla and let cool at room temperature, without stirring, to about degrees F. This should take about 1 hour. With a wooden spoon, beat until creamy and frosting begins to hold shape. If it becomes too stiff, add a few drops of hot water and beat until creamy.

This recipe for fudge frosting fills and frosts a 9-inch 3-layer cake.

Garnish with two maraschino cherries with stems.

Snow!

Hello, Snow celebrates all the good things about the snow, sunshine, and wind while a young child savors the day building snow people, playing in the snow, and enjoying a cup of hot cocoa. Expand on this book by learning more about how others work and play in the snow

Brunelle, Nicholas. *Snow Moon*. (Viking, 2005)

Buehner, Caralyn. *Snowmen at Night*. Illustrated by Mark Buehner. (Dial, 2002)

Carle, Eric. *Dream Snow*. (Philomel, 2000)

Keats, Ezra Jack. *The Snowy Day*. (Viking, 1962)

Martin, Jacqueline Briggs. *Snowflake Bentley*. Illustrated by Mary Azarian. (Houghton Mifflin, 1998)

O'Malley, Kevin. *Straight to the Pole*. (Walker Books, 2004)

Shulevitz, Uri. *Snow*. (Farrar, Straus & Giroux, 1998)

Deborah Wiles—Tuna Salad Sandwich

Among my favorite food memories as a child are the fried catfish and hush puppies and the packet of Tom's peanuts shaken into a bottle of Coca-Cola ... and tuna fish sandwich picnics.

—Deborah Wiles

Deborah Wiles

Birthday: May 5

Favorite place: Louin, Mississippi, and home

Favorite foods: chocolate, good coffee, pie, eggplant

Family:

    Sons—Jason and Zachary

    Daughters—Hannah and Alisa

Home:

    Childhood—Born in Alabama, lived all over with the Air Force—Maryland, South Carolina, Hawaii, and the Philippines, but Mississippi was "home."

    Now—Atlanta, Georgia

Deborah Wiles was born in Mobile, Alabama. During her childhood, she and her family moved from state to state as her Air Force father was transferred from base to base. However, she often visited her grandparents in Mississippi, and thus, she kept her ties firmly in the soil of the Deep South while moving to Hawaii, Maryland, South Carolina, the Philippines. When she was growing up, she loved *Captain Kangaroo,* riding her bicycle, cloud watching, puzzles, and Dr. Seuss. Later she loved the Beatles, the Monkees, and many kinds of music. She loved words, too, but never once thought that writing could be a career.

She says, "I became a mother when I was still a teenager, and I held an assortment of jobs to make ends meet.... I became a writer by working with words for many years, sitting up in the middle of the night after my children had gone to sleep, reading and writing essays. I loved words ... words were power."

Many bits and pieces of Deborah's life began to show up in her books. Her first book, *Freedom Summer,* used incidents from her summer visits to her grandparents' home in Mississippi. Her book recounts emotional incidents that occurred during the summer of 1964, when the Civil Rights Act decreed that all public facilities should be opened equally to whites and blacks. Rather than allow African Americans to use the pool, the ice cream stand, or the roller rink, many closed—some permanently.

Deborah's own "wacky" grandmother becomes the prototype for the grandmother in *Love, Ruby Lavender,* and Deborah's memories of Hawaii enter the novel as Ruby's grandmother writes Ruby from the island.

Freedom Summer—Going Beyond

Freedom Summer is the story of two young boys—one white and one black—in the 1960s at the height of the Civil Rights movement. Each of the boys likes playing marbles, both want to be firefighters, and both love to swim. But when the courts order that public facilities be opened to blacks as well as whites, the town fathers where the boys live pour concrete into the pool and close it to everyone rather than let the black children swim, too. Use *Freedom Summer* as a starting point to study the pivotal summer of desegregation and the Civil Rights movement. Research that period of history and locate pictures of marches, protests, sit-ins, and other aspects of the movement. Use the pictures to write summaries and poems. Create a wall or bulletin board of freedom, tolerance, friendship, and human dignity.

Books to Read after *Freedom Summer*

Coleman, Evelyn. *White Socks Only*. Illustrated by Tyrone Geter. Albert A. Whitman, 1999.

Crews, Donald. *Big Mama*. (HarperTrophy, 1998)—Note the "Whites Only" sign on the train and discuss segregation.

Lorbiecki, Marybeth. *Sister Anne's Hands*. Illustrated by Wendy Popp. Penguin Putnam, 2000.

Woodson, Jacqueline. *The Other Side*. Illustrated by E. B. Lewis. (Putnam, 2001)

IRISH WAKE CAKE

Every Little Bird Sings features Comfort Snowberger, who with her beloved ninety-four-year-old great-great-aunt, Florentine Snowberger, cowrite *Fantastic (and Fun) Funeral Food for Family and Friends*. The Snowberger family has been in the funeral business for decades, and Comfort has seen more dead bodies than most girls at ten years of age. But their cookbook promises to be something special. Most likely, one of those recipes will be a pie that many people refer to as "Funeral Pie." Communities began to refer to a raisin pie as a funeral pie because raisins were most often available regardless of the season and most often available to make a raisin pie.

This pie was particularly popular in the Amish and Mennonite communities and served frequently at the meal following a funeral. Other foods were also popular as "funeral fare." Funeral food should be something that is familiar, good tasting, and easily transported.

Ham is often served at funeral dinners because it is easy to bake and doesn't dry out as turkey sometimes does. There is an abundance of sweet foods because sweets are traditionally comfort food. Many cultural groups have foods that show up at wakes and funeral luncheons. One such food is the Irish Wake cake.

Irish Wake Cake

Grease and flour a 9-inch loaf pan. Preheat oven to 325 degrees F.

Cream together until fluffy:

- 3/4 cup (1 1/2 sticks) butter (soft but not melted)
- 1 cup sugar
- 2 teaspoons vanilla extract
- 2 large eggs

Add and beat into the egg and sugar mixture until well combined:

- 1 package (3 ounces) cream cheese, room temperature

Set aside the egg, sugar, and cream cheese mixture.

In a second bow, sift together:

- 1 3/4 cups cake flour (sifted)
- 1 1/4 teaspoons baking powder
- 1/4 teaspoon salt

Use 1/4 of the flour mixture and mix in a small bowl with:

- 1 cup dried currants

Stir until the currants are well coated. Mix together the remaining flour mixture with the sugar, egg, cream cheese mixture, and

- 2/3 cup buttermilk

When all ingredients are well combined, add in the dried currants and stir to distribute them evenly throughout the batter.

Pour the batter into the prepared loaf pan and bake until a tester (toothpick) inserted into the middle of the cake comes out clean. Approximate bake time is 1 1/2 hours. When the cake is done, remove from the oven and cool on a rack.

While the cake is baking, prepare the glaze. Mix together:

- 1/2 cup powdered sugar (sifted)
- 2 teaspoons freshly squeezed lemon juice

When the cake has cooled for 10 minutes but is still slightly warm, remove it from the pan and drizzle the lemon glaze over the warm cake. Allow to cool completely before serving. Recipe makes 10 servings.

[I have] favorite food memories as a child … Tuna salad sandwiches are one of my favorites and it's sprinkled thoughout my new book [*Each Little Bird That Sings*], and also one of my favorites is deviled eggs.

—Deborah Wiles

Tuna Salad Sandwich for Picnics in the Cemetery

Mix the following ingredients:

- 1/2 cup mayonnaise
- Grated peel and juice from 1/4 lemon
- 1can (7 ounces) white albacore tuna, drained and chunked
- 1/4 cup grapes, cut in quarters, seeded
- 1/2 red apple, unpeeled, cut in very small pieces
- 1/4 tablespoon finely chopped onion
- 1/4 cup finely chopped celery
- 1 boiled egg, chopped finely
- Salt and pepper to taste

To make the sandwich, place generous portions of the tuna salad between two slices of whole-wheat bread, garnish with a piece of lettuce and cut into two triangles. Serve each sandwich with a dill pickle on the side. Makes 4–6 servings.

Deviled Eggs

- 6 eggs
- 1/2 teaspoon paprika
- 2 tablespoons mayonnaise
- 1/2 teaspoon mustard powder

Place eggs in a water filled sauce pan. Bring water to boil and let eggs cook in the gently boiling water until they are hard boiled—about 10 to 15 minutes. Drain eggs, peel, and let cool.

Cut eggs in half, lengthwise. Remove the egg yolks and mash the yolks together in a small mixing bowl. Mix in the mayonnaise and dry mustard. Spoon mixture into the empty hole left in the egg whites by the removal of the yolks, cool, and serve.

Selected Books Written by Deborah Wiles

Each Little Bird That Sings. (Harcourt, 2005)

Freedom Summer. Illustrated by Jerome Lagarrigue. (Harcourt, 2001)

Love, Ruby Lavender. (Harcourt, 2001)

One Wide Sky: A Bedtime Lullaby. Illustrated by Tim Bowers. (Harcourt, 2003)

Linda S. Wingerter—Broccoli Chicken Pasta

> *My style of art has changed a lot over fifteen years, but occasionally I'll paint a tree that bears some resemblance to broccoli. I'm especially thinking of the very green Lovejoy apple orchard in The Water Gift and the Pig of the Pig—not at all unlike the little trees on your dinner plate, when you think about it.*
>
> **—Linda S. Wingerter**

Linda S. Wingerter

Birthday: May 26

Favorite place: The fountain of Edgerton Park in New Haven, Connecticut

Favorite foods: lemons

Family:

    Spouse—Karl Gasteyer (actor, writer, director, and very good cook)

Home:

    Childhood—South Paris, Maine, and Wilmington, Vermont

    Now—West Haven, Connecticut

Her great-grandfather painted church murals in Russia, her grandfather was a puppeteer, her grandmother was a miniaturist, her father was a graphic artist, and her mother a book designer. Linda S. Wingerter, at age four, saw some illustrations created by Trina Schart Hyman and decided she wanted to become an illustrator. By the time she was thirteen, a drawing she created of a paper dragon had been published in *Cricket* magazine. After studying at the Rhode Island School of Design (and graduating in 1996), she began illustrating for magazines, book and album covers, opera posters, and children's books. While preparing to illustrate *One Grain of Sand,* a book written by musical talent Pete Seeger, she discovered that her grandparents had designed posters to announce a concert by Seeger in their hometown during the 1960s. When she is not creating illustrations, she is working on renovating her eighty-five-year-old house, making dolls, figure skating, and playing the fiddle and musical saw. Periodically she and several artist friends meet at the Eric Carle Picture Book Museum in Amherst, Massachusetts, to view the changing exhibits and to discuss their own work.

Booklist

Selected Books Illustrated by Linda S. Wingerter.

Ashman, Linda. *What Could Be Better Than This?* (Dutton, 2006)

Martin, Jacqueline Briggs. *The Water Gift and the Pig of the Pig.* (Houghton Mifflin, 2003)

Milford, Susan. *Tales Alive! Bird Tales from Near & Far.* (Williamson, 1998)

Seeger, Pete. *One Grain of Sand.* (Little, Brown, 2003)

Sherman, Josephan. *Magic Hoofbeats: Horse Tales from Many Lands.* (Barefoot Books, 2004)

Thompson, Lauren. *One Riddle, One Answer.* (Scholastic, 2001)

I come from many generations of artists of all kinds, church muralists, puppeteers, miniaturists, book designers and illustrators. My family spoke to each other largely in visual terms. My mom's favorite trick when I was small was to make scenes from the foods on my plate she wanted me to eat. The one I was most mesmerized by, that I still remember looking at with magical interest, was the broccoli my mom called "little trees." When broccoli is steamed nicely and gets that rich gorgeous green, you've got a whole enchanted forest on your plate.

—**Linda S. Wingerter**

BROCCOLI

Broccoli is a cruciferous (a word that means "crosslike") vegetable, meaning it's a member of a family of plants that often have four petals that look like a cross. Kale, cabbage, kohlrabi, cauliflower, broccoli, and Brussels sprouts are all the same species of plant. Each variation is the result of selective propagation. Broccoli was developed in the sixteenth century in the northeastern Mediterranean and southern Europe areas.

Broccoli was not brought to North America until the early 1920s, when Italian immigrants introduced the plant here. California was the first state to grow the plant commercially. The first shipment east was made in 1924. Crop production was not significant until after World War II. Today, the United

States is the leading producer of broccoli in the world. Ninety percent of the broccoli grown in the United States is produced in California. Lesser crop production takes place in Arizona, Texas, Oregon, and Pennsylvania. In the 1990s, broccoli gained in popularity, perhaps because of its health benefits. Broccoli can be steamed, boiled, pan-fried, or cooked in a microwave. The broccoli florets (little flowers), tops, and stems should be cooked until just tender but crisp to maintain the bright green color, about 3 to 6 minutes. Broccoli florets can be served as a vegetable, in stir-fries, salads, crepes, casseroles, soups, omeletes or with dips. Scientists think that broccoli is high in nutritional value and can help prevent cancer; broccoli has even been touted as the "miracle food."

Illustrations by Linda S. Wingerter.

I took these little trees to heart and drew them into my pictures. I found inspiration in the illustrator of my favorite children's book, Nicole Claveloux of *Forest of Lilacs*, whose beautiful trees rendered in exquisitely detailed pen and ink looked a lot like broccoli, too. I imitated this style with my own little trees, and these pictures helped me get accepted to the Rhode Island School of Design where I would study children's book illustration.

—Linda S. Wingerter

There is only one meal that I can make well, that is not instant oatmeal or soup in a can, the one I rely on when company comes over—broccoli chicken pasta. It's a lovely dish I learned how to cook during years of restaurant jobs after graduating from the Rhode Island School of Design, when I was trying to get my first children's book. An Italian woman named Antoinette was the cook at Sal's in Westbrook, Connecticut, where I was a hostess, and she graciously showed me how to make it.

—Linda S. Wingerter

Chicken Broccoli Pasta (An Unprecise Recipe)

Note: the amount of chicken, broccoli, and pasta is dependent on how many guests you intend to serve, and the proportion of chicken to broccoli, and pasta. Estimate a half chicken breast cut and chunked, 1/2 cup cooked pasta, and 1/2 cup broccoli per serving.

Simmer a tablespoon or two of olive oil in a pan with chopped garlic, and add small chunks of raw chicken. Cook the chicken, adding oregano, rosemary, pepper, or whatever is on hand that smells good and a splash of red wine

Add the broccoli and a good handful of chopped Italian olives. Put the pan on low and simmer, as you boil up a pot of hot water to dunk the fresh linguini pasta for just one minute. Strain and (this is the important part) put the pasta into the pan with the oil and chicken and broccoli, sprinkle on fresh basil leaves, and fry it for just a minute so it soaks up all that good stuff. Serve with fresh parmesan cheese, grated.

Signature Recipe—Linda S. Wingerter

Sugar Cookies to Eat by the Numbers: 1*2*3 Cookies for Me!

Make cardboard templates for each of the numerals 0–9 (or locate and purchase numeral cookie cutters), and use the template to guide the cutting of each cookie. After rolling and cutting out the cookies, sprinkle sugar on the surface of each cookie before baking, and then reinforce the number value of each cookie by placing four chocolate chips on top of a "4" cookie, five raisins on a "5" cookie, and seven Red Hots, so on. Colored M&M's can also be used. Younger children can "eat" their house number or telephone number, and older children can bake and eat addition and subtraction equations. Use the following recipe.

Ingredients

- 2 1/2 cups butter
- 2 1/4 cups sugar
- 3 eggs
- 1 tablespoon vanilla
- 1 teaspoon lemon juice
- 3 teaspoons lemon zest (finally grated lemon peel)
- Pinch of salt
- 1/4 cup ice water
- 7 1/2 cups flour

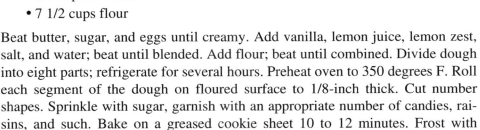

Beat butter, sugar, and eggs until creamy. Add vanilla, lemon juice, lemon zest, salt, and water; beat until blended. Add flour; beat until combined. Divide dough into eight parts; refrigerate for several hours. Preheat oven to 350 degrees F. Roll each segment of the dough on floured surface to 1/8-inch thick. Cut number shapes. Sprinkle with sugar, garnish with an appropriate number of candies, raisins, and such. Bake on a greased cookie sheet 10 to 12 minutes. Frost with ready-made icing. Makes about twelve dozen.

One Riddle, One Answer is a Persian folktale that includes a princess's quest for the perfect husband, and it all revolves around a riddle solved only with number sense. The mathematical solution involves place value, fractions, and multiplication. Wingerter uses a rich palette of color to create illustrations with numbers appearing in the clouds, on the sides of horses, and in the desert sands. Use this book and those listed here as springboards to focus on numbers and mathematical concepts.

Hopkins, Lee Bennett. *Marvelous Math: A Book of Poems*. Illustrated by Karen Barbour. (Simon & Schuster, 1997)

Neuschwander, Cindy. *Sir Cumference and the Great Knight of Angleland: A Math Adventure*. Illustrated by Wayne Geehan. (Charlesbridge, 2001)

Pinczes, Elinor J. *A Remainder of One*. Illustrated by Bonnie MacKain. (Houghton Mifflin, 1995)

Schwartz, David. *If You Hopped Like a Frog*. Illustrated by James Warhol. (Scholastic, 1999)

Credits

Photograph Credits

Photograph of Sue Alexander by Nancy Yamin. Courtesy of Sue Alexander and Nancy Yamin.

Photograph of Berthe Amoss, courtesy of Berthe Amoss.

Photograph of Marsha Diane Arnold by Fred Arnold. Courtesy of Marsha Diane Arnold.

Photograph of Tom Birdseye by Bob Crum. Courtesy of Tom Birdseye.

Photograph of Maribeth Boelts, courtesy of Maribeth Boelts.

Photograph of Roger Bradfield, courtesy of Roger Bradfield.

Photograph of Marlene Targ Brill by Sharron L. McElmeel.

Photograph of Craig Brown by Sharron L. McElmeel.

Photograph of Don Brown, courtesy of Don Brown.

Photograph of Joseph Bruchac by Michael Greenlar. Courtesy of Joseph Bruchac.

Photograph of Betsy Byars by Ed Byars. Courtesy of Betsy Byars.

Photograph of Stephanie Calmenson with "Harry" at the apple stand by Ronnie J. Schultz, copyright 2005. Courtesy of Stephanie Calmenson.

Photograph of Elisa Carbone by Sharon Natoli. Courtesy of Elisa Carbone.

Photograph of Nancy Carlson by Peter Beck. Courtesy of Nancy Carlson.

Photograph of Penny Colman, courtesy of Penny Colman.

Photograph of Diane deGroat by Amanda Latrell. Courtesy of Diane deGroat.

Photograph of Norah Dooley, courtesy of Norah Dooley.

Photograph of Lois Ehlert by Lillian Schultz. Courtesy of Lois Ehlert.

Photograph of Jill Esbaum by Mark's Place, Eldridge, Iowa. Courtesy of Jill Esbaum.

Photograph of Jean Fritz, courtesy of Jean Fritz.

Photograph of Wendy Halperin Anderson by Sharron L. McElmeel

Photograph of Will Hillenbrand by Altman. Courtesy of Will Hillenbrand.

Photograph of Deborah Hopkinson by Rebekah Hopkinson. Courtesy of Deborah Hopkinson.

Photograph of Carol Otis Hurst by Karl Meyer. Courtesy of Carol Otis Hurst.

Photograph of Johanna Hurwitz, courtesy of Johanna Hurwitz.

Photograph of Jennifer R. Jacobson by Jake Jacobson. Courtesy of Jennifer R. Jacobson.

Photograph of Helen Ketteman, courtesy of Helen Ketteman.

Photograph of Eric A. Kimmel, courtesy of Eric A. Kimmel.

Photograph of Sandy Lanton, courtesy of Sandy Lanton.

Photograph of Laurie Lawlor, courtesy of Laurie Lawlor.

Photograph of Loreen J. Leedy by Andrew Schuerger. Courtesy of Loreen J. Leedy.

Photograph of Cynthia Leitich Smith by Greg Leitich Smith. Courtesy of Cynthia Leitich Smith.

Photograph of Cynthia Leitich Smith and Greg Leitich Smith by Frances Hill. Courtesy of Cynthia Leitich Smith and Greg H. Leitich.

Photograph of E.B. Lewis, courtesy of Earl B. Lewis.

Photograph of Peter B. Mandel by Kathy Mandel. Courtesy of Peter B. Mandel.

Photograph of Rafé Martin by Ariya Martin. Courtesy of Rafé Martin.

Photograph of Ann Morris, courtesy of Ann Morris.

Photograph of Robin Pulver by Don Pulver. Courtesy of Robin Pulver.

Photograph of Candice Ransom by Frank W Ransom. Courtesy of Earl B. Lewis.

Photograph of James Ransome and Lesa Cline Ransome, courtesy James Ransome.

Photograph of Connie B. Roop and Peter Roop by Martha Roop Turner. Courtesy of Connie B. Roop and Peter Roop.

Photograph of Nicole Rubel by Geoff Shapiro. Courtesy of Nicole Rubel.

Photograph of Claudia Rueda by Jorge Giraldo. Courtesy of Claudia Rueda.

Photograph of Pam Muñoz Ryan, courtesy of Pam Muñoz Ryan.

Photograph of Diane Stanley by Karen Sachar. Courtesy of Diane Stanley.

Photograph of Hope Vestergaard by Deb Pilutti. Courtesy of Hope Vestergaard.

Photograph of Deborah Wiles, courtesy of Deborah Wiles.

Photograph of Linda S. Wingerter, courtesy of Linda S. Wingerter.

Illustrative Credits

All line drawings in this book were created by Deborah L. McElmeel except as noted below.

Roger Bradfield
Self-portrait of Roger Bradfield as a painter created by Roger Bradfield in pen and ink and watercolor, used here with his permission.

Brown, Craig
Pen and ink sketch of farm yard created by Craig Brown, used here with his permission.

Halperin, Wendy Anderson
Pen and ink hand-drawn recipe pages created by Wendy Anderson Halperin. Used with permission.

Leedy, Loreen
Pen and ink drawing of cookies by Loreen Leedy. Used with permission.

Rubel, Nicole
Illustration of matzo ball soup in a bowl created by Nicole Rubel, used with permission.

Rueda, Claudia
All illustrations of the big-bottomed ants were created by Claudia Rueda and are used with permission.

Wingerter, Linda S.
Linda S. Wingerter created the sketches of the "broccoli trees" and the crests that show the round trees, and they are used with permission.

Quotation Credits

All quotes from books or letters are used with the permission of the authors.

Alexander, Sue. *Witch, Goblin, and Ghost Are Back*. Pantheon, 1985.

Alexander, Sue. Letter to the author, 2004.

Amoss, Berthe. *A Cajun Little Red Riding Hood*. More Than a Card, 2000.

Arnold, Marsha Diane. *The Bravest of Us All*. Dial, 2000.

Arnold, Marsha Diane. Letter to the author, 2005.

Birdseye, Tom. *Attack of the Mutant Underwear*. Holiday House, 2003.

Boelts, Maribeth. *Firefighter's Thanksgiving*. Putnam, 2004.

Boelts, Maribeth. Letter to the author, 2004.

Bradfield, Roger. *Pickle Chiffon Pie*. Purple House Press, 2004.

Bradfield, Roger. Letter to the author, 2004.

Brill, Marlene Targ. *Allan Jay and the Underground Railroad*. Carolrhoda, 1993.

Brill, Marlene Targ. Letter to the author, 2004.

Brown, Craig. Letter to the author, 2004.

Brown, Don. Letter to the author, 2005.

Bruchac, Joseph. "Bill Greenfield's Breakfast" in *Hoops Snakes, Hide Behinds* and *Side-Hill Winders: Tall Tales from the Adirondacks* by Joseph Bruchac. The Crossing Press, 1991.

Bruchac, Joseph. Letter to the author, 2005.

Byars, Betsy. *The Pinballs*. HarperCollins, 1987.

Byars, Betsy. Letter to the author, 2004.

Calmenson, Stephanie. *Dinner at Panda Palace*. HarperCollins, 1991.

Calmenson, Stephanie. Letter to the author, 2005.

Carbone, Eliza. Letter to the author, 2005.

Carlson, Nancy. Letter to the author, 2004.

Colman, Penny. Letter to the author, 2004.

deGroat, Diane. Letter to the author, 2004.

Dooley, Norah. Letter to the author, 2005.

Ehlert, Lois. Letter to the author, 2005.

Esbaum, Jill. Letter to the author, 2005.

Fritz, Jean. *George Washington's Breakfast*. Putnam, 1998.

Fritz, Jean. Letter to the author, 2004.

Halperin, Wendy Halperin. Letter to the author, 2004.

Hillenbrand, Will. Information from letter to the author, 2004.

Hopkinson, Deborah. Letter to the author, 2005.

Hurst, Carol Otis. Letter to the author, 2005.

Hurwitz, Johanna. *A Llama in the Family*. HarperCollins, 1994.

Hurwitz, Johanna. Letter to the author, 2004.

Jacobson, Jennifer R. Letter to the author, 2005.

Ketteman, Helen. *The Great Cake Bake*. Walker Books, 2005.

Ketteman, Helen. Letter to the author, 2005.

Kimmel, Eric A. Letter to the author, 2005.

Lanton, Sandy. Letter to the author, 2004.

Lawlor, Laurie. Letter to the author, 2005.

Leedy, Loreen. Letter to the author, 2005.

Leitich Smith, Cynthia and Greg Leitich Smith. Letter to the author, 2005

Lewis, Earl B. Phone interview and letter to the author, 2004.

Mandel, Peter. Letter to the author, 2005.

Martin, Rafe. Letter to the author, 2005.

Morris, Ann. Letter to the author, 2004.

Pulver, Robin. Letter to the author, 2005.

Ransom, Candice. Letter to the author, 2005.

Ransome, James, and Lisa Cline Ransome. Letter to the author, 2005, from James Ransome.

Roop, Connie R., and Peter Roop. *Keep the Lights Burning, Abbie*. Carolrhoda, 1984.

Roop, Connie R., and Peter Roop. Letter to the author, 2004.

Rubel, Nicole. Letter to the author, 2005.

Rueda, Claudia. Letter to the author, 2005.

Ryan, Pam Muñoz. Letter to the author, 2005.

Stanley, Diane. Letter to the author, 2005.

Vestergaard, Hope. Letter to the author, 2005.

Wiles, Deborah. Letter to the author, 2005.

Wingerter, Linda S. Letter to the author, 2005.

Acknowledgments of Recipe Sources

Except as noted, all recipes in this book were developed and tested by Deborah L. McElmeel (with the help of other culinary assistants). McElmeel is a culinary expert with two decades of experience in the cooking field. She holds a graduate degree in science and used her knowledge of chemistry and her extensive experience in the restaurant industry to develop and adapt the many recipes in this book.

Alexander, Sue—Goblin's Fudge Recipe from a family friend, "Tim's Mother." Compliments of Sue Alexander.

Amoss, Berthe—Pralines. Compliments of Berthe Amoss.

Arnold, Marsha Diane—Mak Kuchen. Compliments of Marsha Diane Arnold.

Boelts, Maribeth—Firehouse Grilled Pork. One of the firehouse chefs, Rick, provided this recipe which comes to us compliments of Maribeth Boelts.

Brill, Marlene Targ—Jabicove Smazenky (Apple Fritters). Compliments of Marlene Targ Brill.

Byars, Betsy—Chocolate Mayonnaise Cake. Compliments of Betsy Byars.

Calmenson, Stephanie—Mark's Apple Cake. A family recipe often baked by Calmenson's husband, Mark. Compliments of Stephanie Calmenson.

Colman, Penny—Penny Colman's Delicious Delightful Concoction. Compliments of Penny Colman.

deGroat, Diane—Diane's Favorite Sugar Cookies. Compliments of Diane deGroat.

Esbaum, Jill—Granny's Cinnamon Rolls. Compliments of Jill Esbaum.

Halperin, Wendy Anderson—Dazzling Bread. Compliments of Wendy Anderson Halperin.

Hopkinson, Deborah—Russ Hopkinson's Baking Powder Biscuits. A family recipe compliments of Deborah Hopkinson.

Hurst, Carol Otis—Carol's Favorite Fried Chicken. Compliments of Carol Otis Hurst.

Hurwitz, Johanna—Blueberry Soup. A recipe from the llama trek guide in Vermont and passed along compliments of Johanna Hurwitz.

Jacobson, Jennifer R.—S'mores. A traditional recipe passed along compliments of Jennifer R. Jacobson.

Ketteman, Helen—Old Time Jam Cake. Compliments of Helen Ketteman.

Leedy, Loreen—Spritz Cookies. Compliments of Loreen Leedy.

Pulver, Robin—Szegediner Goulas (Gypsy Goulash). Compliments of Robin Pulver.

Roop, Peter and Connie R. Roop—Clam Chowder. Compliments of Peter Roop.

Rubel, Nicole—Matzo Ball Soup. Compliments of Nicole Rubel.

Rueda, Claudia—Toasted Big Bottomed Ants. Compliments of Claudia Rueda.

Stanley, Diane—Blackberry Pie. Compliments of Diane Stanley.

Sources for More Information

Many of the authors and illustrators featured in this book, *Authors in the Pantry: Recipes, Stories, and More,* also host their own Web sites, which provide additional information about them and their books. Hot links to those sites may be found on the Author Links page at http://www.mcelmeel.com/curriculum/authorlinks.html.

In addition, a companion page for this book is available at http://www.melmeel. com/writing/authorsinthepantry.html. On this site, you will find hot links to a variety of Web pages that may provide you with additional information to topics connected to various books and recipes in this book.

General Index

Recipe Index